THE PAST AND FUTURE
PEOPLE

Romola McSwain

THE PAST AND FUTURE PEOPLE

PEOPLE

Tradition and Change on a
New Guinea Island

MELBOURNE
OXFORD UNIVERSITY PRESS
LONDON WELLINGTON NEW YORK

Oxford University Press

OXFORD LONDON GLASGOW NEW YORK
TORONTO MELBOURNE WELLINGTON CAPE TOWN
IBADAN NAIROBI DAR ES SALAAM LUSAKA ADDIS ABABA
KUALA LUMPUR SINGAPORE JAKARTA HONG KONG TOKYO
DELHI BOMBAY CALCUTTA MADRAS KARACHI

© *Romola McSwain 1977*

First published 1977

NATIONAL LIBRARY OF AUSTRALIA CATALOGUING IN PUBLICATION DATA

McSwain, Romola

The past and future people: tradition and change on a New Guinea island.

Index.
ISBN 0 19 550521 2.

1. Karkar Island, Papua New Guinea—Social life and customs. I. Title.

995.5

PRINTED IN AUSTRALIA BY BROWN PRIOR ANDERSON PTY LTD
PUBLISHED BY OXFORD UNIVERSITY PRESS, 7 BOWEN CRESCENT
MELBOURNE

CONTENTS

MAPS

TABLES

FIGURES

PREFACE

PAPUA NEW GUINEA became a nation in September 1975. Although she was one of the world's last large colonies, her achievement of independence rated relatively little public attention, even in Australia, the responsible metropolitan power. Yet for over a hundred years after she first came under the direct influence of the West, she had a chequered and therefore fascinating history. She was already within the orbit of European traders, planters, and missionaries in the early 1870s but was not formally annexed until November 1884: Papua by Britain, and north-east New Guinea by Germany. After World War I, Australia had control of both territories, receiving Papua as her own possession from Britain in 1906 and a mandate from the League of Nations in 1921 over German New Guinea, which she had seized in 1914. Early in 1942, the Japanese invaded Papua New Guinea, and they were evicted only after a campaign the bitterness of which was not in proportion to its small scale. Australian administration was re-established after 1945 but policy changed. The Labor Government in Canberra saw Papua New Guinea no longer as a perpetual dependency but as a territory to be developed towards self-determination with Europeans playing an important role as permanent settlers. There was a long period of argument and indecision about the form self-determination should take, but by the middle 1960s there was general agreement that it had to lead to the creation of a completely separate nation rather than perpetuate any formal political association with Australia apart from joint membership of the Commonwealth. This debate notwithstanding, the new policy involved a massive programme of economic, political, and educational development. Within thirty years, starting virtually from scratch, the Australian Administration established most of the institutions essential for a new state. Possibly because of the speed with which this was done, the years before final independence witnessed regional unrest: sporadic tribal fighting in the Highlands; turbulence in Rabaul after the formation of the Mataungan Association; and threats of secession by the Trobriand Islands, Bougainville, and members of the political faction, Papua Besena.

Amidst this recent ferment, the Madang District remained outwardly calm. It rarely featured in such international media

vii

reports as there were. Yet it has never been a backwater. After the Germans abandoned Finschhafen in 1892, they made it their main centre of administration for nearly a decade. Stephansort (Bogajim) was their capital until 1897, and Madang from 1897 until the turn of the century, when the Government moved first to Kokopo and then to Rabaul in New Britain. Even then Madang remained an important centre under both the Germans and the Australians. It was from Madang that administration spread to the Highlands after 1930. In the Madang District the problems besetting Papua New Guinea's development programme after 1945 became obvious very early: contradictions between the indigenous and introduced economic, political, and educational institutions, and a cargo movement that has lasted for over a hundred years.

There is now an extensive, if not exhaustive, literature on the ethnography, colonial history, and problems of development in the Madang District. Between 1920 and 1942, Lutheran and Roman Catholic missionaries—the Reverend Dr E. F. Hannemann, the Reverend R. Inselmann, the Reverend J. F. Mager, and Father A. Aufinger, S.V.D.—carried out pioneer work, the immense value of which is apparent from its contribution to later field research. The first professional anthropologists in the District were myself, working among the Garia near the Ramu and among the Ngaing near Saidor since 1949, and Professor K. O. L. Burridge, who went to the Tangu near Bogia in 1952. After 1966, this early work was greatly augmented by younger scholars who came to the field with more modern training and techniques, and new ideas that had grown with the expansion of anthropology since the war. Dr Romola McSwain went to Karkar Island, Dr Louise Morauta to Kauris near Madang, and Dr Peter McLaren to Bongu on the Rai Coast. More recently Mr David Eisler and Ms Leslie Conton have completed work at Usino village near the Ramu. This research is now beginning to be published. Dr Morauta's book *Beyond The Village* (Athlone Press) appeared in 1974. Dr McSwain's book is now available. As she has done me the honour of inviting me to write a preface to it, I shall try to set it in two sociocultural contexts: the pre-contact situation in the Madang District and the post-contact situation in the whole of Papua New Guinea.

In doing this, I am following the plan of Dr McSwain's book, which falls into two parts. First, she presents the traditional ethnography of the Takia (and, to a more limited extent, the Waskia) of Karkar Island, thereby making an important contribution to our knowledge of the peoples of the District. Second, she offers a careful examination of colonial administration, missionary endeavour, and modern development, which will rank highly among other similar studies of Papua New Guinea published since 1945.

We cannot yet offer a detailed survey of the traditional sociocultural systems of the Madang District, although we now know enough to delineate some of the main areas of similarity and difference. The socioeconomic similarities are well known. Indigenous societies are virtually stateless and tend to lack economic specialization, occupational groups, centralized authority and, with the one reported exception of Manam Island, systems of rank or class. They have subsistence economies, and are organized on the principles of kinship, marriage, and descent. Traditional religions are based largely on beliefs in deities whose activities are recounted in myths and who are credited with the creation of the natural environment, economy, society, and culture, and in spirits of the dead who protect the interests of their living relatives. These superhuman beings are thought to be the source of all true knowledge and power, which they reveal to men.

Yet there are differences between these societies, especially in socio-political and religious forms. The bulk of coastal societies are patrilineal: language groups are divided into bush or island groups or, as now seems more likely in view of Dr McSwain's evidence, phratries, which are subdivided in turn into generally exogamous clans. There are three other main variants. To the north around Bogia, where there was a marked tradition of migration and warfare before the German annexation, social structures seem always to have geen a good deal looser than in the south. Both genealogical patterns and local organization are profoundly irregular. In the southern inland area between the Gogol and Ramu rivers, social structures are distinctly cognatic: local organization is again indiscriminate, although genealogical structure, while recognizing descent in many lines, is regular. (Along the Ramu Valley itself, there is probably greater emphasis on patriliny.) Finally, on the Rai Coast inland from Saidor, there are several societies organized on the principle of double unilineal descent.

The Karkar belong squarely to the first category, patrilineal societies. The phratries which Dr McSwain describes are clearly the functional equivalents of the bush and island groups described for the Ngaing, Neko, Sengam, and Som of the Rai Coast (Lawrence 1964a), and the Yam of Madang (Hannemann n.d.).

The designation of bush group for the Ngaing and Neko is justified: the group is merely an aggregation of patriclans without a further common ancestor. Yet Dr McSwain has validated her use of the term phratry for the Karkar by careful reference to the Kulbob-Manub origin myth, which provides the common ancestors of the major constellations of patriclans. I have no doubt that more detailed research will demonstrate the same for the Yam and many other peoples of the littoral, at least as far as the Saidor area, who share this myth. This is no mere academic pedantry but underlines the feeling of common identity enjoyed by these coastal groups in respect of the myth, an identity given practical expression in the trading network which reached from the Huon Gulf via Siassi to the Rai Coast, Madang, Karkar, and places further north, which has recently been described by Harding (1967), and to which he estimates that about a quarter of a million people belong. Regional associations of this kind, however loose, are not without significance for the new nation-state.

Traditional religious forms differ in one main respect. On the subcoast and in the hinterland, the concept of a primal god or great gods seems either to be lacking or to be little stressed. Creation is attributed to a pantheon of deities, to none of whom is accorded any great pre-eminence. Along the seaboard between the Madang and Saidor regions, however, the concept of a primal deity or great gods is well developed. The great gods are Kulbob and Manub (or, to use more common spellings, Kilibob and Manup), who, near Madang, are often associated with a shadowy first originator, Anut or Dodo, sometimes vaguely described as their father. The Karkar belong to this second tradition, although they do not believe in Anut or Dodo. This seaboard concept of a primal god or great gods was probably important after contact in that (despite a period of resistance in some parts of the mainland coast) it facilitated conversion to Christianity.

Dr McSwain's main theme, however, is her description and analysis at the local level of the postwar economic, political, and educational development programme to which I referred at the outset. She endorses the largely secular approach to economic problems by such anthropologists as T. S. Epstein, Finney, and Salisbury: unless radical change is imposed ruthlessly—which so far it never has been in Papua New Guinea—economic development is at the mercy of the traditional economic system and social structure, which allow it to take place only within the limits they impose. The Karkar have achieved a fair measure of economic progress, but the antithesis of their kinship ethic to European economic concepts creates problems which frequently force them into a symbiosis with European settlers, who alone can guarantee them the cash and constant advice they need in their numerous business ventures.

This symbiosis spills over into the political field: the new multiracial Local Government Council and the House of Assembly. Dr McSwain shows how the Karkar have had to grapple with new political forms that do not always fit easily with their own social institutions. Once again they turn to Europeans to sustain them as members of the Council and to represent them in the national parliament. Interracial co-operation is, of course, admirable but the danger of overdependence is all too obvious.

Nevertheless, certainly in the Madang District, this kind of analysis on its own is not enough. These economic and sociopolitical problems—difficulties in modern economic development, in the assimilation of new political processes, and in relations between indigenes and European settlers—cannot be understood in purely secular terms. Such an explanation by itself is a Western imposition, cultural imperialism. We have to try to see these issues through Papua New Guinean eyes. This brings us immediately into the field of indigenous religion and epistemology, the cargoist interpretation of the modern world, which Dr McSwain explores with consummate skill. In the traditional situation, deities were assumed to guarantee in perpetuity for man a cosmic system with material concomitants of living that were his by the mere right of birth. In the same way, after annexation it came to be accepted that there had to be a comparable cosmic order with the new material concomitant of living introduced by Europeans: cargo. The people's problem, therefore, was to discover the identity of the deity or deities who provided the new wealth and thereby guaranteed the new cosmic system in perpetuity for man. The discovery of this superhuman guarantee would solve all modern economic and political problems, and regulate relationships with Europeans on the basis of equality and equivalence.

Two things should be stressed here. First, the tremendous importance attributed to religious thought in the southern Madang District has been attested by a number of virtually independent witnesses. By July 1950, when I had completed my first period of research, I had come firmly to this conclusion. I learnt afterwards that Dr Hannemann had anticipated me by well over a decade. Dr Morauta and Professor Harding have both told me that, although at the outset they had doubts about this view, they accepted its validity by the end of their field work in the 1960s. Dr McLaren endorsed it for Bongu. Dr McSwain appreciated its true relevance only during her third and fourth visits to Karkar, when she discovered many of the facts she has set out in this book.

I make this point by no means as a matter of self-congratulation. What is at stake is the general nature of a regional epistemological system and, for this, it is inadequate to rely on the testimony of any one scholar, however careful and objective he or she may be. Our conclusions must be weighed exhaustively against new discoveries before they can be finally accepted, especially when it is remembered that many anthropologists still cling to the timid, conservative opinion that people's stated beliefs have no instrumental role in their daily lives and do nothing more than symbolize their social relationships or subconscious. Yet if, as I believe it does, the evidence from the Madang District supports intellectualist inquiry, the credit should go to Dr Hannemann. He first recorded and appreciated the people's epistemology. He is the giant on whose shoulders we have stood to peer a little further into the unknown.

Second, Dr McSwain does not merely duplicate earlier work, such as Professor Burridge's astute analysis of social values and race relations, and Dr Hannemann's and my own work on epistemology. We examined cargo beliefs in a situation almost entirely lacking modern socioeconomic development—at best, one in which such development was in its infancy. Implicitly or explicitly, we regarded this as the root cause of the cargo belief, which would disappear when it was rectified. This one-to-one relationship has proved to be unfounded. It is here that Dr McSwain makes a signal contribution. She has shown convincingly that the cargo belief can coexist with a fair measure of economic and sociopolitical development: traditional and modern institutions operate side by side, sometimes in harmony, sometimes in conflict.

This must help correct a great deal of literature that stresses cargo cult as a condition quite distinct from normal living. The old idea has been that prophets arise, proclaim doctrine, and institute ritual that inevitably fails, after which the cargo phenomenon fades away. It is implicit in Dr McSwain's work that cults as such are relatively unimportant. What is important is the general condition of cargoism, which is interwoven with everyday events. It impinges on economic activities, on sociopolitical activities, and on intellectual life.

There is nothing unique about Papua New Guineans holding

cargoist views while at the same time experimenting with practical development based on secular lines. For a start, the distinction between religious and secular may have little meaning for them. It is ourselves, twentieth century Europeans, who make this distinction—and then only after a long series of historical accidents. Moreover, our own history is full of comparable, barely more sophisticated examples. In the 1650s, eminent parliamentary soldiers such as Major-General Harrison and Colonel Rich could hold their belief in the imminence of the Fifth Monarchy, the personal rule of Jesus Christ in England, ultimately in the face of what was perhaps the world's most barbarous form of execution. Also in the seventeenth century, John Ray, a Fellow of Trinity College, Cambridge, and Thomas Burnet, a Fellow of Christ's College, Cambridge, Master of the Charterhouse, and finally Chaplain-in-Ordinary to William III, were physicotheologians who wrote geological histories based on ideas drawn partly from the Bible and partly from the new scientific discoveries of the age. 'Enlightened' Parisians who endorsed the apparently rational experiments of 1789 could also pay serious attention to the charlatan, the self-styled Count Cagliostro. In the nineteenth century, much to the contempt of Frederick Engels, Wallace, who put forward a theory of evolution similar to that of Charles Darwin, argued that spiritualism was a demonstrable reality.

Once again this is no mere academic comparison but has direct relevance for the current situation in Papua New Guinea. It stresses the argument with which Dr McSwain begins her book. She comments that both Professor Peter Worsley and I endorse the mistaken view I have already outlined. Worsley assumes that cargoism will give way quickly before the onslaught of secular economic and political progress. Although allowing it greater powers of resistance, I too agree that it will eventually disappear in similar circumstances. Yet Dr McSwain has described the kind of situation which both Worsley and I envisage—village cash crops, trade stores, trucking businesses, a local government council, and a national parliament—but which has not materially affected the cargo belief. She suggests wisely that we should look at the nature of introduced institutions. It seems that so far the people have been able to equate the developments we have brought them with comparable aspects of their own culture. They have incorporated them within, and assimilated them to, their own conceived cosmic order, explaining and legitimizing them as being guaranteed by a deity, either the Christian God or the traditional Kulbob. By way of contrast, we should not forget that the sociopolitical and intellectual conflict of the seventeenth century in Europe led to the triumph of science and technology: the Industrial Revolution. We may well ask at what point development in Papua New Guinea will be qualitatively so different that it will create a similar revolution in human production and relationships, and in the interpretation of the natural environment. In theory, gigantic enterprises such as Bougainville Copper, the Ramu Hydroelectric Scheme, and the projected Purari industrial complex should have this effect. If this happens, the question will be whether these enterprises must transform Papua New Guineans into yet another version of twentieth century industrial man or whether Papua New Guineans will stamp the enterprises with their own idiosyncratic *nescio quid*. But it is not entirely inconceivable that cargoism will survive even the modern commercial leviathans, especially if they are manned by a limited skilled work force and ordinary villagers are not personally involved. In that case, Dr McSwain's experiences and analysis will have practical meaning for a long time to come.

PETER LAWRENCE
University of Sydney

INTRODUCTION

THIS IS A study of a New Guinea people's social and intellectual system which has remained basically unchanged in a rapidly changing economic and political environment. It investigates specifically whether apparent material progress in response to official schemes of economic, political and educational development indicates the villagers' parallel acceptance and understanding of the concepts upon which such schemes are based.

As Barnett (1953) shows, in situations of change some groups retain much of their old culture, and others almost nothing. Yet examples of persisting traditions abound in the literature on modernization in contemporary societies: Holmberg (1952) records this persistence for the Viru Valley in Peru, Steward (1967) for some African groups, Wolff (1965) for the Malay Peninsula, and Shils (1962) for new states in general. Similarly, a number of scholars have emphasized the limited effects of European contact on fundamental aspects of New Guinea societies. Among them, A. L. Epstein (1969), while acknowledging significant changes in Tolai economic and political institutions, draws attention to continuing traditional structural features and the existence of contemporary cargoism. Salisbury (1970), arguing for the dynamic, changing nature of traditional societies, nevertheless notes that the economic concepts of the Tolai in Vunamani village changed little between the 1880s and the 1960s. Lawrence (1964a) illustrates the persistence of traditional beliefs in his study of cargo cult, as does Worsley to some extent in 1957, but more particularly in the introduction to the second edition of his book (1968). Worsley argues that cargo cult will give way before modern economic achievement and secular political institutions in the near future; Lawrence disagrees, claiming that it will disappear later rather than sooner. But like Moore (1965) in his general study of social change, he contends that economic development is a prerequisite for changed socio-political and intellectual systems.[1]

How relevant are these hypotheses for the situation on Karkar? If one accepts the general Marxist proposition that the intellectual system is part of a superstructure based on the economic system of a society, then as the latter changes, so, allowing for a time lag for the superstructure to catch up with the substructure, the intellectual system can be expected to change. This study indicates that for this to happen, economic change must be far more comprehensive than anything so far inaugurated in Papua New Guinea or suggested by Lawrence's analysis. On Karkar, considerable economic, political and educational change has occurred over a relatively long period, yet the traditional intellectual system remains, leading to a situation of potential frustration among the villagers. As A. L. Epstein (1969: 302) points out for the Tolai, and Finney (1968; 1969) for the Goroka people, agricultural development alone, and even entrepreneurial activities, not only permit traditional values to continue, but actually tend to encourage them.

I suggest, therefore, that to avoid further frustration, the nature and process of economic development be re-examined. Less emphasis should be placed on the extent and greater attention given to the kind of development. Planning should be more sensitive to human needs and aspirations. It should take into account existing systems of harmonious relationships among men and between men and the natural environment, which are customary in Papua New Guinea. In the past, developmental planning has been wasteful both in its efforts to destroy existing traditions and in its failure to achieve people's goals.

My field work on Karkar lasted for about eighteen months between December 1966 and March 1969. Visits in May 1970 and 1972, and from December 1973 to March 1974 brought me up to date with subsequent events which are referred to in the notes at the end of the book. I discuss Karkar generally, but concentrate on Takia, the southern half of the island, and on Marup village, where I lived, in particular. I have relied mainly on Mager (1937) for traditional Waskia culture in the north, comparing it with descriptions given to me by contemporary villagers.

I chose Marup village for detailed study because of its convenient location. Situated in the south-western foothills, it presented opportunities to establish regular contact with both mountain and coastal neighbouring villages. Furthermore, it was in a densely populated area, where pressures of modern development could be expected to appear early. Although I concentrated on Marup, I visited and stayed in villages all around Karkar. This enabled me to generalize at times and to distinguish between certain areas at other times.

Methodologically, there seemed to be two possible frameworks of investigation open to me on Karkar. One was the sociologically-inspired consideration of the major institutions: the economic, political and education systems, their interrelatedness and influence on each other, and the effect of their traditional forms on modern ones. The other was the consideration of society as New Guineans themselves saw it, not as distinct institutions, but as one generalized system within a universe comprising the physical, human and extra-human environment. But through their intellectual system, based on a belief in religious technology and superhuman corporeality, New Guineans see even these broad categories interacting more or less reciprocally with each other. This is clear for Papua New Guinea in general, from the work of such scholars as Fortune (1935), Hogbin (1951), Burridge (1960) and Malinowski (1932), and for the central Madang District in particular, from Hannemann (n.d.; 1934), Mager (1937), Inselmann (1944) and Lawrence (1964a).

Although relevant Administration, mission and planter attitudes and policies are referred to, my main concern was with the villagers' point of view. Hence a methodological framework based on the people's own perception of their world seemed not only fitting, but advantageous. I have, therefore, borrowed from Lawrence's approach to the people of the southern Madang District (1964a) and from his and Meggitt's combined approach to both Highlanders and coastal dwellers (1965).

As Karkar responses to change derive from the people's own traditions and their experience of foreign contact, a historical approach, combined with traditional anthropology's participant-observation field method, seemed to be required for this study. Anthropologists commonly write in the historic present. Here, the value of a logical progression from the past to the present through the historical approach outweighed the advantages of the dynamic qualities that would have resulted from using the present tense. With what is essentially a contemporary final analysis, I could not describe warfare as a current phenomenon, then its demise and its after-effects. Nor could I describe purely pagan beliefs and rituals in this way, when they were replaced by Christian forms, however superficial or syncretic. The only solution was to use the past tense throughout and to emphasize that, apart from the notes at the end of the book, reference is to events up to the end of 1968 only.

In a sense, it is presumptuous to attempt to describe a people's intellectual system without having control over their native language. I depended on Pidgin. But the linguistic situation was in my favour. All but the very old people spoke Pidgin and used it a great deal in ordinary daily life for the following reasons: there was some intermarriage between the two Karkar language

B

groups and between Karkar and the mainland; a high proportion of men had grown accustomed to using it while working away from home; Waskia and Takia participated jointly in many activities, making Pidgin the only means of communication on these occasions. It was mainly the language of cargo cult and the Karkar invariably spoke it in other moments of stress, such as deep anxiety, grief, anger or high oratory, and especially during any violence. In addition, the councillor, his assistant, and the Marup pastor usually addressed people in Pidgin in my presence. Nevertheless, I do not claim that the lingua franca, however second nature it may have been, revealed sensitive areas of knowledge and belief as accurately as the native language would have done.

During my research and in the preparation of this book I have incurred debts to many people in Australia and Papua New Guinea. I owe most to Professor Peter Lawrence, who first aroused my interest in Papua New Guinea when he taught me social anthropology at the University of Western Australia. Later, he suggested a specific area of research, visiting me in the field and giving me invaluable encouragement and advice. At a very personal level, my great debt is to the Karkar Islanders themselves, particularly those of Marup village. Among them, Councillor Kabug Bilag enabled me to attend village events at all levels as well as Local Government Council meetings; Bugou, Kidau and Sumal and their husbands, Toani, Kabug Bangan and Kasek respectively, helped me learn Pidgin and Takia and welcomed me unreservedly into their households. If the true spirit of reciprocity is to be maintained, I shall long be obligated to them for their warmth and affection, humour and integrity. More than that, they introduced me to a life-style for which I have only respect and admiration.

In Australia, Mr E. Wolfers criticized the manuscript in detail and made many extremely helpful suggestions. Mr E. E. Savage, Mrs C. Lee and Mrs Tania Tinney prepared some of the maps, Miss A. K. Eckermann and Mrs J. Moses translated from the German literature, and Mrs D. Pedler and Mrs G. Nossek typed the manuscript.

In Port Moresby, I am indebted to officers of the Department of District Administration for their co-operation and especially to Mr W. Tomasetti for his practical assistance. Mr. Loang Mileng, of the Public Works Department and formerly of Karkar, prepared detailed maps of Marup village and its environs. Madang Administration officers gave me access to official documents, Mr John O'Brien generously sharing his experience of six years' administration on Karkar with me. Mrs Elizabeth Sowerby and the late Mr Roy Sowerby were always hospitable.

On Karkar itself, I received many kindnesses. Administration officers patiently bore with me at meetings of the Local Government Council, co-operative societies and demarcation committees. Mr and Mrs E. Tscharke of the Lutheran Hospital at Gaubin, Mr and Mrs R. Middleton of Kaviak Plantation, Mr and Mrs J. Middleton of Kulili Plantation, and Mr and Mrs W. Lloyd of Dogowan Plantation helped me in practical ways and on many occasions. I am indebted to Mr and Mrs W. Middleton and the late Mr A. Barnett for discussions of early European contact on the island.

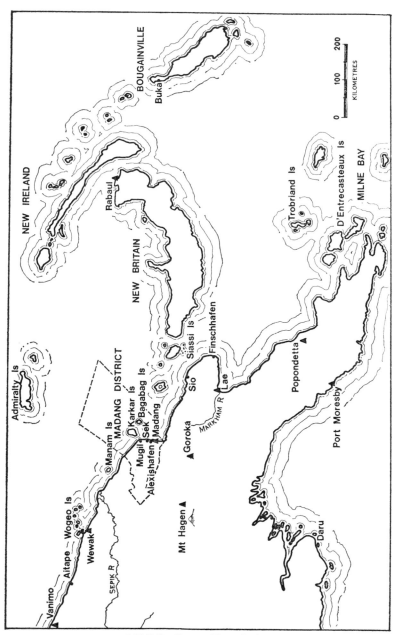

MAP I—Papua New Guinea

KARKAR ISLAND AND THE TRADITIONAL
WORLD VIEW

K ARKAR ISLAND, lying fifty-three kilometres north-north-east of
Madang, is one of a series of volcanoes which has risen above
the sea off the north coast of New Guinea. Roughly eliptical in
shape, it is twenty-four kilometres long and nineteen kilometres
wide, with a perimeter of eighty-eight kilometres and an area of
324 square kilometres. Bagabag Island, nineteen kilometres to the
east, Manam Island, eighty kilometres to the west, and Mugil,
nineteen kilometres away on the mainland across Isumrud Strait,
are its neighbours (Map I). From Madang, Karkar rises purple
and steep from the ocean in a classical pyramidal shape, its peak
wreathed in clouds. Closer, it presents its true colour in lush
green growth tumbling down the slopes and over the coastal
plain to the water's edge. The trees all but hide the villages of
thatched houses, so that, at first glance, the island appears unin-
habited. Yet under this cloak of tranquillity, lives a community
performing its ancient daily tasks and at the same time grappling
with new and disturbing social activities.

The topography of Karkar is a product of its volcanic origins.
The land slopes upwards more or less gently from a narrow
coastal plain and foothills to a height of about 210 metres. Then
the terrain becomes so rugged and steep that above 610 metres it
is largely inaccessible. Roughly in the centre of the island is a
volcanic crater five by four kilometres in diameter, with a base
914 metres above sea level and sheer forest-clad walls over 300
metres from rim to floor (Patrol Report 25, 1960; Cogger 1966:
213). Two small cones, Bagia (after which the crater is commonly
called), and Uluman, rise from the solidified lava floor, but the
largest is an adventive cone on the flank of the main volcano.
This is Mt Kanagioi, which dominates the southern part of the
island at a height of approximately 1,890 metres. Although previous eruptions were severe, the only one in living memory until
1973 was in 1895, when gardens were damaged by falling ash and
one casualty occurred (personal communication from G. A. M.

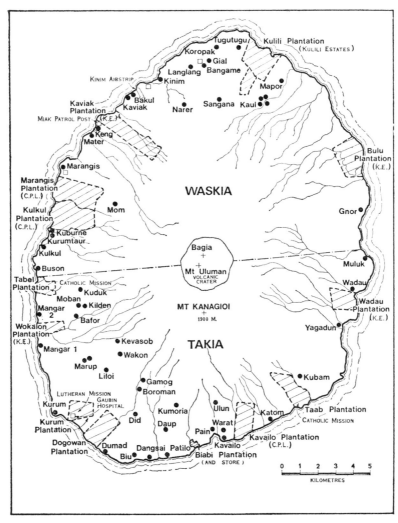

MAP II—Karkar Island showing European Plantations

Taylor). There was considerable volcanic activity in 1973, and tremors are frequent.

The soil on Karkar is very fertile, comprising mostly a friable, dark brown clay loam. It supports primary rain forest on the upper foothills and central mountain area, but vegetation becomes stunted and sparse near the summit. The remaining secondary vegetation on the lower foothills and the coastal plain is rapidly being taken up by subsistence gardens, and European and locally-owned copra and cocoa plantations.

The average rainfall of 3,810 millimetres varies considerably from year to year. The topography and clearly defined wet and dry seasons, accompanied by the north-west (*Taleo*) and south-east (*Rai*) winds respectively, cause micro-climatic variations as well. There is no annual drought period, although 1965 and 1966 were exceptional in that droughts occurred during both these years.[1] Generally the day-time climate is hot and humid. The average daily temperature range is from 21°C to 29°C, with extremes of 18°C to 35°C and significant variations between mountain and coast.

Karkar is inhabited by two language groups: the Melanesian-speaking Takia in the south and the non-Melanesian-speaking Waskia in the north. The 1967 Administration Census gives their numbers as 8,600 and 7,800 respectively.[2] Their territories are roughly equal in area, the boundary running from west to east slightly south of the Waskia villages of Buson and Gnor shown on Map II. Although traditionally interacting only along certain formally defined trade routes, they represent a single fairly homogeneous socio-cultural system. Extensive mission activity, a common Local Government Council and Administration headquarters, and a shared education system, all encourage friendly relations and even intermarriage. A relatively good coastal road encircling the island links thirty-one Karkar villages. It runs through shady plantations, bisecting some coastal villages, where children, chickens and pigs scatter as a vehicle approaches, where friends receive a wave and a shout, and strangers curious stares. At the junctions of rough mountain tracks and the coastal road, villagers often rest, eating betel nut and smoking. Only a few travel on trucks or tractor-trailors, most going in a leisurely manner on foot, enjoying the *camaraderie* and potential excitement of the main road. About 90% of the people are Lutherans and the rest Catholics.

With a few exceptions, the Takia and the Waskia claim their origins, their languages and their characteristic personality differences from two deity brothers. Hannemann (1934: 29) records that the Takia believe themselves to be the children of Kulbob, who, being quick of thought and action, endowed them with their dynamic temperament, their extreme sense of group unity and their 'melodious' language. The Waskia attribute their greater conservatism and 'cumbersome' language to the phlegmatic deity, Manub, from whom they believe they descended.[3] The two peoples themselves made this kind of distinction between their languages: 'Takia', they said, 'lies easy in the mouth and can be learned quickly; Waskia lies heavy and is a difficult language to master'.

Formerly occupying the mountain slopes for security against attack[4] (Mager 1937: 4), the Karkar now live in fifty-nine villages on the rich coastal plain and in the foothills (Map II). Their plantations and subsistence gardens follow the same pattern while the thirteen European and mission-owned plantations hug the coastline. A high natural rate of population increase of 3.43% per annum, with dense concentrations on the north and south-west coasts, plus extensive cash crop planting and land alienation, all contribute to a potentially acute land shortage.

THE TRADITIONAL SOCIAL STRUCTURE AND RELIGION

Traditional social structure, which was identical for Takia and Waskia, was based on ties of kinship, marriage and descent. The people traced their descent, and inherited rights to land, reefs, houses, movable property, magic and ritual, patrilineally.

Karkar society was divided into two great-phratries, one for each language group. These in turn comprised a number of phratries. To use Meggitt's (1965a: 6) terms for the Mae Enga, the great-phratry and phratry were 'categories rather than groups', since neither acted as a corporate body, and hence neither was politically significant. Internal aggression was the norm: even sub-phratries of the same phratry fought to kill, although individual warriors avoided fighting their kindred. The sub-phratry, the genealogical framework of the village, was the widest recognized political unit. It consisted of a number of exogamous patriclans, each comprising several patrilineages.

In Karkar religion, mythology emphasized the value of materialism by explaining the creation of important aspects of the environment and validating the ritual means of communication between humans and superhuman beings by which material goods and physical well-being would be assured (cf. Berndt 1965: 87). By conceptualizing ordinary human social interaction, men maintained a system of quasi-social relationships with deities and spirits of the dead (cf. Horton 1960: 11; Lawrence 1964a: 13).

Traditional religion closely approximated the forms of the southern Madang District (Lawrence 1964a: 1-33) and of the New Guinea seaboard generally (Lawrence and Meggitt 1965: 28-30) in two respects. First, the Karkar believed in a system of reciprocity with superhuman beings: in return for performing ritual and observing taboos, they would achieve success in all activities through divine goodwill. Second, religious beliefs dominated their epistemological system: the deities revealed all knowledge, and sacred rather than technical knowledge was of supreme functional importance (Mager 1937; cf. Hannemann n.d.: 16-22).

A CASE STUDY OF MARUP VILLAGE

The Economy and Social Structure

Contemporary Marup occupies a narrow ridge 1·6 kilometres long and 183 metres above sea level in south-western Takia. It lies between the mountain villages of Kevasob, Wakon and Liloi and the coastal villages of Mangar 1 and Kurum, all from two and a half to three kilometres distant (Map III). Among their fellow islanders, administrators and missionaries, Marup villagers have earned the reputation of being lively, self-confident and quick to involve themselves in new activities. With a population of 864 in 1967, their settlement is the largest in Takia and the second largest on Karkar. The Administration divided it arbitrarily into Marup 1 and 2 for tax collection, but it still appears in census records as one village and has the outward appearance of being so. It comprises 115 houses (many of which are occupied by individual nuclear families), seven trade stores and three bakeries. The road from Marup leads first to the large Lutheran church of Kalul, and thence descends steeply for about one and a half kilometres to the coastal road. Plantations, scattered among secondary forest and subsistence gardens, reach at one point to the sea. A Lutheran Bible school provides some elementary education in the village itself, while, on the coastal road below, a Lutheran central school at Gulfuk and an Administration school at Namau are within easy walking distance (Map III).

Following the usual pattern for coastal New Guinea, the traditional subsistence economy comprised agriculture, pig breeding, fishing, hunting and collecting, and trade. The people also kept dogs and jungle fowl. Above all, they were gardeners, for the rich volcanic soil and favourable climate produced bountiful

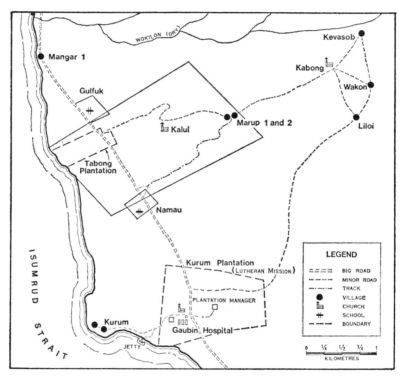

MAP III—Marup Village and Environs

crops and permitted the same ground to be planted at least twice. Their staple was taro *(Colocasia esculenta)* but they also grew yams *(Dioscorea* spp.), sweet potatoes *(Ipomoea batatas)*, sugar cane *(Saccharum officinarum)*, 'pitpit' *(Saccharum edule)*, and various bananas and coconuts *(Cocos nucifera)*. Planted among the food crops were tobacco, pepper vine *(Piper betel)* and betel palms *(Areca* sp.). They reserved pigs, the only domestic animal of importance, for ceremonial purposes, exchanges and trade. Coastal villagers supplemented their diet with fish and crustaceans, and mountain people hunted wild pig, marsupials, certain reptiles, and birds. Because of the rich rewards from collecting bush products, some of the associated activities were formalized. Every large tree (both food producing and otherwise) had its own name and owner, as did gourd vines. When clearing land, gardeners left valued nut and fruit trees standing. Formal and communal arrangements dictated the harvesting and breaking of galip nuts *(Canarium* almond), which were ceremonially and economically important. *Mon, aila, talis* and other nuts, collected casually, staved off hunger during the day. Breadfruit trees provided a useful basis for meals for up to five months of the year, and a great variety of ferns, shrubs, vines, berries, fungi, large insects and grubs found their way into the cooking pots.

The characteristics of economic activity on Karkar were those Stanner associated with New Guinea economies in general:

> (It is) non-individualist and distributive . . . what is by definition 'economic' is inextricably interwoven in the social life of actuality with magic, ceremonial and ritual practices on the one hand and with the discharge of social and kinship obligation on the other. (1953: 7-8, 10).

Roughly equal access to resources and the fact that everyone was expected to perform all tasks kept specialization to a minimum. True, some men were experts in performing ritual, some excelled at carving and manufacturing woven shields and one man in each settlement undertook the removal of pigs' tusks. In Takia, at the village level, Kevasob and Gamog specialized in making fine hand drums and wooden bowls, and Boroman alone produced dogs' teeth ornaments.

Lack of profit motive in the Western sense further encouraged a generalized economy. Dependence on the co-operation and reciprocity of kin and quasi-kin made equivalence in the exchange of goods and services inevitable. This, in turn, safeguarded trade relationships and the highly valued ceremonial and peace links they provided.[5] Ambitious men did envisage profit, but in terms of prestige achieved through display and distribution, and through the extension of social relationships beyond the agnatic or local group. In an environment less competitive than Highlands societies, they nevertheless sought to make political capital out of economic activities (cf. Barnes 1962: 9; Sahlins 1963; Schwartz 1963: 79; Berndt 1964: 183; Harding 1967: 248-50; Finney 1969: 10 and others).

Because of the subsistence basis of the economy and the adequacy of their simple technology for food production,[6] the villagers' needs and desires changed little. To produce beyond these needs when there were no means of storage would have made wasteful inroads on a man's energies and the store of obligations owed him by other people. It would also have put undue stresses on his co-operating group, whose members might consequently have withdrawn their assistance (cf. Sahlins 1963: 293). The fact that people believed in an original extra-human source of all skills and material goods in their finished form plus the relative absence of specialization and profit motive, engendered little tendency for change in the economy. In other words, emphasis on change for its own sake was not built into values about the economy. Change came about so gradually as to be absorbed without stress.

At the broadest level of the social structure, the Marup belonged to the great-phratry coincident with the Takia language group. Locally, they were members of a phratry which comprised the villages of Wakon, Liloi and Marup itself. Their sub-phratry, which, as noted, occupied the village area, divided into five major and three emergent clans. The major clans consisted of two or three lineages each and the emergent clans of single lineages functioning in the same way as clans. War refugees from the former neighbouring village of Medan occupied four houses in Marup, but retained their original clan identity.

Although great-phratry members shared a common putative ancestor, territory and culture, they undertook no joint activities. In fact, warfare within the great-phratry was frequent, but occurred between the two language groups as discrete entities only on the borders where contact, and therefore conflict, were common. Otherwise, Takia men fought the Waskia only at the request of their Waskia trading partners.

A myth of a common male ancestor, called Marup, and of a former common settlement bound the three phratry villages of Wakon, Liloi and Marup in an emotional sense. Cognatic ties brought them together, although not exclusively, for initiation, marriage and mourning ceremonies, pig exchanges, and trade with the coastal villages of Kurum and Mangar. Nevertheless elements of hostility and competition between them were only temporarily contained in fluctuating military leagues and frequently exploded into aggression.

The sub-phratry of Marup derived its solidarity as the widest recognized political group not only from its claim to a common ancestor, its coincidence with the compact village residential area, and its occupation of common territory, but also from a variety of non-agnatic factors. A high degree of endogamy within the sub-phratry led to a dense network of local affinal and matrilateral ties. The Marup acted in concert at pig exchanges with neighbouring mountain villages, in trade with coastal and mainland villages, and as hosts for initiation and other religious ceremonies. Aggression within the sub-phratry was proscribed and relatively harmless methods of protest existed to relieve tensions when they occurred. The only exception to this prohibition was the slaying of men believed to have murdered by sorcery, which custom required to go unrevenged. Against outsiders, the Marup acted corporately as a permanent war-making group, their only consistent military allies being the people of Kurum and Mangar, with whom they regularly traded.

Among Marup's eight clans, there existed a subtle ranking system (cf. Hannemann n.d.: 15) based on their order of emergence, which, according to tradition, is shown in Figure I. The clans of Babu and Lul expressed their seniority in the possession of male cult houses, and outstanding leaders. In other respects, each clan was relatively autonomous and extraordinarily cohesive. Except in the matter of defence, it was the most significant of all descent groups. The Takia word for the clan (and also for its cult house) was *gugoi*, but villagers referred to it familiarly as *nug tain*, meaning the children of brothers. In fact, this was an ideal, since beyond the lineage level, relationships were putative. Consistent use of the name of the clan strengthened identification with it:[7] 'All Lul is going . . . This land belongs to Lul . . . This is where Lul lives . . .' (cf. Meggitt 1965a: 26-7). The customs of the clan expressed its cohesion. Members occupied a common residential area within the village, with men eating and sleeping in the clan men's house, while their wives and children occupied separate houses surrounding it. They held land in common and acknowledged a hereditary peace chief and a war chief. They shared a clan deity, heraldic totem, mythology and ritual.

10

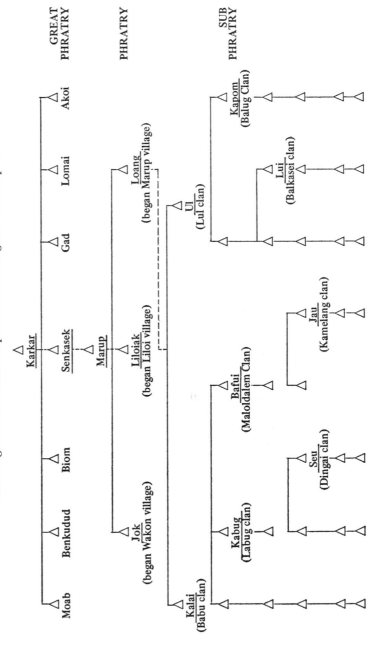

FIGURE I

The Origins of the Takia People and the Emergence of Marup Clans

The clan maintained its unity through the practice of exogamy, patrilineal inheritance and co-operation. Although partners in twenty-five of a sample of 268 marriages in modern Marup 1 broke the rule of exogamy, it seems likely that traditionally, clan exogamy was the rule as it was in the similarly constituted clans in Madang (cf. Hannemann n.d.: 15). I base this conclusion on the fact that people in four of the nine Takia villages where I took genealogies, and in all numerically small clans, considered clan endogamy to be deviant. Certainly everyone subscribed to exogamy as an ideal, by emphasizing the stability of males on patrilineally inherited land and the dispersal of females after marriage. Because they supported uniliny in theory and because intra-clan marriages were a minority, I use the term 'patriclan' rather than 'descent category' or, as Hogbin (1970: 25-6) puts it in reference to the Wogeo, 'cognatic descent group' or 'residents of a housing cluster'.[8]

Clansmen co-operated in amassing food and wealth for the bridal exchange and received the return gifts as a group. They arranged the exchange of women in marriage and acknowledged joint responsibility for the incoming bride and her future offspring through the institution of the levirate. In this case, a man ideally married his older brother's widow and was acknowledged as the progenitor of further offspring (cf. Murdoch 1949: 118).

The ideal and usual pattern of patrilineal inheritance, providing continuity and stability for the patriclan, involved five major categories: rights to residential sites; to land, reefs and canoes; to houses; to movable property and to myths and ritual. A man automatically inherited rights through his father to build a house on lineage land within the clan residential area, to cultivate a section of lineage land within clan gardening land, and to hunt, collect and cut timber on clan bush land. While individuals and the lineage were free to make decisions over the use of their land and to give temporary rights of cultivation and usufruct to others, alienation required the permission of the clan as a whole.

Unlike land, reefs and adjacent fishing waters belonged to the corporate clans of coastal villages. There was no further subdivision into lineage and individually owned areas. One could fish by basket trap in one's clan section, and with spears on any part of the sub-phratry reef. Coastal dwellers inherited rights to send trade goods to the mainland in the big clan-owned canoes.

When a lineage was too small to cope, clansmen co-operated in clearing and fencing gardens, building the men's house, hunting wild pigs and providing food for ceremonial feasts. The clan expressed its uniqueness by not eating its own pigs and validated this custom by placing them in a kind of kinship category. To obtain pigs for their own consumption, big men organized pig exchanges on behalf of their clan members, joining with other Marup clans to exchange with Kevasob and Wakon. In the same way, they traded with mainland villages through their coastal trading partners, upon whom they relied for canoe transport. Most men of consequence inherited trading partners from their fathers but only important traders undertook the journey across Isumrud Strait to the mainland. Since all clans in the sub-phratry participated in overseas trading simultaneously, they were able to take advantage of clement weather and to provide sufficient numbers and goods for impressive feasts and dancing.

Clansmen also co-operated in mourning and initiation cere-monies which were centred on the cult house. Theoretically, the cult house, as its general name *gugoi* suggested, symbolized the clan and its unity. But people described it as 'one house with several doors': as new clans split off, they changed their names but not their allegiance to the parent cult house. In a system comparable to that described by Kaberry (1965-6: 344-5) for the Abelam, the senior clans organized the construction of cult houses, naming them after important ancestor spirits, and per-mitting offshoot clans to use them. Although men helped build them on a multi-clan basis, they used carved totems of men, fish, frogs and birds, representing their own clans, as supporting posts and major roof rafters.[9] Contemporary Marup villagers insisted that these were not ancestor totems but heraldic devices or means of clan identification.

Aggression within the clan was absolutely prohibited. Ideally, clansmen expressed a consensus of opinion on important matters, undertaking joint responsibility for the actions of fellow members and joint revenge for offences against them. There were two kinds of leaders in each clan: a peace chief with hereditary status and a war chief who achieved his position. According to the Takia, the system of inheritance to the office of peace chief was that of agnatic primogeniture. The Marup found inconceivable the possibility that the chief's eldest son might not wish to under-take the position, suggesting, as does Schwartz (1963: 65-6) for the Manus, that his life to this stage had been a process of gradual training, if only by example, for leadership.

The institution of peace chief, validated by his inheritance of clan ritual and sole right of access to the clan deity, contributed to internal harmony (cf. Mager 1937: 19-20) and the Takia called

him *maroltamol*—the man of peace and custom, or *kautamol*—
the man who offered *kau* or lime to his clan's enemies to symbolize his peaceful intent and willingness to mediate over shared
betel nut and lime. Presiding over all recurring peaceful activities
and mediating between clans and villages, he was the most respected man in his clan. As Read says of the Gahuku Gama
leader, he was the 'voice of the group's collective conscience'
(1959: 432). He was superseded only in matters of warfare.

The title of clan war chief in Takia was *yugumulang*—head
of the spear, or *agertamol*—enemy or foe. He achieved his position
by personal expertise, prestige and charisma, in much the way
noted by Barnes (1962: 9) and Sahlins (1963: 289) for New Guinea
leaders or big men generally. Sometimes he opposed the peace
chief, ignoring village mores and acting in a headstrong fashion.
Such behaviour could lead to his deposition by a more powerful
candidate or to his demise by sorcery. In this situation of con-
trasting ascribed and achieved leadership, the peace chief provided stability and some balance to the powers and excesses of the
war chief, while the achieved status of the latter gave scope for
ambitious men to compete for power without endangering the
fundamental unity of the clan.

In connection with the lineage, the eldest able man, by his
seniority and representative functions, was a respected figure and
focal point for lineage members. From both emotional and practical points of view, lineages, especially small ones, were inviol-
able units. Once they became large it was necessary to think in
Fortes' (1967: 7) terms of 'maximal lineages' and 'Major Seg-
ments', with the latter co-operating most closely. All lineages,
despite their uneven growth, expressed their unity in the following ways: they practised exogamy, lived patrilocally and gardened
on lineage land, co-operated in daily tasks, and supported members at all times.

CROSS-LINKING RELATIONSHIPS

Clearly, patriliny was the primary organizing feature of the
descent system, which, at sub-phratry, clan and lineage levels, exhibited a high degree of solidarity through political cohesion, co-
operation and reciprocity. Nevertheless, unilineal groups inevitably interacted with non-agnatic kin, thereby linking one
patrilineal group to another of the same order. When necessary,
they entered into alliances with unrelated persons, frequently by
drawing them into established behaviour patterns as if they were
kin. The Karkar forged such links through marriage and its sub-

C

sequent special kin relationships, adoption and certain kinds of land inheritance, ceremonies (especially those marking *rites de passage*), and trade and military alliances.

MARRIAGE AND ITS SPECIAL RELATIONSHIPS

The best way to approach the role of bilateral kin is through the kinship terminology, which is a variant on the Iroquois type (see Figure II). The variation lies in that ego's cross-cousins of the opposite sex are classed with siblings and parallel cousins of the opposite sex, instead of being distinguished from these categories as are cross-cousins of the same sex.[10]

The Karkar claimed the following three marriage rules as the logical accompaniment of this system: a prohibition on marriage with true and close parallel and cross cousins,[11] the practice of the levirate and the sororate, and the exchange of women.[12]

The effects of these rules were as follows: The prohibition of cross cousin marriage established formal cross-linking ties through a single marriage with more clans than would otherwise have been the case. Since mothers' brothers arranged the marriages of their sisters' offspring, at least four patriclans were intimately involved. The form of the levirate practised gave ego's mother's brother's son *(kol)*, as well as his parallel cousins and siblings, rights over ego's widow. This linked his mother's clan to his own in a particularly complex way. The Karkar envisaged the exchange of women (preferably sisters of the marrying males) as a payment in kind to the incoming bride's clan for rights over her offspring (cf. Reay 1966: 168), and as a double insurance against the possibility of rivalry between patriclans (cf. Lévi-Strauss 1969: 84-93) and future disruption of the marriage. It ensured the safety, status, and well-being of a wife, and the children's membership in their father's clan, in return for similar security for her husband's sister. The exchange was not necessarily made simultaneously but the clans concerned symbolized their goodwill on the occasion of each marriage by the equivalent ceremonial exchange of food and gifts. Even in 1968, the villagers always spoke in favour of woman exchange and opposed any marriages proposed on the basis of a bride-price only.

Initial inter-clan ties forged through marriage were strengthened by important relationships between affines and, in the next generation, non-agnatic kin. These can be traced through by reference to Figure II. Highly formalized behaviour characterized a man's affinal ties with his wife's parents and his wife's brother. He addressed her mother and father only by the formal terms of

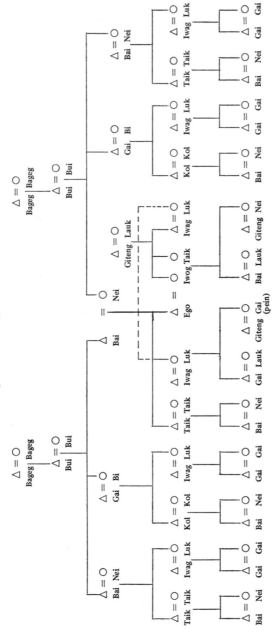

Figure II

Kinship Terminology—Terms of Address

All members of the second generation descending from Ego are Bui.

lauk and *giteng* respectively, and her brother by *iwag*. He showed them great respect and gave them his hospitality, support and protection. Since, by the process of woman exchange in marriage, he and his wife's brother had ideally married each other's real or classificatory sisters, each would support the other's sons in initiation and arrange their marriages. The relationship was therefore a delicate, but strictly symmetrical one. A man's interaction with his children's spouses was simply a reversal of the pattern between him and his wife's parents, with him receiving their respect and assistance.

From affinal links grew important consanguineal ties, the main ones being with a mother's brother (*gai*), mother's brother's son (*kol*) and sister's son (*gai*). As a man's mother's brother behaved towards him during his lifetime, so he, in turn, behaved towards his own sister's son, as the use of reciprocal terms suggest. From the time of a child's birth, his *gai* took a close interest in him, and could, in fact, demand the child as his own if the bride price had not been satisfactorily paid. Usually, the father paid the *gai* a small pig on the birth of the child, and thereafter received reciprocal gifts each time the child achieved some significant social undertaking for the first time. A *gai* exacted immediate obedience from his sister's son, but in return contributed much towards his upbringing, supported him during the rigours of initiation, arranged a suitable marriage, and frequently gave him access to his fruit trees and even permanent rights to some of his land.

The formal respect relation between a man and his *gai* relaxed into a relationship of mutual informal friendship between that man and his *gai*'s son (or his cross cousin). They were initiated together, could marry each other's widows and equated each other's sons under the single term *bai* or son. These sons themselves called each other *taik* or brother and so brought to a close the formality of the initial affinal cross-clan tie, in a classificatory sibling relationship.

Adoption of children from one clan to another also contributed to inter-clan ties since the connection with true parents was always maintained. Adoption had three main functions: to facilitate future marriage arrangements by balancing the number of male and female children, to supply an heir for a childless couple, or to provide a substitute marriage payment for a woman. Although the ideal pattern of adoption was by a child's father's brother, almost twice as many adoptions in Marup traced in 1967, were to mother's brothers in lieu of bride price, the child, as a representative of its father's clan, going in exchange for its mother to her clan.

Similarly, in respect to land tenure, the ideal patrilineal inheritance of rights to land was not always followed. Because of the Karkar concept of personal rights over the use of land, the transfer of rights of usufruct established links of an individual rather than a communal nature. People gave such rights freely, usually to daughters, sisters, and sister's sons to be inherited in perpetuity by their patrilineal heirs. Furthermore, whoever helped a man clear and fence a large garden area could establish a plot of his own in a spot designated by the owner and could return for some years after the main crops were exhausted to harvest bananas and pawpaw.

Alienation of land or the permanent transfer of full personal rights over land was politically far more important than the transfer of rights of usufruct and temporary rights to cultivate because it involved corporate clan groups as donors and receivers and resulted in scattered land holdings. There were three common ways of alienation: giving land to a daughter on her marriage, when it was administered by her husband and ultimately inherited by his sons; giving land to a sister's son, when he might or might not be incorporated into the donor's clan; giving land to a son on his adoption into another clan. Full alienation of land from one clan to another usually occurred only when a payment (token though it may have been) was accepted by the original owners.

The custom of holding land rights in two (or more) clan areas at one time was a powerful incentive for a man to identify with members of both, and a valuable asset in extending social relationships. For emotional as well as practical reasons, people particularly valued ties formed through non-agnatic inheritance.

SPECIAL CEREMONIES

Wider links than those afforded by kinship resulted from joint participation in special ceremonies, and trade and military alliances. Where possible, people based them on existing cognatic and affinal ties. Otherwise they negotiated with non-kindred.

Of all the ceremonies linking otherwise exclusive groups in peaceful celebrations, initiation was the most important. About once every ten years in each village, mature men initiated youths from all clans of the sub-phratry, as well as their cross cousins from neighbouring villages. Although initiates from further afield rarely attended, adult males came from all parts of Takia and beyond. In November 1891, for example, Kunze (1892: 196-207) while in charge of the first Lutheran Mission Station, saw from 2,000 to 2,500 men, including Bagabag Islanders, at the closing initiation ceremonies in nearby Kavailo village. Age mates undergoing this ordeal together established life-long bonds of friendship which cut across those of clan and sub-phratry. Other ceremonies attracting many visitors were those which marked the opening of a new cult house, and the installation of a clan's new slit gong.

Trading on Karkar was of three kinds: between villages of the same linguistic group, between Waskia and Takia, and between Karkar and the mainland. Mountain villagers exchanged vegetables, betel nut and small game for the fish and lime of their neighbours on the coast, and certain specialists, such as the Gamog and Kevasob people, traded their fine wooden bowls locally. Waskia and Takia traded goods common to both areas but with seasonal variations, and Waskia obtained mainland clay pots through south coast Takia middlemen. Most trade with the mainland was for goods for use in ceremonies and, in the case of clay pots, for further exchange in local transactions. Like most Takia villages, Marup traded red, black and white ochres, woven arm bands, dogs, pigs, galip nuts, betel nut and wooden plates and drums to the mainland. Some Karkar also traded elaborate woven shields *(Koloniales Jahrbuch* 1898: 9; *Zeitschrift für Kolonialpolitik* 1904: 858).

The frequent food exchanges between mountain and coast were organized on an individual basis. All other trading combined three levels of negotiation simultaneously between individuals, clans and villages (cf. Barnes 1962: 7). While all men of any status had trading partners or *tisan* (as they were called in Takia) in coastal and mainland villages, the collection of sufficiently large quantities of goods for the annual trading expedition to the mainland, and the arrangement of transport in the coastal villagers' canoes, required communal contributions and communal representation.

The Karkar called the trade route the 'road of peace'. They modelled their trading behaviour along kinship lines[13] and inherited their partners patrilineally, a man's partner standing in the category of brother to him and the partner's son as his own child. This enabled them to operate within a predictable set of rules for personal safety and economic reciprocity. Like the Siassi to the east (Harding 1967), they aimed not to amass profit, but to create and maintain trade relationships and to fulfil social obligations. They sought equivalence in exchange, thereby reducing the possibility of conflict, which might have cut off supplies and hence reduced opportunities for achieving and maintaining prestige. They sent dogs to Malala whence they obtained dogs' teeth, traded for bark cloth when they made their own, and, internally, received galip nuts from mountain partners in return for imported goods: 'We had our own galips', the coastal traders in Biu admitted, 'but it was for trade'! (cf. Harding 1967: 54).

New Guineans generally closely associated economic with military activities (Schwartz 1963: 68-9; Berndt 1964: 183). On Karkar, economic alliances provided the only stable political extensions of the village unit (cf. Berndt 1964: 194-5). Takia units of alliance included both Waskia and Takia trading partners: 'Trading friends were fighting friends', said an old Marup man. 'That is how Waskia and Takia sometimes came to be fighting so far inside each other's territory. When trading partners called, we would go to their help'. Marup's allies were Kuburne in Waskia, and Mangar and Kurum in Takia. Kurum and Mangar also maintained peace with Kevasob, Wakon and Liloi through their economic relationships. Further, like the Waskia, many Takia villages had peaceful relationships with the east coast village of Wadau, whose products, according to legend, were superior to all others.

Apart from these leagues, military contacts were a constantly fluctuating system of alliance and hostility dictated by the exigencies of the moment (cf. Schwartz 1963: 68-9; Brown 1964: 351). Kinship, although an obvious factor for non-aggression, was at variance with a major characteristic of warfare on Karkar: its usual occurrence between neighbours (cf. Berndt 1962: 234; 1964: 193; Brown 1964: 336; Meggitt 1965a: 234). This meant, as Brown points out for the Chimbu (1964: 336, 354), that while the rule of non-aggression toward kin was strictly maintained on a more-or-less individual basis, it was not necessarily practised between descent groups as wholes.

Marup men avoided affines and matrikin during fighting but, as noted, frequently fought fellow phratry members. As with the Tsembaga (Rappaport 1969), joint participation in ceremonies functioned to limit warfare and reduce associated anxieties to some extent, yet these occasions also offered opportunities for making new alliances and permitting the host village to display its strength and unity to outsiders. Therefore, like all contact, it too contained the seeds of strain and subsequent aggression.

Changes in military alliances resulted mainly from three factors: an understanding that an alliance be maintained only long enough for the instigator of an attack to reciprocate with assistance to his partners in military undertakings of their own; an increasing population pressure on land and reef resources (cf. Brown and Brookfield 1959: 42; Meggitt 1965a: 256) which induced intolerance of what might otherwise have been minor irritations; and an egalitarian dislike and fear of one village becoming more powerful than the others (cf. Read 1959: 429; Berndt 1964: 193).

When the Germans initiated the *pax Germanica*, they crystallized the existing land distribution, enabling some villagers to continue to prosper economically, leaving others to suffer deep resentment over losses they were henceforth forbidden to redress, and sentencing yet others to an unenviable future as unwanted, landless refugees in neighbouring villages.

So comprehensive were the gains and losses in warfare experienced by some villages, that I suggest that consistent success or defeat helped shape the modal personality and general characteristics of political groups. It is conceivable that the self-confidence of the Marup people, as well as their large population, resulted in part from three aspects of warfare: feelings of security arising from their last overwhelming victory just before the Lutheran missionaries arrived and the fact that they appear never to have experienced defeat (cf. Berndt 1964: 200); the rich land they had acquired; and their successful peace negotiations with the vanquished owners.

To sum up, while the people's ideology of their society was one of unadulterated patriliny, in fact, Karkar society operated on a recognizable agnatic core with minor modification. Individuals extended their network of relationships by means of strong secondary affiliation to their matrikin, formalizing their interaction with their affines, and creating permanent and temporary alliances with unrelated groups. The manner in which they increased and took advantage of their personal non-agnatic ties fitted Barnes' (1962: 8) term, 'New Guinea network cohesion'. (See also Brown 1962; Kaberry 1967, and de Lepervanche 1967). But, as Schwartz (1963: 68-9) warns for the similarly structured society of the Admiralty Islands, the formal and essentially unilineal nature of the social organization should not be underestimated. Although the Karkar had a cognatic network like, for example, the Garia, it was very different from the essentially cognatic Garia structure. Even their unrelated trading partners were incorporated as pseudo-agnates to enable a broader set of relationships to be usefully incorporated into society than those dictated by marriage and descent.

Social Control

Social control among the Takia was broadly typical of the general Papua New Guinea system (cf. Malinowski 1926; Read 1950, 1955; Burridge 1957 and Lawrence 1965-6, 1969), in which mechanisms for social control were built, not into offices of leadership, but into the broader social system through religious beliefs, processes of self-regulation (cf. Nadel 1953) and self-help or retaliation. Earlier accounts of social control describe leaders as having no permanent, effective means of enforcing conformity or punishing deviance. Religious sanctions were both positive and negative: ideally mythology ensured conformity through validating the existing social order and ritual means of communication between men and deities (cf. Fortes and Evans-Pritchard 1940:11; Nadel 1953: 267; Berndt 1965: 79-98; Meggitt 1965a: 25, and 1965b: 108). It also carried moral injunctions about proper conduct (Berndt 1965: 82; Lawrence and Meggitt 1965: 16). On the negative side, the deities and ancestor spirits punished offences against the religious code such as performing incorrect ritual or ignoring taboos, by causing crops to fail or inflicting sickness, deformity and even death (Lawrence 1965-6: 381 and 1969: 26). The only religious offence in which men intervened was where a woman or child observed the ritual or paraphernalia of the male cult, for which the punishment was said to have been death.

In respect to offences against human beings, social control was a secular matter: self-regulation, learnt through socialization, encouraged acceptance of social values and mores. It was based on reciprocity arising from self-interest, which dictated the content of positive, face to face relationships. Self-interest gave rise to feelings of moral obligation towards those with whom one interacted regularly. Shame and fear of public criticism operated to maintain such obligations where they were most pertinent within the framework of the sub-phratry, clan, lineage, kindred and trade alliance. The more distant and less frequent the interaction, the less compelling these sanctions were.

Retaliation enabled the rehabilitation of offenders through the payment of compensation (Nadel 1953: 271), and the release of tensions against outside aggressors through revenge, usually in the form of a blood feud. Like self-regulation, its extent and degree varied according to the effective social ties, based on kinship, marriage and trade, between the disputants (Read 1955). Thus intralineage quarrels, which would seriously affect customary close co-operation, were speedily resolved through the mediation of close kin, and the *status quo* restored by the payment of compensation. Mutual kin of the protagonists usually achieved a similar result in intra-clan disputes so that peaceful reciprocal relationships could be resumed. On the other hand, inter-clan dissension, sometimes involving disputants who were not related to each other, was more difficult to overcome and called for the intervention of kin neutral to both parties, and mediation on the part of clan leaders. Quarrels between members of different or remote settlements usually resulted in violence which often took the form of a lengthy blood feud. Since these groups did not come into frequent, close contact, it was not imperative that peace be quickly restored, and it was less likely that there were neutral kin to mediate.

The Takia social control system conformed fairly closely to this general pattern, except in respect to leadership. Its dual leadership organization, described earlier, resembled that of the Tolai (cf. Salisbury 1964: 225-6) in that hereditary peace chiefs, like the *lualua*, were clan heads who concerned themselves with peaceful activities, and war chiefs, like the Tolai *luluai*, were aggressive, ambitious men, who achieved positions of power and influence by violence and personal skill. Peace chiefs sometimes carried their influence beyond their own clans and sub-phratries, as successful arbitrators able to achieve a consensus of public opinion (cf. Read 1959). On the other hand, war chiefs, while they could achieve personal control over several or all of the clans of a sub-phratry, were unable to develop an inter-village following because of the unstable nature of military alliances and the uncertainty of tenure of office caused by their own frequently ruthless efforts at despotism which led their own followers ultimately to depose them. As among the Tolai, people regarded them with a mixture of fear, disapproval and admiration. On Karkar then, leaders do seem to have achieved a measure of authority, although it was accompanied by few special privileges and did not truly extend into the judicial field.

In common with other peoples of the Madang District, the Karkar feared religious sanctions and severely punished unauthorized observance of *barak* or secret male cult activities, to the extent, the Waskia claim, of wiping out entire villages. In their practice of self-regulation, self-interest over-rode even sibling ties: 'If my brother worked with me, I helped him', said a Marup clan leader. 'If he was a lazy man, he was not my brother'. Reciprocity was a complex matter, involving appreciation of what Nadel (1953: 267) calls focal or multivalent activity, upon which a series of other important relationships depended. Thus, a man reciprocating with his wife's brother simultaneously maintained obligations to him as his sister's husband, and as the major figure in his own son's initiation and marriage arrangements. Finally, the idea of disharmony and retaliation occurring within the lineage so appalled the modern Takia that they denied its very possibility. They emphasized the influential role of the peace chiefs when offences occurred between clan members and between clans of the sub-phratry. In the latter case clan members assuaged their anger by lining up in clans and, at a given signal, hurling spears once at each other amid great shouts. The prohibition on violence was so crucial for the political survival of the sub-phratry that, when an offence did occur, it was usually by devious means. For example, in Marup, members of Babu clan, plotting to annex land from Labug clan, persuaded their matrikin in Kevasob village to ambush Labug and kill its leaders. Demoralized, Labug acceded to Kevasob's demands for land which, according to the agreement, was later handed over to Babu. The instigator of this plan, Babu's war chief, Sob, was notorious for his violent interference in village matters. Hence his death, presumed to be by sorcery, soon afterwards. At phratry level and beyond, retaliation was openly violent, being either in the form of blood feud or outright warfare and often with the ulterior motive, as mentioned, of gaining new territory.

Religion

The Karkar envisaged extra-human beings as being present in their immediate environment and their relationships with them as permeating all their endeavours. For the sake of convenience in discussing them, however, I separate this interaction artificially from other social institutions under the label of religious beliefs and practices.[14]

RELIGIOUS BELIEFS

Karkar mythology postulated the existence of deities, spirits of the dead, and fiends alongside humans in the physical universe. Some deities were creative, some protective, and others regulative. Pragmatists as they were, the people were little concerned with the creation of their physical world, but with factors of current material significance to them. They did not bother to examine contradictions within their belief system and hence were able to hold two main sets of creation myths simultaneously. In the first, the major creator deities, as mentioned earlier, were Kulbob and Manub, the progenitors of the Takia and Waskia respectively.[15] Born in Takia, Kulbob lived at Urit near Kavailo and Manub at Bangpat near Patilo. After Manub's wife inveigled Kulbob into committing adultery with her, Kulbob incurred his brother's violent anger. He avoided being murdered through a series of adroit manoeuvres which humiliated and aggravated the dour Manub. Myths about these conflicts emphasized the superior physical appearance, skills, wit and charm of Kulbob and the clumsy, imitative efforts of Manub (Hannemann n.d.).[16] After the brothers quarrelled they left Karkar. But Kulbob sailed first, with his sister Kamgi, to the village of Wadau on the east coast, where he left his gifts of food crops, and house- and canoe-building skills. He continued eastwards to Bagabag Island and thence to Madang, where he created the mountains and the offshore islands. He made his way along the Rai Coast to Tami Island and thence to Siassi and probably to New Britain. Manub sailed along the north-west coast. As each travelled, he created people and distributed his characteristic goods, skills and languages, thus creating the cultural and linguistic variations to be found along the mainland coast. People believed that neither Kulbob nor Manub returned.[17]

The second series of creation myths refers to the origin of modern man on Karkar. It is similar to one Hannemann (n.d.: 14) relates for the Yam of Madang. People claim that long ago, a tidal wave or a flood covered Karkar. It was followed by a volcanic eruption which few of the inhabitants survived. Then the first ancestor, a being called Karkar, arrived, or came into existence on the island, marking the transition from superhuman to human ancestors (cf. Burridge 1965: 242). As the Takia put it: 'He was close to being like us'. Because of his partly mortal state, the people felt that they could claim reasonably precise descent from him (cf. Meggitt 1965a: 6). His descendants spread out and populated Takia and probably Waskia. The genealogy in Figure I refers in particular to Senkasek, from whom Wakon, Liloi and Marup phratry members claimed descent. It illustrates the segmentation that resulted in modern Marup clans.

Two non-creative deities, Misken and Kaulok, lived in or near the crater Bagia, the ultimate home of spirits of the dead.

They appeared in a variety of forms to men crossing the mountain, with Kaulok favouring the guise of a large, bony rooster. They were guardians of the ancestors' home and warned travellers when a death had occurred in their villages during their absence.

A third category, also non-creative, but vitally important, consisted of the clan deities and the sub-phratry war god. Clan deities lived in pools, springs, large trees and rocks in the bush or sea. In Marup, Keng of Labug clan, pointed out the large stone where his clan's deity dwelt on a point of land overlooking the sea. Its goodwill ensured success in all economic activities, such as gardening, pig-rearing, canoe building, and trading. Each sub-phratry had its own war god which lived in a spring or pool.

Ancestor spirits were mainly protective. Mangar villagers described them as follows: everyone had two spirits, *buga* and *ngutun*.[18] In life, *buga* was incorporated into a man's shadow and visited other people in dreams (Hannemann n.d.: 18; Kunze 1897; Mager 1952: 44; cf. Burridge 1965: 244; Lawrence 1965: 207; Valentine 1965: 166). After death, it remained in the village concerning itself with the activities of its descendants. *Ngutun* was soul substance which people believed adhered to anything that belonged to a person or had been in contact with him (Mager 1952: 225). After death, it proceeded to Bagia, or, in the case of some coastal villages such as Mangar, to the mainland. As among the Yam and Amele people, whose ancestors were conceived to live east of Saidor and Erima respectively, this in no way interrupted their communication with the living (cf. Lawrence 1964a: 24 fn. 2): the success of important religious ceremonies, particularly initiation, depended upon their presence and co-operation.

As an adjunct to the powers of clan deities, ancestor spirits contributed to the health, strength and fertility of humans, animals and crops, and to the safety of their living descendants during trading journeys or warfare. *Buga* sometimes played the role of tricksters, appearing in human form to tease relatives with whom they stood in joking relationships in life. They were known to be *buga* by the peculiar greasy condition of the skin and by the whistling sounds they made. If offended, they showed their displeasure by withholding their protection from their descendants and by inflicting sickness or even death upon these descendants' enemies.

Two other kinds of beings, which I group under the heading

of fiends, lived on Karkar. The first, inhabiting dark swamps or rocks on dangerous reefs, were constantly evil, and people avoided them at all costs. The other beings were the *wargumargum*. Although Hannemann describes them as 'monstrosities, the embodiment of evil', modern villagers insisted that they were small, timid creatures, half animal and half man. They lived harmlessly on the upper mountain slopes, existing on uncooked possums and stolen pawpaw.

The Karkar performed no ritual to the creator deities, whose work was completed and who had, in any case, sailed away. They feared the guardian deities of Bagia but, since these were concerned with spirits of the dead only, they merely observed taboos of respect and silence and, if possible, avoided their dwelling place. To spirits of the dead, they showed the simple courtesies of observing correct burial rites, inviting them to the ceremonies and feasts of all their *rites de passage*, leaving food and other gifts on their graves, and respectfully asking for their protection. Each cult house (or *gugoi*) of the secret male cult was named after one of these beings. Apart from wearing sweet-smelling leaves to ward off danger, people practised no ritual in connection with fiends: harmful fiends were inherently evil, and the *wargumargum* aroused no anxiety. However, they conceived the goodwill of the clan deities and war god to be crucial to their existence. By the rule of reciprocity they expected their material welfare to be guaranteed in return for the performance of correct ritual and the observance of taboos.

Although varying from village to village, forms of ritual were all believed to have derived from Kulbob. At planting time, the peace chief of Labug clan would call all clansmen together at night near the stone called Tabong where their clan deity lived. He burnt dry coconut fronds at its base and whispered a spell. The following morning, he planted the first taro and afterwards others could follow suit. Without these initial observances, planting was believed to be in vain.

Ritual for success in war belonged to the sub-phratry as a whole, being taught to boys during initiation. War chiefs performed the major ritual which, in Marup, consisted of visiting the war god's pool or spring, reciting an esoteric formula, and throwing some of the water in the direction from which the enemy would come. This was believed to cause the ground to shake and the attackers to be repelled.

Some Takia men claimed that the ancestors obtained knowledge of contagious and sympathetic magic from their mainland trading partners, who had received it from their deities. Its divine source accounted for its power. The practice of contagious and sympathetic magic lacked the concept of reciprocity inherent in relationships with deities and spirits of the dead. Since the aim was to influence humans secretly through the agency of impersonal occult forces, it gave rise to anxiety and suspicion. There were two general categories of magic: *baz pau*, which had no evil connotation and comprised such things as love magic and magic for rain, and *naiz pau*, which was harmful to humans and can be labelled sorcery. Knowledge of them could be inherited from parents or bought. The Waskia people performed love magic by making incantations over a mixture of discarded betel nut (containing the *ngutun* of the victim), tobacco, coconut oil and a small insect. This was then given to the desired person to smoke. The Takia mixed ginger with the same ingredients, placing it on a path where the object of their attentions would have to step over it. The technique for sorcery was manipulating human refuse. Kunze relates how the sorcerer '. . . picked up all things lost, made a fine thread of it, invisible to the human eye, and bound the soul of that person who had thrown it away or lost it. The bound person then had to die' (1925: 35).

KARKAR VALUES AND EPISTEMOLOGY

As in other societies in New Guinea, both coastal (Lawrence 1965: 214-21) and Highlands (Berndt 1965: 93-4; Bulmer 1965: 156-7), Karkar religion related to basic aspects of the social structure and to the community's main problems (cf. Hogbin 1958: 71, 163). As we have seen, the people served the important value of materialism through the practice of reciprocity, equivalence and co-operation or communalism. Kin groups and the wider network of relationships provided a framework within which these concepts worked, and were themselves maintained by them. On the one hand, religion supported the social values through myth and ritual. On the other, it provided an intellectually satisfying explanation of those areas of life which induced anxiety, by postulating the divine source of all knowledge.

Mythology stressed the value of materialism in two ways: it described the deities' roles as creating material goods and guarding the physical welfare of the people, and it contained the divinely inspired ritual, by which human beings could obtain these benefits. The villagers believed that the performance of correct ritual obliged the deities to reciprocate favourably, and that incorrect ritual meant failure in important undertakings.

This belief validated existing general values of co-operation and equivalence.

The epistemology, derived from mythological explanation of the physical and social environment, served to inspire further confidence in the social system. Briefly it was this: all knowledge derived from Kulbob and Manub. They alone created the material and the non-material culture and gave it to the ancestors in its completed form. New knowledge could be obtained only through dreams or revelations, or by purchase, but not through human intellectual enterprise. In a limited sense, the deities made provision for individual decision-making (cf. Firth 1951: 61): men could decide when and where to plant gardens, whether to plant extra crops for feasts or to depend on clan members for donations, and whether they should undertake the arduous work necessary to compete for 'bigmanship' or the role of war chief. Within this range of choice, there were only two general kinds of activities, sacred or ritual and technical. Both were gifts of the deities and together they were necessary in every undertaking. But secular technology, informally acquired, was, as noted, useless without ritual. 'True knowledge' was the ability to perform ritual to the relevant superhuman beings to ensure automatic success (cf. Lawrence 1964a: 30-3 and 1965: 217).

In the favourable physical environment of Karkar, most ritual appeared to achieve the required results. Only in warfare was failure inevitable for one group of participants and people blamed incorrect performance of ritual for this. In spite of changing human actors, limited opportunities for individual choice resulted in the epistemology remaining constant: all knowledge had a divine source, and for material success, man had to address himself to this source.[19]

2

THE HISTORY OF EUROPEAN CONTACT

FROM 1885 the people of the central Madang District were exposed to the impact of Western culture with its significantly different form, functions, values and beliefs. The implicit European concept of society was, of course, one of institutional, individual specialization and centralized authority: Europeans saw the economic, political, and religious systems as discrete entities;[1] individuals involved themselves in only one aspect of the economy and acknowledged a hierarchical system of control. The fundamental value was still materialism, but based on empiricism and influenced by inbuilt social pressure for change and expansion. A largely secular orientation divided sacred from technical knowledge, and emphasized the causal role of human intellectual effort.

Each agent of contact, Administrations, missions and planters, had its own emphasis, goals, and what the villagers saw as a relatively superior way of life. There were eight successive Administrations:[2] the colonial Administrations, consisting of the German New Guinea Company (1885-99), the Imperial German Administration (1899-1914), the Australian Military Administration (1914-21), and the Australian Mandate Administration (1921-42), each mainly supported policies facilitating outright economic exploitation:[3] ANGAU[4] (1942; 1944-45) and the Japanese Command (1942-44) were preoccupied with military matters. The Australian Provisional Administration (1945-49) concentrated on bridging the period between the folding up of the Military Administration and the return to civilian government. The Australian Trusteeship Administration, which succeeded the Provisional Administration on 1 July 1949, set out to atone for previous colonial policies through progressive development programmes.[5]

The Lutheran and Catholic Missions began work in the area in 1887 and 1904 respectively and on Karkar in 1890 and 1930. They restricted their activities almost entirely to religious and educational change. German planters came in 1892 and had their heyday from 1905 to 1914, exploiting land and labour for their own economic goals.

Because the Karkar were inevitably influenced by events in the mainland Madang District, I begin this chapter with an outline of European contact there until the 1950s or the beginning of local development programmes.

EUROPEAN CONTACT IN THE CENTRAL MADANG DISTRICT (1885-1952)

Administrations

In the economic field, the German New Guinea Company carried out an energetic policy of European plantation development, exploiting indigenes as cheap labour and alienating much land under questionable circumstances. The Imperial German Administration tried to ameliorate the crudeness of this programme by planning indigenous participation in the cash crop economy, reforming labour laws and supporting existing land laws. Nevertheless, heavy labour demands, supported by the imposition of a head tax and land alienation, continued and were the presumed causes of revolts in Madang in 1904 and 1914. The Germans retaliated by exiling the Madang people and confiscating their land.

The Australian Military Administration repatriated German officials, but allowed planters to remain in the interests of the economy. The effect of this was that the planters interpreted German law under which the colony still functioned. Inevitably, this favoured further European expansion at the expense of the recently formulated German development plans. The succeeding Australian Mandate Administration, depending for its budget entirely upon royalties from copra and gold, also favoured European commercial interests. It expropriated German properties and sold them to Australian ex-servicemen, and imposed a head tax of $1 on all adult males, except indentured labourers, mission students and workers, and village headmen. In the interests of the villagers, it placed some limitations on further land alienation.

Representatives of both ANGAU and the Japanese provided little more than wartime caretaker administration. The Australian Provisional Administration, which eventually became the Australian Administration under the Trusteeship Agreement of the United Nations Organization, combined with the Administration of Papua to receive an annual subsidy from the Australian Government. This allowed the implementation of schemes which dependence on local revenues would never have permitted. In 1952, economic development policy began.

The Imperial German Administration extended its political control through pacification patrols and appointing headmen or *luluais* over groups of villages, with *tultuls*, men who were fluent in Pidgin, to assist them.[6] By 1919, legislation had banned all flogging but Field Punishment No. 1, which consisted of tying offenders up by the thumbs, could still be applied in serious cases with the permission of the Administrator. In 1922 all disciplinary punishment by employers was prohibited. After 1921, the Australian Administration appointed *luluais*, *tultuls* and medical *tultuls* to each village brought under control, and a salaried paramount *luluai* to some areas. It prohibited recruitment of more than one-third of village adult male populations, and set up a District Court and a Court for Native Affairs, with provision for indigenous representation. After 1945, the Provisional Administration and later the Trusteeship Administration and the Australian Government drew up plans to include New Guineans on the proposed Legislative Council in Port Moresby and to establish local government councils with elected councillors. The first Council (Ambenob) was proclaimed in 1956 and Karkar followed in 1958.

The first Administration school in Madang opened in 1941 only to be closed a year later after the beginning of the Japanese war. Post-war plans for a system of primary and later secondary schools began to bear fruit in 1952.

Missions

The Lutheran Mission, with headquarters since 1946 in Lae and administered by the American Lutheran Church, was an amalgamation of the Rhenish and Neuendettelsau Missions. The Catholic Society of the Divine Word established a bishop's seat at Alexishafen. Each mission divided its area into congregations under the supervision of European missionaries, with the Lutherans delegating responsibility for congregational affairs to councils of elders, in accordance with their plan for establishing an independent Lutheran Church of New Guinea. The Evangelical Lutheran Church of New Guinea, known as ELCONG, came into being in 1956.

Apart from alienating large areas of land for plantations, the missions avoided disrupting the traditional economy. On the socio-political side, lay missionaries could administer corporal punishment to workers until 1915, while indigenous teachers and evangelists often wielded considerable power. Official policies restricted interference by missionaries in traditional social customs to seeking to prevent sexual offences and sorcery.

The Administrations encouraged missions to assume responsibility for the colony's education programme. By 1942, all large Lutheran villages had a teacher and an evangelist in charge of the school and church, while in Catholic villages the catechist ran both. Each mission had a central secondary school, the Lutherans including carpentry and mechanical work in their courses. Here, teaching was in English, but the Lutherans used Graged (the language of the Yam people of Madang) and the Catholics used Pidgin in all their other schools. This monopoly over secular and spiritual education brought considerable power and prestige to the missionaries. They re-established their institutions after the Japanese war.

Planters

As noted, the need to support the planters determined the Administrations' exploitative economic policies. By introducing Western goods, planters created new needs which, with tax pressures, forced the villagers into economic relationships with them. Their political significance lay in their consolidation of European control near their plantations and their powers of trial and punishment. These powers fostered the European belief in inherent indigenous inferiority, which led to the unsatisfactory race relations still existing in 1950 (Lawrence 1964a: 60; cf. Hastings 1969: 105 and *passim*).

EUROPEAN CONTACT ON KARKAR (1885-1968)

The relative isolation, compactness, and high economic potential of Karkar resulted in somewhat different aspects of contact being emphasized from those Lawrence (1964a) describes for the mainland Southern Madang District. His main concern is with the impact of Administrations and missions, although he includes planters in a general way in connection with land alienation and race relations. With the missionaries, the planters on Karkar occupied a position of power and status overshadowing by far that of the Administrations. Only after 1950 did the Administration approach them in importance when it began implementing progressive policies. From this time onwards the clear distinction between Administration influence and the response of some villagers is difficult to maintain, since indigenous officials took increasing responsibility in Administration-inspired programmes. This was one of the major features distinguishing contact during the colonial period before 1950 from that during the period from the 1950s to 1968 when the Government introduced programmes to foster development.

Administrations

THE ECONOMIC FIELD

The economic field was crucial for all later development. Like the mainland Southern Madang District, Karkar experienced eight colonial Administrations, although with considerably less personal impact. Indentured labour and land loss characterized the first four Administrations' economic policies; *Deutsches Kolonialblatt* (1905) reports the recruitment of Karkar men before 1905 but gives no figures. Four Karkar properties listed by the Custodian of Expropriated Property in 1926, plus an estimated 198 hectares controlled by the Lutheran Mission, amounted to 1,422 hectares of land alienated by 1921 (Table I). Like many grants made at the outbreak of war, titles for Karkar plantations were not finalized (cf. Mackenzie 1942: 277). Lyng, the Australian Military Administrator in Madang, describes adjudicating in a dispute between two Germans at Kavailo who '. . . had not acquired any right to the land upon which the plantation stood' (1925: 76). Nevertheless, under expropriation procedure, three properties, Kavailo, Marangis and Kulkul, reported to be surveyed but not entered in the German Ground Book, were granted title and sold as freehold (cf. Rowley 1958: 28) ostensibly to Australian ex-servicemen, but possibly to 'dummies' for the company of W. R. Carpenters Pty Ltd (cf. Rowley 1967: 80). Mr W. M. Middleton, an ex-serviceman and a member of the Expropriation Board, bought the fourth, Kulili, on a ninety-nine year lease.

As elsewhere, the Mandate Administration's head-tax forced the Karkar into indenture. They worked mainly on local plantations and, until 1931, in New Britain where labour was in great demand (cf. Epstein 1968: 58). Then, because of heavy labour demands from local settlers, and concern over the absence from their homes of many villagers, the Administration restricted recruitment of the Karkar to work on their own island *(Annual Report* 1931-2), but withdrew this limitation the following year. Alienation of a further 1,359 hectares of land after 1921 brought the area under European control to approximately 2,781 hectares.

Leasehold title only was granted for the six new plantations. In 1937 the Administration closed the island to further alienation.[7] It also required every villager to plant sixty coconut palms for home use.

When the Japanese bombed Madang in January 1942, the settlers left Karkar and the plantation economy lapsed. The

TABLE I

*Land Alienated to European Planters and Missionaries**

Name of Plantation	Area alienated before 1921	Area alienated after 1921	Name of current owner
Kurum	198 hectares		Lutheran Mission†
Kavailo	202 hectares (approx.)		Coconut Products Ltd (Carpenters Ltd)
Kulkul	400 hectares		Coconut Products Ltd (Carpenters Ltd)
Marangis	350 hectares	26 hectares	Coconut Products Ltd (Carpenters Ltd)
Kulili	272 hectares	107 hectares (approx.)	Middleton Family (Kulili Estates)
Bulu		200 hectares	Middleton Family (Kulili Estates)
Kaviak		336 hectares (approx.)	Middleton Family (Kulili Estates)
Wadau		150 hectares	Middleton Family (Kulili Estates)
Wokalon		90 hectares	Middleton Family (Kulili Estates)
Dogowan		209 hectares	A. Barnett (W. Lloyd Manager)
Tabel		27 hectares	Catholic Mission
Taab		207 hectares (approx.)	Catholic Mission
Biabi		7 hectares (approx.)	N. Goodyear
TOTALS:	1,422 hectares (approx.)	1,359 hectares (approx.)	

GRAND TOTAL: 2,781 hectares (approx.)

* These figures are from the records of the Custodian of Expropriated Pro-perty (1926) and from Karkar Island Noting Map and Surveyor's Charts, Valuer General's Branch, Department of District Administration, Port Moresby.

† A further thirty-seven hectares (approx.) have been alienated to the Lutheran Mission and ELCONG at Anul, Narer, and Kulbob, and the Mission has numerous small blocks of land scattered about the island.

Japanese arrested the three Lutheran and Catholic missionaries in April and May 1943 and sent them to Alexishafen. Some fifty soldiers occupied the island. They made heavy demands on the people for food and labour for themselves, and for the Japanese in Madang, but otherwise did little harm. The real damage to the island was done by the Allies after the Japanese withdrawal in March 1944 (Dexter 1961: 807). After heavy strafing and bombing, members of the 37/52 Australian Infantry Battalion landed at Bison Bay with five ANGAU officers on 2 June. These officers distributed food rations, and began medical patrols and building and planting programmes. They recruited 35% of the men to work on local European plantations under the supervision of the Production Control Board,[8] at the army sawmill set up on Dogowan plantation, or in Lae or Jacquinot Bay in New Britain with the Allied armies.[9]

The post-war Administration concentrated on rehabilitation rather than on indigenous development.[10] Short term benefits to the Karkar included the payment of $8,608 to 1,409 claimants of war damage compensation and of lump sums in wages to recruited labourers returning from two years' work with ANGAU.

From its succession on 30 October 1945, the Provisional Administration made efforts to plan the implementation of broad development programmes in the economy, in politics, education and health. But apart from fair success in getting the Commonwealth Reconstruction Training Scheme under way, it was not until 1950-51 that encouraging results began to appear in any number throughout Papua New Guinea. For Karkar, however, this was a period of unfulfilled promises: the proposed Commonwealth Reconstruction Training Scheme, although recommended there, never began (Patrol Report 1. 1946-47); nor was there any sign of other improvements; for the first time an official report (Patrol Report 1948) commented on the inhibiting effects of European employment and European expansion on village development, but a recommendation for the appointment of a Native Projects Manager to train promising individuals failed.

The year 1952 marked the beginning of tremendous changes on Karkar. It was three years after the Provisional Administration was superseded by the Trusteeship Administration. An increase in the annual subsidies from the Commonwealth Government and certainly unrest in the form of numerous small cargo cults on the island itself led to the introduction of the development plans designed in 1945-46. The Administration based its economic programme on copra and cocoa production, encouraging interest through the introduction of co-operative societies (1952), organized planting (1959), land demarcation (1966), and a loan service through the Papua New Guinea Development Bank (1967).

In 1952, a co-operatives officer seconded from the Administration established nine native societies on Karkar. Renamed co-operative societies by ordinance in 1965, they were members of the central Madang Association of Native Societies, known as MANS. With their buying points scattered around the coast, the societies were to buy and market copra from village coconut palms. Cocoa production, being too low to warrant building fermentaries for indigenous producers alone, was sold to European planters. The Madang Association trained clerks in simple buying and book-keeping procedure. Later, as well as buying copra, these men opened sixteen retail society stores. At first, the Karkar co-operatives achieved great success but, in 1963, they began to decline. In spite of the appointment of a resident indigenous officer in 1964, they ceased to operate in December 1968.[11]

Until 1959, the Administration discouraged people from planting cocoa because of problems of disease and pests. That year a resident agricultural officer arrived to organize and supervise both coconut palm and cocoa planting, which had previously been carried out in a haphazard fashion. At first, cocoa growers had to register to ensure regular inspection, but by 1956 widespread and extensive planting and adequate supervision made this unnecessary.

The strain the expanding plantation economy placed on land resources produced a spate of disputes during the 1950s. Consequently, Waskia and Takia were gazetted as adjudication areas for demarcation under the Land Titles Commission Ordinance of 1963-65. 'The ultimate objective was to introduce a single system of land holding . . . providing for secure individual registered titles after the pattern of the Australian system' (Hasluck in *Parliamentary Debates* 1960: 1021). The people had three alternatives: to continue holding land by customary tenure, to register communally-held land with the Registrar of Titles, or to apply to have land converted from customary tenure to individual registered title. Demarcation committees for each adjudication area comprised a presumably impartial chairman from the neighbouring language group, a vice-chairman, and representatives from each clan concerned in defining boundaries at any one time. Theoretically, both chairmen were to attend meetings to decide boundaries between Waskia and Takia border villages.

Since neither man was personally involved in border areas, it was presumed he would remain as impartial here as elsewhere. In the case of disputes, the committee '. . . had power to note boundaries in accordance with its own view' (Land Titles Commission Circular 24.4.1966: 7), or could refer the matter to the Commission. In the last case, the land in question could be placed out of bounds to all claimants. Where representatives reached agreement, they cut boundaries through the bush if necessary and set cement markers in place. Volunteer student workers from Australian universities surveyed village and clan boundaries for several months during Christmas 1966 and 1967, so that the Commission might examine the resulting plans before recording and registering boundaries, but delays caused by disputes among villagers, inaccurate surveying and an inadequate official programme resulted in demarcation being suspended in 1968 (personal communication from the Land Titles Commission in Port Moresby, January 1969). Thereafter, resident Administration officers assisted, on request, to obtain either individual or communal registered title for intending applicants for loans from the Papua New Guinea Development Bank. As a rule, registered title was the only security villagers could offer.

The Papua New Guinea Development Bank opened in July 1967 with capital from the Australian Government under the control of a board of twelve, two of whom were Papua New Guineans. It was an autonomous body devoted to the economic development of the Territory through its lending policy. Administration officers and staffs of other banks acted as field agents, advising and assisting applicants for loans. The bank preferred individual land title, but considered granting aid on communal title, if clan or lineage leaders guaranteed the borrower's rights of use. It considered making loans to a maximum of five clan or lineage members on their own behalf, or as representatives of a large group. Repayments for cash crop development had to be made within five years. The bank considered loans for establishing plantations and services such as transport on Karkar, but it had not fully investigated applications by the end of 1968.[12]

THE POLITICAL FIELD

Until 1957, Karkar was administered from Madang by means of annual patrols. The Germans appointed *luluais* over the west and south coast villages in 1910 (*Deutsches Kolonialblatt* 1905; Kriele 1927: 78). But the Karkar remained a 'thorn in the side of the Madang District Officer' (Hansen 1958: 86) who, therefore, encouraged German settlers as a means of furthering control. Later, the Australian Mandate Administration appointed *luluais, tultuls* and medical *tultuls* to each village, a paramount *luluai* each for Takia and Waskia, and finally a paramount *luluai* for the entire island. The *luluais'* duties were to record all births, deaths and recruitments, to report serious sickness, and to organize labour to clean villages, clear tracks and bridle paths and, after 1935, to keep the eighteen miles of vehicular road in good order.

The small force of Japanese that occupied Karkar brought the people their first experience of consistent contact with an Administration. There were two officers, Maida and Matimoto, who took charge of Takia and Waskia respectively. They forbade their men to interfere with the villagers on pain of death and maintained the *luluai/tultul* system, replacing only those headmen who opposed the new regime. They recruited two hundred men, some from the mainland, as policemen to keep order and to spy on anti-Japanese villagers (Patrol Report 4. 1944-45). In Takia, Maida held courts for minor offences. He allowed special rank and privileges to the pro-Japanese paramount *luluai*, Aitul of Takia, and to his self-appointed headmen, inviting them to confer and dine with him as equals at Dogowan Plantation (cf. Mead 1956: 179). The only violence that occurred was Matimoto's execution of a Chinese in Waskia. The Allied approach towards Madang caused the Japanese to withdraw to Alexishafen on 20 March 1944, accompanied by about fifty indigenous policemen, some with their families.

ANGAU officers, anxious to rehabilitate European plantations, failed to investigate the events of the occupation, and gave important positions to men who had stolen from European stores to curry favour with the Japanese, and had bullied, beaten and stolen from their own people. This, plus bad working conditions imposed by the Production Control Board, led to much unrest which ANGAU officers interpreted as 'a type of anti-British campaign' (Patrol Report 4. 1944-45). They responded with a programme of anti-Japanese propaganda in which they explained British methods of government, built a model village to inspire reconstruction, and dismissed village officials installed by Aitul's henchmen. They charged twelve men with assaulting their fellow villagers during the occupation and sent them to Madang for trial.

ANGAU control passed to the Provisional Administration on 30 October 1945. The latter established a patrol post in 1946 and promised local government councils at an early date, but staff shortages caused it to close the post after only six months. Eleven years passed before local government began during the succeeding Trusteeship Administration.

As in the economic field, the 1950s marked a significant change in Karkar socio-political history. Since 1957, the people have moved from the old system of direct rule through *luluais* and *tultuls*, policed annually by an impersonal patrol officer from Madang, through separate local government councils for Takia and Waskia to a single wealthy and relatively successful multi-racial Karkar Local Government Council under an indigenous president, and with an Administration adviser. They have participated in two elections for the Papua New Guinea House of Assembly.[13]

The Administration planned to achieve its ends of establishing representative, centralized government and concepts of nationalism through a series of intermediate stages. As a preliminary step, in 1957, it established Karkar's first permanent patrol post at Miak in Waskia. In October, Local Government Councils for Takia and Waskia were gazetted (Gazette No. 52), with twenty-six members for Takia and twenty-five for Waskia. Voting was by 'whispering ballot', whereby voters whispered their choice of candidate to the returning officer who recorded it and deposited the completed ballot paper in the ballot box. Initially councillors held office for one year and this was extended to two years thereafter. They elected a president and vice-president from among their number. From the early 1960s, each councillor had an assistant at the village level, known in Pidgin as the *komiti*, who was informally elected by the villagers. He helped the councillor organize and direct labour for roads, schools and village upkeep.

The two Karkar Councils amalgamated and incorporated Bagabag Island in 1962. Administration officials favoured the union on grounds of economy and efficiency and as a positive step towards removing traditional parochialism (Annual Report 72/3/1). The Karkar Native Local Government Council (which became the Karkar Local Government Council in 1965) met at the former Waskia Council Chambers at Bakul. The first system of representation proving unsatisfactory, the following arrangement was reached in 1966: Karkar was divided into twenty-five wards and Bagabag comprised one. Wards had one councillor each and were based on a population of roughly 500, proximity and, where possible, traditional ties between villages (Map IV).

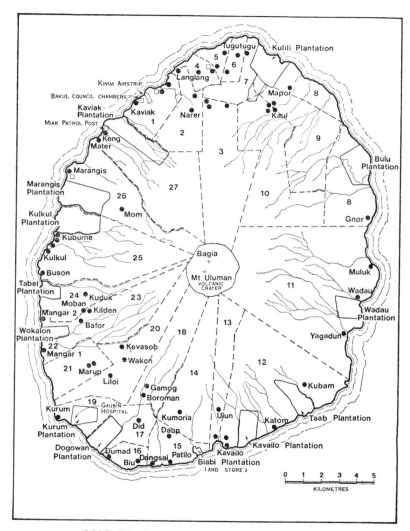

MAP IV—Local Government Council Wards

A ward might consist of up to four small villages or of one large village like Marup. In 1956, voting became preferential.

In 1958, the Karkar Council employed a total of sixty people, including casual road labourers. The Administration Officer-in-charge attended meetings in an advisory capacity. Two clerks registered births, marriages and deaths, and prepared civil claims which a visiting indigenous magistrate heard at monthly Courts for Native Affairs at the Council Chambers.

The Karkar Local Government Council Inspection Report for October 1968 notes that apart from Finschhafen, Karkar had the largest revenue and expenditure on public works of any council in the New Guinea mainland region for 1967-68. In the year ending June 1968, total revenue was $59,304. This came from Council tax of $9 per adult male on Karkar[14] and $7 on Bagabag; $21,140 grants-in-aid for roads, bridges, airstrip maintenance, low-income mileage on Council vehicles, aid-post orderlies' wages, and education; and $21,175 profit from Council liquor sales, for which a licence was granted in 1965. This budget was $20,000 less than the previous year when the Council obtained loans to purchase a grader and a boat, the *Watabag*.

Councillors divided their heavy works programme between six committees. These were Executive, Finance, Health, Education and Agriculture Committees and, in 1968, a Roadworks Committee. The Finance Committee consisted of five members, the rest of four, two each from Waskia and Takia. They patrolled the island regularly on inspection and met once a month in preparation for the Council's general monthly meeting. Committee members had the right to charge offenders against Council rules concerning village hygiene, maintenance of school grounds, truancy, and care of gardens and crops against pests and disease.

In 1967, the councillors agreed to the Administration's recommendation for a multi-racial Council, having opposed it the previous year, when they feared that undesirable Europeans might gain control. They divided the single ward of Bagabag into two, and included alienated land in the existing wards. In August 1968, the Administrator of the Territory proclaimed the new constitution and area of the Council. This gave an additional 360 'foreigners', including twenty-six Europeans, the right to vote. At the general elections in November, two Europeans were successful. The Karkar Multi-Racial Local Government Council held its first meeting in December.

Some Karkar councillors took part in the 1967 Legislative Council election, but the 1964 House of Assembly elections introduced the Karkar people as a whole to the concept of national politics. Administration officers carried out a political education campaign to explain the work of the House and Karkar's involvement in two electorates: the Madang Open Electorate, in which both indigenes and Europeans could nominate and vote, and the Madang-Sepik Special Electorate, which only Europeans could contest. A Waskia councillor, Suguman Matibri, stood successfully for the Madang Open Electorate.

Political education on Karkar for the 1968 House of Assembly elections came almost entirely from councillors and candidates. This time there was to be a Regional Electorate comprising the entire Madang District and a number of component areas called Open Electorates. Karkar and the adjacent mainland coast comprised one such electorate, Sumkar. Preferential voting took place simultaneously in Waskia and Takia with facilities for the 'whispering ballot' provided. John Middleton, of Kulili Estates on Karkar, won the seat for Sumkar, while Jason Garrett, a surveyor living in Madang, was successful in the Regional Electorate. This campaign is discussed in more detail from the Karkar point of view in a later chapter.[15]

THE EDUCATIONAL FIELD

In the general area of educational development, I include formal education through the official school system, and health education through hospitals and aid posts. The informal educational aspects of agricultural extension and political programmes will already be apparent.

The first purely secular teaching began with the construction of eight Administration schools between 1957 and 1962. Seven of them expanded to include standard VI, while the eighth took students to standard IV. Europeans supervised all but the last school and all teachers held teacher training certificates. They taught in English, following a syllabus approved by the Education Department and recently adapted, to some extent, to Territory Primary School needs (cf. Hastings 1969: 141-2). Hence, these schools were called Primary 'T' schools as opposed to multiracial Primary 'A' schools in the major towns where mainly European and Chinese staff followed the N.S.W. syllabus.

The Administration gave all mission schools, other than Bible schools, financial assistance provided they offered similar improved standards of teaching and accommodation. At the end of 1968, work began on temporary buildings for a high school near the patrol post at Miak in Waskia. This was to cater for primary school graduates in 1970 and to expand by one form annually until it reached form IV.[16]

The following limited opportunities for technical education existed on Karkar. The Department of Agriculture, Stock and Fisheries (DASF) officer accepted five students as trainees for positions in his department. An unqualified European tradesman, assisted by a former technical school teacher from Bagabag, taught building and carpentry to thirty-two youths at an Administration training centre in the old Takia Council Chambers near Biu village. Graduates of the two year course, which began in 1965, received certificates. All recognized Primary 'T' schools and the two technical schools are shown on Map V.

Health education increased gradually after 1950 with improved training programmes on the mainland for aid post orderlies (the former medical *tultuls*). By 1967, there were eleven aid posts catering for groups of villages all over the island. A small Administration hospital for minor illnesses opened in Waskia, first under the supervision of a European medical assistant, and later under a Papua New Guinean graduate from the Papuan Medical College. A Public Health Department officer from Madang made occasional patrols, addressing assembled villagers on hygiene, and inspecting latrines, garbage disposal, housing and water supplies. The Council Health Committee also carried out village inspections.

In all three fields of economic, political and educational development, the Australian Administration eventually assumed an important role on Karkar. Yet, once new schemes were set in action, European officers in departments such as District Administration, Trade and Industry (Co-operatives), Agriculture, Public Works, Education and Public Health concerned themselves increasingly with refining or reformulating regulations, training programmes, finance and output. Actual Administration devolved to a great extent on the local indigenous officers and Council members, for, contrary to their officially postulated roles as decision-makers, the latter soon found that their villagers as well as their local Administration officer depended on them to disseminate information and implement new ideas. This situation suggests the need for expanding the categories of administrators and administered to include an intermediate one of indigenous officers and councillors who belonged to both.

Missions

Mission influence was the most powerful, pervasive and con-

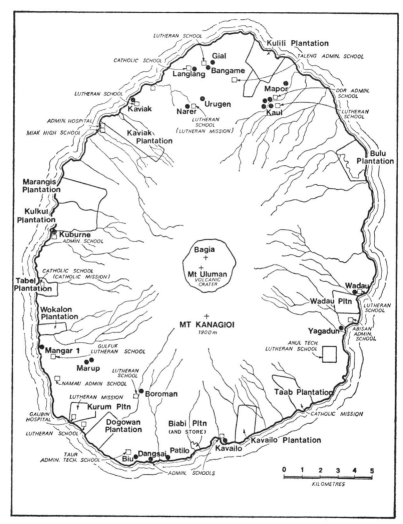

MAP V—Primary 'T' Schools: Administration and Mission

tinuous alien force on Karkar for forty years (cf. Burridge 1960: 12). This resulted from the slight influence of the various Administrations until the 1950s and the self-interest of the planters, who interacted with the people as employers and buyers, but because of their presumed superiority, avoided them socially. It arose, as well, from the missionaries' concern with the villagers' personal welfare and their relationships with the supernatural. Not only did the Lutheran and Catholic Missions provide all schools until 1957, but the Lutherans introduced villagers to active representation and participation in a hierarchical system of control through the congregational structure, and involved them in an extensive health service. Since it claimed the adherence of approximately 90% of the population, I concentrate on the Lutheran Mission and refer only briefly to the Catholic Mission.

THE LUTHERAN MISSION

In 1890, the German Lutheran missionary Kunze and two companions established the first European settlement on Karkar at Kavailo in south-eastern Takia. It survived for five years, before being abandoned in August 1895, after a volcanic eruption followed by a smallpox epidemic. In 1911, Eckershoff and George set up a permanent station and plantation beside the all-weather harbour at Kurum. The Australian occupation in 1914 had little effect on them: they signed an oath of neutrality and remained on Karkar. After 1922, when the American Missouri Synod took over control of the mission, newcomers were mainly American, but the Germans stayed on.

The arrival of a Catholic missionary at nearby Mangar village in 1932, spurred the Lutherans to renew their efforts in Waskia, where evangelization had never progressed as successfully as it had in Takia. The following year, Mager founded Narer station high on the Waskia mountain slope, and it became the administrative headquarters. Three Samoan evangelists from the London Missionary Society settled in Kaul, Bangame and Buson, to further the work in Waskia on behalf of the Lutherans and a European lay-worker took charge of the mission plantation at Kurum.

After the Administration withdrew from Madang in 1942, the Lutheran and Catholic missionaries made energetic efforts to gain control of each other's congregations, causing ill-will and even violence between their respective followers (Patrol Report 4. 1944-45; personal communication from Father J. Tschauder). The Japanese arrested first the two American Lutherans, then

E

the German priest in 1943, and imprisoned them on the mainland. During the next three years schools and churches collapsed from neglect and bombardment. Hence, the immediate concern of post-war missionaries on the island was the reconstruction of these buildings.

In 1946, a lay missionary and former army medical assistant, Mr E. Tscharke, with the help of the Takia villagers, built a hospital of bush and disused army materials on reclaimed swamp land at Gaubin near the old Kurum station. He replaced it in 1967 with a permanent 200 bed building largely financed by a German organization, Bread for the World, but initiated by a contribution from the Middleton family. As well as modern hospital and training facilities, the Lutherans provided a number of general facilities at Gaubin. These included a post office with radio link to Madang, a branch of the Commonwealth Bank, a venue for a large Saturday market, a basketball field, a place for church leaders to meet each week and the Karkar Circuit Office. The main Lutheran church was opened there in 1960. Gaubin Hospital, in an easily accessible part of a densely populated area, was almost continuously under the supervision of the same person after its inception. On the other hand, Narer, in the remote Waskia highlands, came under five missionaries from 1946-68. Not surprisingly, Gaubin rather than the official headquarters was the spiritual and secular focus for villagers.

THE ECONOMIC FIELD

The Lutherans affected the local economy through land alienation and employment of local labourers: at Kurum they alienated approximately 198 hectares of land from the Musob villagers, who had been defeated and dispersed in warfare. They established a coconut plantation and driers and, after the Japanese war, interplanted with cocoa, employing men from nearby villages as labourers, drivers, fermentary and drier attendants, carpenters and storemen. Occasionally they encouraged the people to plant coconut palms but only to increase their subsistence output. Even a sawmill built in Takia in 1946 and supervised by the missionary at Gaubin was seen as a means of providing timber for re-building churches and schools, rather than as a business enterprise.

THE POLITICAL FIELD

The hierarchy within the Lutheran Mission and congregation was, in a broad sense, a political structure. First, it developed some concept of membership in a unit extending beyond Karkar's boundaries to include the Lutheran Mission field in New Guinea generally. Second, in view of the occasional nature of official administration, it became a medium of social control at village level. Third, it offered new possibilities of leadership (cf. Rowley 1965: 142, 145).

In 1937 the organization of the Lutheran congregations was as follows. Church elders in each village assumed responsibility for the moral welfare of the people and for supervising the work of the village teacher and evangelist. They elected one of their number as chief elder. Seventy to eighty elders from both Takia and Waskia met at a general conference four times a year under the chairmanship of a leading elder or the missionary, and elders representing all the districts in the Madang area attended an annual mainland conference. The Mission Conference surmounted the entire structure.

Mager (1937: 34) notes that the missionaries, in their perceived roles as chiefs, leaders and guides, planned to re-organize Karkar society, which they considered had disintegrated by contact. They encouraged morning and evening communal religious services, mid-weekly meetings of the village congregation as a whole for private and public confessions, and regular Sunday services in the village church.

As noted, the development of indigenous leadership was part of a long-range plan for an independent Lutheran church in New Guinea. 'The more the congregation grows in leadership, the greater should be [the missionary's] withdrawal', comments Dr Reitz, soon after the war against Japan ended, in a Report for the Lutheran Mission (n.d.: 15). He referred specifically to Karkar, but echoed ideas behind the successful policy of evangelization instigated after 1899 by the Reverend C. Keyszer of the Neuendettelsau Lutheran Mission at Finschhafen. Because of anxiety over increasing secularism through Administration development schemes and Catholic inroads on Lutheran congregations, the Mission accelerated this policy after 1950. The first two Karkar pastors were ordained in 1954 and eight were appointed three years later. In 1956 the Lutheran Church of New Guinea (ELCONG) came into being. The old Lutheran Mission in New Guinea (LMNG) remained as a separate body concerned with training and supporting European missionaries, handling overseas grants, and controlling income from mission enterprises in Papua New Guinea.[17]

On Karkar, the European missionary continued to administer the circuit from Narer and to be the ultimate authority on all

moral and Church matters. He also undertook to reorganize the
Lutheran schools system to meet the Administration's demands
for higher standards. In 1968 he handed over control of the Circuit to Pastor Gubag of Takia. Indigenous church leaders faced
great problems in administering the formal organizations (especially schools) they inherited, but the missionaries' attitude
reflected that of the late Reverend F. Henkelmann: 'If we wait
for great ability, we will wait in vain. The congregation will
first collapse' (Report to the Lutheran Mission n.d.: 15).

The new congregational structure was as follows: every
village, with its elders, pastor's assistant and teacher formed a
fun medaeng or village congregation. Several villages made up a
named congregation called a *badim medaeng*, which was represented by an elected member on the Church Council of Karkar.
Takia had nine *fun medaeng* and Waskia seven, each of which
met every month. From 1967, congregations joined into three
wider groups called North, West and South Areas, each under
an ordained indigenous pastor, who presided over triannual
meetings. Areas in turn comprised the Karkar Circuit in the
charge of its president, Pastor Gubag. Nine neighbouring circuits
combined to form ELCONG Madang District, headed by a Takia
pastor, Stahl Mileng, in Madang. Finally, six New Guinea districts were members of ELCONG, with a European bishop and
headquarters at Lae.[18] Thus, a new hierarchical system of leadership, but based on broad village participation and opinion, involved the Karkar in responsibility for all local church affairs and
in policy-making for ELCONG itself.

THE EDUCATIONAL FIELD

As appears the common experience in the southern Madang
District (Lawrence 1964a), the Lutheran Mission controlled not
only all formal but also much informal education until 1957. In
1890 Kunze built the first school on Karkar. After his station was
abandoned, the missionaries continued to teach young Takia men
at their headquarters on Graged Island in Madang harbour.
These contacts assisted their return in 1911 and the rapid expansion of their influence to most villages by 1918. According to
Wagner (1963: 12), the missionaries aimed to bring people
'. . . the fact of salvation in Jesus Christ'. They envisaged schools
as a means of achieving this aim and established four kinds for
the purpose: village and middle schools, a seminary, and catechumenical or Bible schools. Mager (1937: 35-8) describes them
as they were in 1935. Teaching was in Graged, which, as noted,

the mission established as its lingua franca in the Madang District. A small press set up at Kurum in 1924 produced mission literature in Graged for schools throughout this District. In the forty-four village schools, fifty teachers taught reading and writing, Bible stories and Luther's Small Catechism, simple arithmetic, names of days and months, how to tell the time, hygiene, games, and singing. Learning was by rote. For example, students memorized Bible stories, which the teacher then related to some desirable value or behaviour, and finally they memorized the relevant part of the catechism.

Graduates from village schools could attend middle school at Kurum, where indigenous teachers and evangelists gave preliminary training for the seminary. The missionary and four indigenous assistants taught sixty-eight seminary students from Karkar and Graged Island near Madang. The four-year course comprised extensive religious instruction, composition, public speaking, physical hygiene, some knowledge of the treatment of disease, geography, and carpentry. At the catechumenical schools for adults, evangelists and teachers held classes in religious instruction and its application to everyday life several times a week.

After 1935, the missionaries transferred the seminary to Graged Island, and the middle school to their new Karkar headquarters at Narer. Following the Japanese war, successive missionaries re-organized village and Bible schools and began a technical training school on leased land at Anul on the south-east coast.

Education Department officers investigating mission schools preparatory to inaugurating their education programme found the standards unacceptable (Karkar Circuit Report 1956; Patrol Report 1. 1958). If the Lutherans wished to become part of a recognized schools system and to receive financial aid, they would have to employ qualified staff, teach in English instead of Graged, and follow the Primary 'T' syllabus. The mission's efforts to meet these requirements resulted in the Education Department registering five of its new schools, assisting nine existing schools with equipment, and accrediting thirteen teachers. Yet considerable conflict arose from what Karkar Circuit Reports in 1960 describe as 'critical and negative attitudes' of Administration officers in opening schools adjacent to major Lutheran ones and refusing financial assistance to Lutheran schools in areas where the Catholic Mission provided the only alternative opportunities for education.

In order to retain some influence under the new conditions, the Lutheran Mission instituted a policy of centralization. By

1968 only eight Lutheran primary schools remained out of a previous total of about sixty, and only one of these, Narer, prepared pupils for secondary education. The mission employed one European and twenty-seven certificated indigenous teachers, whose wages and teaching supplies the Education Department provided. From 1966, a mission education officer and inspectors visited schools annually. Neighbouring congregations continued to provide teachers' houses and land for gardens, school buildings and furniture, except in the case of Narer, which the Karkar Circuit as a whole supported.

Bible schools continued in many villages, remaining outside the jurisdiction of the Education Department. Their uncertificated teachers trained at Ameron near Madang or at Rintebe near Goroka. They prepared young people for Communion and gave limited elementary education to children who, for various reasons, did not attend Primary 'T' schools.

In short, the Administration's demands for higher standards and the introduction of its own schools ended the Lutheran Mission's monopoly of education on Karkar. It resulted in fewer and larger schools with better qualified staff dependent on Administration supervision and financial support. When European missionary control ended in 1968, the Karkar Circuit president assumed the task of maintaining the new educational standards.

Apart from its medical services and the general facilities already mentioned, Gaubin Hospital played an important educational role: it provided a training school for nineteen staff members and informally educated the villagers on hygiene and the nature of disease. Formal teaching, which was entirely in English, covered general as well as medical subjects for nursing trainees mainly from Narer school. In a sense, therefore, it was an extension beyond primary education. In the broad field of health education, the hospital staff waged constant battle against disease and traditional beliefs associated with it. By 1968, infant welfare and prenatal clinics contacting every village controlled almost all fatal illnesses of children. The increase from thirty-five to 192 annual births in hospital over ten years reduced infant mortality significantly while tuberculosis decreased by half during the same period. In villages, at the outpatients' clinic at Gaubin, in the general and tuberculosis wards, nurses discussed hygiene, diet and the causes of current diseases. Tscharke wrote in Pidgin and illustrated an amusing hygiene booklet, which he distributed widely among the people.[19]

In 1967, the Karkar Circuit agreed to elect representatives to a board, with senior hospital orderlies, to meet every few months under Tscharke's guidance to deal with Gaubin's affairs. A major problem was paying the staff, who in the past worked for little more than a token wage. Consequently, as well as school fees levied since 1958, medical charges were made for the first time in 1967. That year school fees to assist in building and maintenance costs were $1 per family (as well as the Administration fee of $1 per pupil). Hospital fees were $1 a month for in-patients except tubercular patients (for whom the Public Health Department provided a grant) and widows, and ten cents a month for any number of visits to the daily clinic. The aim was to introduce people gradually to the idea of paying for the services they received, and thus decrease their dependence for social benefits on the Lutheran Mission.

THE CATHOLIC MISSION (S.V.D.)

The first resident Catholic missionary, following earlier lay workers, arrived at Mangar in 1932. Father Hubers came in response to appeals from Mangar men who were angered by the harshness of indigenous Lutheran teachers to their children. In spite of threats and actual violence from the Waskia Lutheran congregation, he established a permanent station at Tabel on the border of Takia and Waskia, for at this time many Waskia villagers, although influenced to some extent by the Lutherans, were not baptized.[20] After the notoriously harsh and unpopular Samoan evangelist, Jerome, withdrew from the border village of Buson, Catholic influence spread northwards to Buson, Kulkul, Kurumlang, Kuburne, and to the fringes of the mountain villages of Moban and Kuduk.

When Father Tschauder, a German priest, took over in 1939, he found a Catholic congregation of approximately 500. His intention was to win the entire population for the Catholic Church. Again, reacting against the harsh and reputedly irresponsible behaviour of Lutheran teachers, six more Waskia villages asked for conversion. Refused permission by the European planter at Kulili in the north to build a chapel there for recruited Catholic labour, Father Tschauder approached the two neighbouring villages. They agreed to give him land for this purpose in return for a church and school. But before these gains could be consolidated the war intervened.

In the competition between the Lutheran and Catholic missionaries referred to earlier, '. . . a situation arose over which the white missionaries lost control and an era of lawlessness reigned'

(Patrol Report 41. 1944-45). The arrival of the Japanese put an end to this confrontation. Ultimately four of the six promised villages returned to the Lutherans and only half of the inhabitants of another became Catholic. In 1968, seven villages on the west coast were Catholic, while another four were partly Catholic. After the war, the Catholic Mission initiated a vigorous building programme paid for by the bishop at Alexishafen. The north Waskia village of Langlang became a sub-station.

Like the Lutherans, the Catholics affected the local economy through land alienation and plantation employment. They planted twenty-seven hectares at Tabel and 206·8 hectares at Taab on the south-east coast, where a lay brother was in charge. But by the very nature of the Catholic Church's rules, they could create no hierarchical, responsible, congregational structure, and mission headquarters continued to control churches, schools' catechists, and their wages. The priest permitted catechists to read devotional services in lieu of mass and to baptize, but he made them directly responsible to him and he alone heard confessions and administered the sacraments.

Before the war, education and intellectual development among the Catholics centred around the main church and elementary school at Tabel. By 1967, there were five new churches, the major ones being at Tabel and Langlang. Two schools at Tabel and Langlang took pupils to standards VI and III respectively. Certificated teachers followed the Primary 'T' syllabus and received financial aid from the Education Department. Pupils paid the Administration fee of $1 and contributed two coconuts weekly towards a school fund. The congregations were not obliged to provide or maintain school buildings or equipment.

With their longer experience in the mission field, the Catholics were less demanding of individuals than were the Lutherans. Private records made available by Father Tschauder show that, although they waged constant war against polygamy, sexual licence, and intermarriage with Protestants, they impinged little on secular life. Catholics depended on Gaubin's medical services and general amenities, and established relationships with the Lutheran Mission workers there.

Planters

The planters followed closely on the heels of the missionaries in 1912 to provide, except during the Japanese occupation, constant inter-racial contact until the present. Primarily, their presence meant land alienation (to which I referred earlier in connection with official economic policies), labour demands, and power, consisting in early years of jural authority to punish, and later of *de facto* power to command. Contact with planters had the inevitable latent functions of informally educating the villagers and moulding their ambitions.

There were three clearly defined planter periods: the German (1912-21) which includes the German-Australian transition period (1914-21), the early Australian (1921-42), and the second or current Australian (from 1946). The Germans pioneered plantations on Karkar and continued under the Australian Military Administration. From 1921-28 caretaker managers were appointed while the Australian Government expropriated German properties. During 1926-42 the early Australian planters expanded and consolidated the plantation economy. After the Pacific war until 1952 the Australians mainly tried to restore the old socio-economic *status quo*. But in 1952 they began to compete with each other in exploiting the new economic avenues offered by indigenous primary production and to make gestures of goodwill to the villagers, in both economic and political fields, as insurance against a possibly uncertain future in an independent Papua New Guinea.

This description concerns mainly planters who resided permanently on Karkar. Thus I refer first to the Germans, then to the Middleton family, which owns five plantations known as Kulili Estates, to Mr A. Barnett of Dogowan plantation and his manager since 1960, Mr W. Lloyd, and to Mr N. Goodyear, a relatively recent arrival, who owns a small plantation and an extensive trade store enterprise at Biabi (see Map II). I give little emphasis to W. R. Carpenter Pty Ltd (later Coconut Products Ltd), because its European employees had almost no contact with the villagers. Not only were they transient, but were prohibited by Company policy from employing or trading with the Karkar. For convenience, I adopt the local custom of referring to the three Carpenter properties as 'Company' (in Pidgin, *Kompani*) plantations.

THE ECONOMIC FIELD

Both German and early Australian planters believed that the economic future of the villagers lay in their absorption as labour into the European economy (cf. Miles 1955-56: 109). This entailed considerable land alienation and labour recruitment.

The first arrival was a Prussian, Paul Schmidt. An experi-

enced planter from New Britain, he claimed that Governor Hahl
in Madang asked him to 'tame and develop' the island in accordance with the popular belief that plantation labour was a suitable substitute for warfare (Hansen 1958: 86). Schmidt, who
settled on the west Waskia coast near Marangis in 1912, was
later joined by Schwartz and Eidelbach. Between them, they
planted Marangis, Kulkul and Kavailo plantations. In 1917,
on the assumption that it would be exempt from expropriation,
Schmidt established Kulili. Most planting only began in 1914,
continuing, as noted, throughout and after the war until 1921
(Table I). By this time the Europeans had planted 132,644 coconut palms on 1,421 hectares of alienated land. As well as palms,
Schmidt introduced 10,000 cotton trees and small areas of cocoa
(Custodian of Expropriated Property 1926; Hansen 1958: 86).

The villagers reported that the German planters' only interest
in them was as a source of labour. In 1926, 267 of them worked
locally as indentured labourers, but as three of the four properties were by then fully planted previous figures were probably
higher. The Germans paid leaders and later *luluais* in knives,
axes and blankets for their co-operation in getting labourers. The
Karkar claimed that, if necessary, they recruited by force, that the
work was onerous, the hours long and their employers stern and
repressive.

Australians took over the expropriated German properties in
1926. Kulkul, Marangis and Kavailo, sold, as mentioned, with
freehold title ostensibly to returned soldiers, soon passed into the
hands of W. R. Carpenter Ltd. Marangis was later extended by
twenty-six hectares. Mr W. M. Middleton, with a ninety-nine year
lease of Kulili, negotiated through his neighbour, Paramount
Luluai Salum of Waskia, for another 883 hectares during the next
ten years. This provided for extensions to Kulili and for four new
plantations at Wokalon, Kaviak, Wadau and Bulu. In 1926 the
Musob and Kagil villagers, dispersed by warfare, sold 209 hectares
of their unoccupied land in Takia for another plantation, Dogowan, which Mr. A. Barnett took over in 1932. Finally, a Chinese-
owned trade store at Biabi on Takia's south-east coast came into
European hands in the 1940s with approximately seven hectares
of land suitable for planting.

In all, as set out in Table I, planters obtained a further
1,125 hectares of land and established six new plantations during
the first eleven years of the early Australian period. With the two
Catholic plantations at Taab and Tabel amounting to roughly
284 hectares this made a total of 1,359 hectares, an area almost

equal to that alienated to Germans. In accordance with the 1921 Land Ordinance, title was restricted to leasehold. It is generally maintained that the Australians did not alienate land on a grand scale in New Guinea generally. In fact in 1932, they caused 4,400 hectares of virgin land to be returned to the original owners in Madang (Phillips 1932). But on Karkar, in spite of the Imperial German Administration's plans and the 1917 Copra Ordinance providing measures for indigenous involvement in organized primary production, they removed a relatively large part of the rich but limited arable coastal land from indigenous use. In 1956-57 Patrol Report 1 estimated a total of $12\frac{1}{2}\%$ of Karkar's cultivable land occupied by Europeans.

Some of these resented Administration legislation protecting local land owners. In 1934, one planter complained in the journal, *Pacific Islands Monthly* (1934: 32-3) about having to obtain the owners' consent for their land to be sold. In 1937, when a complete prohibition against alienation of any kind seemed imminent, another exclaimed in a letter to the same journal: 'Balderdash! . . . the natives are never likely to require half of the remaining land' (vol. 7: 46).

As the question of land alienation became increasingly vexed, Europeans began to compete for land. For example, a bitter dispute arose over land at Bulu, which both the Kulili and Dogowan planters coveted. Paramount *Luluai* Salum secured it for his Kulili neighbour, who had made an exceptional gesture in helping him establish his own European-style plantation in 1933. Consequently, Salum was forbidden ever to set foot on Dogowan Plantation again. The antagonisms between planters, missions and certain Waskia and Takia people resulting from this rivalry are discussed later.

Local men provided 80-90% of indentured labour (or contract labour as it was called after World War II) until the Company plantations began to employ mainland labourers exclusively (private communication from Mr J. Middleton). According to Mager (1937: 39), 300-400 Karkar men worked on local European plantations in 1935. The planters approved the Administration's limitation, in 1933, on recruitment except for local employment because it safeguarded their own labour needs. A published letter from one of them illustrates how restriction of recruitment was used as an argument for the continuation of land alienation: '. . . if it is kept and enough plantations formed to absorb the population it would be of benefit to the Karkar native' (*Pacific Islands Monthly* 1934: 32-3). Clearly, development for the villager in his own right was not envisaged.

After the Australians returned to their plantations in 1946, they concentrated on restoring their economy, a task already initiated by ANGAU and the Production Control Board. Gradually the villagers began to experiment in making copra, and the planters gave them limited assistance in building driers, together with advice on processing. What was more important, they provided the only marketing outlets for copra before the advent of co-operatives.

After 1952 the planters, realizing that there were rich profits to be made by trading for the increasing village production of coconuts, copra and cocoa, co-ordinated and organized the enterprise.[21] Eventually, nine of the thirteen plantations on Karkar, including those of the missions, provided buying and processing facilities. In so doing, they actively contributed to the collapse of the co-operatives: they collected copra or green coconuts right in the villages, whereas the co-operatives had no transport at all; they were in a sufficiently strong position financially to gamble against a fall in world prices by offering a steady and immediate price for copra, which the co-operatives were unable to do; some of them openly criticized and undermined members' confidence in the co-operatives.[22]

Nevertheless, since the co-operatives did not handle cocoa, the planters provided a valuable service in buying wet cocoa beans in spite of the low prices they paid (Agricultural Report D. 1966-67). By 1968 they controlled the entire cocoa output and had regained 75% of the copra trade. Competition between them became so fierce that it was known on the island and in Madang as the 'copra and cocoa war'. In an effort to contain the situation, the Kulili and Dogowan planters met and agreed upon boundaries within which each would operate. Having installed expensive fermentaries to cope with the rapidly increasing cocoa production, they consistently opposed Administration proposals for a native growers' cocoa marketing and processing association (cf. Reay 1969b: 65). So uncompromising were they, that a visiting Administration officer compared them with 'medieval mercantile fiefdoms' (Co-operatives Extension Survey 30.7.1968). Company plantation managers, on the other hand, confined their activities to their own plantations; and the two missions, while continuing to buy, practised more restrained business methods.

By 1956, the Karkar showed a marked preference for cultivating their own rather than European-owned cash crops

(Patrol Report 1. 1956-57). Consequently the planters had to employ 'foreign' (non-Karkar) contract labourers or offer less binding conditions than those of indenture to the local people. In 1968 they employed approximately 640 recruited men, mainly from the Highlands, including 332 working on Company plantations. They complemented their permanent work force with local people working on a casual basis. There were two systems: the villagers worked by the month for wages, or the planters paid for the amount of cocoa harvested or copra cut and smoked, but left working hours and the composition of work groups entirely to the people themselves. Limited sharefarming was attempted on Dogowan. A very few Karkar men performed semi-skilled work as carpenters, drivers and storekeepers and, relatively recently, as produce buyers and trade store managers handling large sums of money and assuming some degree of responsibility.

While financial independence through cash cropping freed the villagers from having to work for Europeans, they still looked to them to divulge important economic knowledge. As Reay (1969b: 68) points out, employment that neglected training in management and organization was not good enough. Finney (1969: 63) too, questions the adequacy of economic opportunities offered by Europeans. Ambitious Karkar men, frustrated by their failure to achieve wealth by the methods available to them so far, sought advice about setting up their own enterprises. The planters, apprehensive of their future, especially after the 1964 House of Assembly elections, responded positively, provided their own financial concerns were not jeopardized.

It was, in effect, a bargain: they wanted a new image in return for their co-operation (cf. Finney 1969: 64). They helped promising men build and stock stores and bakeries, and arranged the purchase of vehicles on terms from Madang, sometimes guaranteeing payments themselves and making loans towards the deposit. When disaster threatened these ventures, as it so often did, they occasionally took over the supervision of stores and transport businesses. One planter even hired out his 'foreign' labour line, so that village plantations would not suffer through the owners' pre-occupation with Council or other duties. Although banking facilities already existed, another opened a branch of a private bank and started a schools' banking system, under which he or his wife regularly visited every school on the island. He imported breeding pigs and poultry from Lae with the intention of gradually improving village strains through this stock. Sometimes efforts of this kind were unsuccessful, but the planters overcame the loss of face and finance this caused by evolving simple, fool-proof methods of preventing local entrepreneurs from getting into serious debt.

Once again, initial gestures of goodwill developed into profitable ventures. The planters built up lucrative businesses carrying stock from Madang to village stores on their boats and tractor-trailers, or selling stock direct from their own trade stores. Their general trading expanded as the people adopted the custom of frequently spending small amounts of money on non-essentials. In 1966 two planters acquired licences to sell liquor, and two years later one of them obtained an agency for trucks and tractors.

Thus, instead of the outright exploitation or, at best, the remote paternalism of the past, the planters now made determined efforts to involve themselves in local changes. As in the land disputes and produce 'wars', they vied fiercely in currying favour with the Karkar. In Takia, they competed with each other in their own trade store businesses, apparently blind to the dangers inherent in their expansion at the inevitable expense of indigenous enterprise (cf. Curtin 1968: 22; Crocombe 1969a: 55-6). Yet the owner of Biabi, now more a trader than a planter, while extending his store at a phenomenal rate, acknowledged that his future depended on unlimited local economic development, and implemented some democratic ideas founded on this concept. The most striking was the formation of his own business into a company with a small group of progressive villagers as joint shareholders. This was the reverse of the usual pattern set by long-established planters, which had evoked the following official comment: 'Expatriate private enterprise is not actively seeking indigenous participation as shareholders, partners or in management, therefore the Administration must!' (Co-operatives Extension Survey 30.7.1968).[23]

THE POLITICAL FIELD

The economic success of the German planters depended on their ability to extend pacification. The Karkar received Schmidt peaceably enough, but later they attacked him in protest against his increasing appropriation of essential gardening land, seriously injuring him and killing some of his Buka and New Britain workers. Overt hostility ceased only after punitive measures by the Australian Military Administration in 1915. To the people, the settlers represented the law, and a law they deeply resented, which permitted them to assess offences and punish by flogging.

The German caretaker managers from 1921 to 1926 and the Australian planters who succeeded them in 1926 continued to impose their will on their labourers, but flogging was now forbidden. Former employees claimed that although the Australians were more lenient than their German predecessors, violence, prejudice, and intolerance of local custom persisted. Therefore, it was only in a comparative sense that the people referred to this era as the 'good time' (in Pidgin, *gud taim*). Yet in 1941, when the Karkar abandoned work on the plantations during a widespread cargo cult known as *Kukuaik*, the planters were outraged. With production virtually at a standstill, they sent to Madang for Administration intervention. At an informal hearing at Dogowan in December 1941, they joined with the resident missionaries in recriminations against their ungrateful labourers. They experienced a good deal of satisfaction when the presumed leaders were sent to Madang for trial, and lesser supporters were gaoled or otherwise punished (Henklemann n.d.; personal communications from A. Barnett, W. Middleton and Father Tschauder). A month later, the planters left Karkar for the duration of the war against Japan.

Bad working conditions under the Production Control Board, and the settlers' efforts to restore pre-war master-servant relationships led to a situation of unrest in 1946 and later (cf. Mair 1948: 216-7): W. M. Middleton left Kulili to be managed by only a skeleton staff for a year because of labour difficulties,[24] and in 1951 the manager of Dogowan charged his Takia employees with boycotting work to participate in a cargo cult. Administration investigators traced the trouble to the manager's disregard of his promises and to his inability to maintain good relations with the people (Patrol Report 17. 1951-52). It is worth noting again that the annual Government subsidy allowed the Administration to take measures now which dependence on local revenue would never have permitted.

The establishment of a patrol post during the current Australian planter period curtailed the settlers' powers even more. Yet, as Finney (1969: 65) found in Goroka, the belief that indigenous labourers could understand only toughness and intransigence persisted, especially, on Karkar, in connection with unsophisticated indentured workers from the mainland. The new casual employment systems allowed the villagers relative independence from plantation regimentation, and in any case, payment on the basis of output made strong-arm tactics unlikely. The 1964 House of Assembly elections emphasized the point that, despite their superior status, the planters did not, in fact, represent the law. Hence, for the same reason as they became involved in indigenous business ventures, European planters entered the political field: they wanted the villagers to recognize their involvement in and contribution to Karkar's interests.

At first they were unsuccessful. J. Middleton[25] of Kulili Estates was defeated in 1964, when he stood, with Government urging, for the Madang-Sepik Special Electorate[26] and, as noted, the councillors rejected a proposal for a multi-racial Council because they 'had opportunities to form realistic, if unflattering opinions of what "multi-racial" involves' (Regional Local Government Report 42.75.1). But in 1968, Middleton won the seat for the Open Electorate of Sumkar in the House of Assembly Elections, and in the same year a multi-racial Council was established. Apart from motives of self-interest, Middleton hoped to prevent the election of unsuitable Europeans from the mainland, but would not have opposed a capable aspirant who was reasonably certain of success. In fact, President Sibon and Vice-President Jongale claimed that they had considered standing until his nomination caused them to abandon the idea. Middleton has made intensive efforts to keep his electorate informed on matters discussed in the House of Assembly and to increase leading councillors' awareness of national politics by taking them in turn to Port Moresby to observe House of Assembly proceedings at first hand.

In the elections for the first Karkar Multi-Racial Council, three Europeans nominated and two were elected. They were Tscharke, of Gaubin Hospital, and W. Lloyd, manager of Dogowan Plantation for eight years. By dissuading his European manager on Kulili from opposing the popular vice-president, Middleton endeared himself to the villagers and avoided creating a cadre of political influence at Kulili out of all proportion to that possible for his Dogowan protagonist. At the first meeting of the Multi-Racial Council, Tscharke accepted election to the Health Committee and Lloyd to the Agriculture Committee.[27]

Thus in the changing economic and political situation on Karkar, the planters made a fairly successful bid to play new, prestige-building roles. In the process, two factors emerged: their unwillingness to surrender any of their financial interests without a struggle, and increasing competition between them in proportion to the growing complexity of life on Karkar.

At the same time as the planters tried to improve their image, they obstructed increased indigenous income by opposing the establishment of a Karkar-owned cocoa marketing association and by competing against indigenous small businesses. Their new roles as economic and political advisers provided them with excellent opportunities subtly to present their views. For example, when a group of Takia villagers asked about the benefits of the proposed marketing association, they received the undeniably true but evasive answer: 'Why should you want to change things? You've never been better off than you are now!'

The divisions among the planters increased and inevitably involved others. The relative newcomer at Biabi rendered useless the agreement of the other two parties to divide the island into two defined areas for trading. Since he was not involved in these arrangements, he traded freely everywhere, but because he lived in Takia, he constituted a greater threat to the Dogowan planter and hence upset the former rough balance. Each European, trying to enlarge his own faction and sphere of influence, tended to stress differences between Takia and Waskia, and between areas in each language group, at a time when the people themselves were overcoming local animosities. Even each missionary passively supported the planters of his choice.

THE EDUCATIONAL FIELD

Although the planters have only recently seen themselves in the role of teachers, they have been informal educators in the relatively closed Karkar community from earliest contact (Mager 1937: 19): until 1952, they unwittingly provided the only practical economic education, thus enabling their labourers to experiment with cash crops (cf. Epstein 1968: 167); and Salum's achievement of a European-style plantation aroused ambition among other Karkar men. When the planters realized the potential of trading in village produce they encouraged widespread planting as a means of economic expansion for themselves (Agricultural Report D. 1966-67). A small minority of their employees learned specialist skills such as driving, storekeeping and carpentry. Perhaps most important of all, the relatively large number of plantations enabled the people to become acquainted with many European culture traits, and to aspire to make the planters' way of life their own.

As we have seen, after 1964 the planters deliberately provided informal education in small business enterprise. This involved new relationships which constituted yet another phase in the island's fifty-seven years of race relations. As elsewhere in coastal New Guinea, race relations on Karkar were based initially on

F

Europeans with political power exploiting indigenous land and labour. Then the villagers, with slowly increasing political representation, attempted to exploit the skills and knowledge of Europeans. The order of these events is important: the arrogant master-servant relationship created by the early settlers and Administrators hardened into what Finney (1969: 63) calls 'caste-like relations', which even the improved economic and political fortunes of the Karkar and the good intentions of some Europeans could not easily dissipate. The people saw themselves as a deprived group in comparison with the economically superior and powerful Europeans, whom they regarded with an ambivalence born of both need and envy.

Like planters everywhere in long-settled coastal areas, the German and early Australian planters made clear to the Karkar their concept of essential indigenous inferiority (Lawrence 1964a: 57-61; Rowley 1965: 14, 76; Inglis 1968: 30). This contrasted with the people's own interpretation of obvious differences as a cosmic accident. The published letters of European planters on Karkar mentioned earlier suggest that the 'commercial viewpoint' anonymously presented in 1937 for an unspecified district, could also have been theirs. 'Anyone not blinded by maudlin humanitarianism', runs the letter, '. . . must see that the European must necessarily be master and the native the servant—a condition which is an integral part of the natural order of human society' (*Pacific Islands Monthly* 1937: 43-4). Race relations on Karkar reflected this suggestion.

As noted, the Germans regarded the people merely as 'units of labour' (cf. Rowley 1967: 72) and avoided involvement with them outside this context. In spite of their own alliances, they considered native women 'merely a necessary evil' (Lyng 1925: 179). Early Australian attitudes were scarcely more sympathetic. Lyng (1925: 181, 189), the Australian Military Administrator in Madang mentioned above, concluded that a European could scarcely have affection for his half-caste offspring. Moreover, in hearing a charge of forced recruitment against a Chinese, he considered that the silence of the villagers must be accepted as acquiescence in order to maintain the economic machinery of the colony. The Lutheran missionary Henklemann (n.d.), in his report of the *Kukuaik* cult, criticized the planters sharply for postulating one set of rules for themselves and another for the Karkar, and for the unnecessary harshness and outright antagonism they and Administration officers from Madang exhibited during *Kukuaik*.

After 1952, race relations were tinged with a degree of superficial *bonhomie*. At the same time the villagers voiced dissatisfaction over their continuing general subordination. While scrupulously and patiently observing their obligation to hand over as much responsibility as possible to indigenous public servants and councillors, resident European Administration staff remained socially remote. The heavy demands of the new education system and expanding health services made personal contact with congregation members all but impossible for mission personnel and helped maintain the old paternalism. While the settlers made overt gestures of generosity and sometimes of hospitality to important men, their attitudes ranged from acknowledged racism through paternalism to acceptance of and relative involvement in the local scene. The last, at Biabi, may be explained in part by the fact that this settler, being mainly a trader, was more dependent on the villagers than were the other Europeans. His marriage to a Takia woman facilitated friendly and informal interaction. Yet even here, his ambitious and extensive business interests limited relaxed social relationships. Long-established planters, while acknowledging the economic and political emergence of the Karkar, only cautiously acknowledged them socially, and when they did, it was from a sense of necessity. At the very best it was a self-conscious effort, rather than the spontaneous result of a natural growth of friendship.

The difficulties of both Europeans and indigenes in building up rapport on a friendly and informal level, after more than half a century of virtual social segregation, should not be underestimated. There was no social field common to both, on which they could meet and exchange small talk, and a further obstacle to a genuine relationship was that the people themselves sought in such an association the secret of economic success. In my own case, some admitted their hopes of obtaining knowledge of this secret from me. Burridge (1954: 935-9; 1960: 8) had the same experience among the Manam, and Lawrence (1964a: 2-3) among the Garia.

The other Europeans on Karkar not mentioned so far were the employees of private and Company plantations. The former, comprising manager, accountants and mechanics, numbered about nine in 1968. On the whole, they participated in the new trends as much and no more than their employers required. Their ignorance of local traditions, values and problems, and the prohibitions the planters placed on them made their influence negligible. Managers of Company plantations, having almost no economic contact with the villagers, were almost completely isolated from them. They took little or no interest in local matters and, with rare exceptions, seemed unaware of the delicate issues at stake.

These then were the major features of European contact. In spite of the changes in the influence of the Administration, missions and settlers as groups, and in spite of the economic and political modernization the Karkar achieved, a great material and intellectual gap still existed. The people characterized Europeans as wealthy, powerful and knowledgeable and believed that they derived their superior way of life from a sacred source. Their efforts to attain European standards of living are the subject of the following chapters.

3

KARKAR REACTIONS TO EUROPEAN AND
JAPANESE CONTACT TO 1952[1]

THE KARKAR characterized the German and Australian Administrations until 1952 as exploitative, harsh and openly racially
prejudiced; 1952-68 was a period of modernization with some
benign elements. From the Karkar point of view, the Japanese
war changed their world outlook and eventually led to their
improved fortunes (cf. Inglis 1968b: 29; Hastings 1969: 81).

This chapter deals with Karkar responses to contact as it impinged on the traditional economic, political and educational
systems until 1952. During this period, land alienation and plantation labour only modified the traditional economy, but from
1946 to 1952 the people began to make their own changes. In the
political field, European Administrations prohibited warfare, imposed taxation and appointed *luluais* and *tultuls*. The Lutheran
Mission imposed its congregational structure on the traditional
socio-political system. For a period from 1946, Yali 'boss boys'
controlled some areas. But much of the former political structure remained, with lineages, clans and phratries retaining
their cohesion under traditional leaders. Finally, as demon-
strated in the *Kukuaik* cult in 1941 and a few minor cults after
1946, the villagers modified but did not replace their traditional
belief system by the incorporation of Christianity.

THE ECONOMY

As already mentioned, only planters made a significant economic impact on the Karkar until 1952, while the Administrations and missions had scarcely any effect. Therefore, rather than
treat these three contact groups separately here, I give a general
historical account of responses in the economic field.

The villagers accepted knives, axes, mirrors and blankets for
the land the Germans alienated, without, they claim, appreciating the extent and permanence of this alienation. At first the
Kulkul and Marangis welcomed Schmidt because he promised
them protection from marauding mountain villagers who were

decimating them. But his eventual appropriations deprived them of adequate gardening land, and forced them to negotiate marriage alliances with those of their neighbours who would lend or give them land. These arrangements contained the seeds of dissension which matured during land demarcation proceedings in the late 1960s.

Although they disliked and feared the Germans, the Karkar claimed that most men in nearby villages worked for them at some time until 1921. They gave four main reasons for this. First, they had to earn money to pay head-tax. Second, they coveted European goods, not only for their usefulness, but for the prestige they brought. Third, the planters' bullying methods of recruitment frequently left the villagers little choice in the matter. Last, they found it difficult to avoid consistently the pressures of their traditional leaders and later, *luluais*, who received payment for securing labourers. When their contracts expired, they received wages in cash and trade goods, such as knives, axes and loincloths. They distributed these to their kindred, who gradually accepted them as a necessary part of village life.

During the Australian Mandate Administration from 1926 to 1942, the alienation of a further 1,359 hectares of land for plantations resulted in increased demands on Karkar labour. While they made good use of the new axes and knives, they remained subsistence gardeners, exchanged pigs in the old way, and, thanks to the ban on warfare, engaged in mainland trade on a wider basis than ever before. But three factors were soon to undermine the old trading system: the Administration prohibited travel to the mainland by canoe in 1934 because of mishaps at sea (cf. Fortune 1935: x); heavy recruitment and the constant presence of Europeans resulted in new perceived needs, which could not be satisfied through traditional channels; and as a consequence of the spread of Christianity and the cessation of the old pagan rites, ceremonial goods, which previously formed the bulk of imports, were no longer in demand. The Takia still exported pigs, wooden plates, galip nuts and betel nut in return for clay pots from Madang, and traded these internally with inland villages as before, but the alliances between the west coast Karkar and people on Mugil and the north coast as far as Malala declined.

The Karkar avoided the extreme insularity, which the Administration ban on sea-going canoes and preference for local recruitment might have created, by buying large boats with oars and sails. Paramount *Luluai* Salum in Waskia, and the villages of

Mangar, Biu and Kurumlang each bought one. The traditional co-traders, Marup, Kurum and Liloi were joint owners of the *Makuli*, named after themselves. Although not of great economic significance, these arrangements indicated a readiness to work on a communal basis in the new money currency. They were the first of a series of activities initiated to achieve European wealth and prestige.

The example of European plantations in their midst, and their experience as labourers, inspired men to try their hand at planting cash crops for themselves. With minor exceptions, they depended on their own initiative. As noted, Salum established Gaum Plantation on eighty hectares near Kaul village with the assistance of W. Middleton. In 1933, Mileng of Marup modelled Tabong Plantation on the Lutheran Mission plantation at Kurum (Map III). He planted coconuts on thirteen hectares of land contributed by himself and the villages of Marup, Mangar and Kurum for the benefit of the local congregation. Yas of Kavailo followed his example. In their capacities as leading mission teachers they both enlisted schoolboy labour to clear the bush and plant. Other men planted the sixty coconut palms required by the Administration for home consumption, but their experiments at cash cropping were of little consequence. Therefore, they continued to work for the settlers under contract to earn cash for the Administration's head-tax.

By 1939, dissatisfaction with working conditions and feelings of social and economic deprivation were widespread (cf. Lawrence 1964a: 87). Although the *Kukuaik* cult of 1941 purported to be a religious revival in its early stages, it quickly became a vehicle for efforts to change economic conditions. *Kukuaik* is described in detail in a later section; here I merely summarize the general nature of its doctrine, as given me by participants (including leaders) in Takia, and supported by an undated, detailed report by the late Reverend F. Henkelmann, who investigated the movement on behalf of the Lutheran Mission.

Respected Lutheran Mission leaders inspired *Kukuaik* initially, with the missionaries' approval. They believed that demonstrations of Christian faith through prayer and public confession would result in congregational unity, harmony, and a state of purity in readiness for the return of Jesus foretold in the Bible (especially in Mark 13 and Luke 18: 25-30; 21: 27-36). After a former mission helper, Kubai of Boroman, claimed to have had a series of startling visions, people emphasized the material aspect of the promised millennium: God would cause

European cargo to appear and would enable them to live in comfort, ease, and harmony for ever.

The Karkar tried to achieve these goals entirely through appealing to the Christian deities through Christian ritual, which they interpreted in terms of their traditional epistemology and placed within their traditional world view. In other words, the form of *Kukuaik* was largely Christian, but the assumptions upon which it was based were pagan. This combination entailed a materialistic and reciprocal view of the relationship between God, Jesus, and man. Like the pagan creator deity Kulbob, God was the source of material wealth, in this case cargo, which he would deliver under certain ritually prescribed conditions. In conformity with the traditional belief that pagan deities lived on Mt Kanagioi, people assumed that the Christian heaven was there also, and turned their bodies and directed their prayers towards it during *Kukuaik* ceremonies.

The almost universal practice of the cult on Karkar devastated the economy. The villagers neglected their gardens, killed and ate many pigs, and destroyed their possessions to demonstrate their confidence that God would satisfy their needs, and their readiness to receive his bounty.[2] In spite of the heavy penalties for breaking labour contracts, they abandoned their work on European plantations, and flocked home to their villages to await the geophysical upheaval that would precede the millennium.

Kubai nominated 1 January 1942 as the day on which Jesus would arrive with a shipload of cargo. Instead, the Lutheran Mission boat, the *Totol*,[3] came into Kurum harbour with two Administration officers on board. Action they instigated against the presumed leaders came to a halt when the Japanese bombed Madang on 21 January, and those awaiting trial escaped and returned to Karkar. Belief in the *Kukuaik* doctrine persisted, but the associated ritual gradually ceased.

Believing that the Japanese arrival in May 1943 was the fulfilment of *Kukuaik* predictions (cf. Lawrence 1964a: 102), most people accepted their promises of future economic prosperity and social equality. The work demanded of them was not hard and they received payment for it, albeit in worthless occupation currency. But hopes for material gain from the occupation faded as food shortages, illness and general debilitation increased (cf. Read 1947: 98). After the Japanese left, the villagers fled to the bush to escape the apparently wanton destruction of their villages and gardens by Allied bombing. They cooked at night what little food they could scavenge and buried the many who died from a dysentery epidemic to which they gave the Pidgin term *pek pek blut*.

ANGAU recruited 445 men in 1944, sending some to work on local plantations and at the sawmill at Dogowan, and the rest to Madang, Lae, and New Britain. Those put to work on Karkar resented being forcibly recruited, mainly because they considered it to be a means of getting them to work out the balance of their pre-war contracts, which they believed the planters' retreat and the events of the war had cancelled.[4] On the other hand, those who went to the mainland relished the prospect of working away from home. It carried some status, and opportunities for travelling and even for learning useful skills such as carpentry. To many, this was the highlight of their lives.

After 1946, the people had more money than they had ever possessed before from their accumulated ANGAU wages and compensation received for damage to houses, trees and pigs. Their imaginations were fired by the apparent wealth and frequent egalitarianism of Australian soldiers, and by the awareness that Administrators, planters and even missionaries were neither infallible nor indestructable. As Inglis concludes from his survey of the literature on this period: 'They [New Guineans] decided that the soldiers were a different race from the Europeans they had known before the war' (1968: 30). The Karkar claimed that largely because of these new and exciting experiences, they hoped for post-war improvements in their socio-economic situation.

But the years from 1946 to 1952 brought only frustration. Intent on its own rehabilitation, colonial society left the villagers to draw on their own resources for development. But their efforts failed because, although financially equipped and eager to undertake European enterprises, they lacked the necessary organizational skills and basic education. This is illustrated by the case of the sawmill which fifteen Takia villages set up with some encouragement from the Lutheran Mission, at a cost of $850.[5] Its main function was to provide timber for Lutheran schools and churches. Hence there was no formal wages system, some people helping because of the prestige involved, and others because they felt obliged to do so. In fact, too many workmen operated the mill at well below its capacity. Furthermore, production was limited by the lack of transport for carting logs. As in pre-war years, boats attracted interest as promising business enterprises. Mileng of Marup collected $5,000 for a pinnace which soon became unseaworthy. Kavailo and its three neighbouring villages with communal funds of $3,400 tried in vain to buy a schooner for trading to the mainland. Kurum had an ambitious plan to install a power plant with savings of $1,000 but it never materialized (Patrol Report 1. 1949-50).

Efforts to increase village cash crop production failed for the same reasons (Patrol Report 1. 1946-47). Even Salum, in spite of his co-operative European neighbour, his eighty hectares of mature coconuts and his copra drier, was unable to organize labour efficiently and his output fell. In 1949, a patrol officer reported cocoa rotting unharvested beneath groves of trees, and few of the post-war copra driers in operation (Patrol Report 3. 1950-51). The following year, in a fresh burst of enthusiasm, people from fifteen villages cleaned their coconut groves, built new driers and sold from one to six tons of copra a month to the settlers. Many abandoned their work on European plantations to follow this example, but so many driers burned down, that at one stage only Salum and Mileng were drying copra. Production fell drastically and coconuts became merely an item for home consumption. Disillusioned, people returned to work as plantation labourers in such large numbers that houses and villages fell into a state of disrepair (Patrol Report 3. 1950-51). A new system of employment at a daily rate of forty-three cents and no rations proved so popular that by 1952 only eighty-three Waskia and no Takia worked as contract labourers. With ample food supplies from their own subsistence gardens, the Takia preferred payment entirely in cash.

The villagers added their current income from labouring, selling a little copra, and marketing betel nut, to their post-war savings, spending little at the European trade stores. They banked between $10,000 and $12,000 in community accounts at a branch of the Commonwealth Bank opened at Kulili Plantation in 1951, appointing their *luluai* and two others as trustees for each village. Administration officers believed that considerable amounts were still being hoarded in villages (Patrol Report 17. 1951-2).

Comparing their own failure in organizing European economic enterprise with the successful rehabilitation of the European economy, the Karkar were disappointed and resentful. With the outright aim of achieving wealth, they tried minor cargo cults, such as the short-lived movement in the Waskia village of Kurumtaur, in which people carved effigies of important ancestors and prayed to them for cargo. They also participated in an island-wide go-slow movement in protest at unsatisfactory plantation conditions. As early as 1946 the Administration itself acknowledged their readiness for modern development by promising them a patrol post, co-operatives and a local government council (Patrol Report 1. 1946-47). But Administration officers were beset by many post-war problems, not the least of which was the pressing need to rebuild Madang which had been destroyed by Japanese bombing, and none of these promises was to be realized for some years.

THE POLITICAL FIELD

European contact entailed the imposition of a centralized, hierarchical socio-political structure upon a stateless or egalitarian one, which, on Karkar, retained its intrinsic traditional form. Although each Administration had been hostile to its predecessor, the Karkar learned to adapt superficially to each with a minimum of fuss and involvement. Hence the patrol officer and *luluai-tultul* system co-existed with, but never replaced, traditional and mission social control. That discontent with the imposed official structure did exist is clear from the political elements of *Ku-kuaik*,[6] the assumption of Administration titles and roles by some villagers during the Japanese occupation, and protest movements on plantations following the return of the Australians. Because the political influence of the missionaries and planters was, in fact, more significant than that of the Administrations, these three agents of contact are examined separately. But it should be remembered that the Karkar themselves did not always differentiate between the powers of these groups, each of which was frequently in a position to assert its authority as it saw fit.

The Administrations

The Karkar villagers saw the *kiaps* or patrol officers as embodying the full power of the Administrations. Their observations about most of these officers, particularly before the 1950s, coincided with the following comments from a young New Guinean writing under the pseudonym of Kokou Warubu:

> The most powerful and disturbing word in the Territory today is the word 'Kiap'. Powerful first for the policing powers that it conjures up; secondly for the inscrutable prerogatives of rudeness and dismissal it embodies. Thirdly, for the arrogance with which the owner of such a title frequently behaves. The word kiap does not convey the notion of pioneer and helpful friend (1968:61).

Because they feared them, people placated the *kiaps* if necessary and avoided them whenever possible.

Reactions to the German system of appointing a *luluai* over a group of villages were negative because the tradition of politically autonomous villages militated against a headman's influence extending beyond this limit.[7] Here was the first example of fragmentation or the traditional concept of statelessness and kinship cohesion operating against that of centralized authority. Yet the trappings of the *luluai*'s office impressed people. When Saleb of Biu and Del of Marangis became the first Takia *luluais*, the caps and carved sticks were regarded not so much as symbols of European law, but as the law itself. 'At this time', said Sibeg of Biu, reverently producing the stick 'the law came to Karkar. Saleb visited many villages and held the head of the king—this stick'![8]

The villagers found the *kiaps* of the Australian Mandate Administration less brutal, if less predictable than their predecessors. Yet they still feared them as arrogant and powerful beings who treated them as if they were 'less than pigs and dogs' (cf. Luana 1969: 18). The people called them 'the thieves from the sea' because they took away their money in the form of tax for some unknown purpose, and they resented their commands to cut tracks and roads which benefited only Europeans (cf. Rowley 1965: 87).

The appointment of a single *luluai* and *tultul* to each village in 1921 met with greater acceptance, but the paramount *luluai* had little influence beyond his own immediate area, and still less beyond his language group. Administration-appointed headmen had varied backgrounds: some were traditional big men, but most were ordinary villagers with more than usual contact with Europeans, or men of only middle status answerable, as Rowley (1965: 84-5) suggests for the system in general, to both the *kiap* and the real village leaders. For example, Paramount *Luluai* Salum, according to his son's explanation, inherited rights to a relatively large area of land, and leadership of his lineage only through the death of his father's two brothers without issue. His prestige derived largely from his relationship with his Australian neighbour and his subsequent relative economic success. He reached the highest political position an indigene could occupy: paramount *luluai* first of Waskia, and later of Karkar. He was awarded the Loyal Service Medal in 1957. Even more remote from the traditional leadership pattern were the appointments of a refugee from Kevasob as *luluai* of Marup 2 and of a Tolai residing in Bangame as *luluai* of that village and right-hand man to Salum.

A *luluai* who was not a traditional leader and who lacked the opportunities and charisma of Salum achieved little power, except, as people admitted with some irony, immediately before the arrival of the *kiap*. In fact, the *tultul*, because of his fluency in Pidgin, frequently superseded him (Mager 1937; cf. Rowley 1954: 772-82, 1965: 84). Not surprisingly, in 1941 most *tultuls* and *luluais* gave way to *Kukuaik* leaders who took control of every aspect of village life.

The *Kukuaik* cult succeeded, where the Administrations had failed, in extending political boundaries from the village to encompass virtually the entire island (cf. Lawrence 1964a: 222). Only Kavailo and its three neighbouring villages under the influence of the Takia paramount *luluai*, Aitul, abstained because of the punishment they had suffered after supporting a revivalist movement in 1926. Defiance of Administration headmen was such that some people suggested sacrificing Aitul for fear his opposition might jeopardize their chances of success (private communication from Father Tschauder). Eventually, as noted, they abandoned activities associated with planters and missionaries as well, in the belief that anybody working for Europeans at the time of the millennium would remain forever a servant of other men. This wholesale contempt for labour contracts led to Administration intervention, but the influence of *Kukuaik* beliefs, while dissipated, was never really broken.

The Japanese landing presented the people with a paradox: on the one hand, they were afraid and, on the other, as we have seen, they believed the event was the fulfilment of *Kukuaik* predictions (cf. Lawrence 1964a: 107, 133). These two main factors conditioned their behaviour during the occupation.

To say that they welcomed the Japanese warmly (Worsley 1957: 214) is not generally true (cf. Burridge 1960: 12). They observed, and some actually experienced, the terrors of the bombing of Madang. After the occupation of the town, they grieved to see their missionaries arrested and ill-treated. Rumours were rife: 'The Karkar tremble with fear of the wild Japanese', Father Tschauder wrote in his diary at Tabel Catholic Mission, 'and they fear, above all, for the young women and girls'. When the troops landed on the island, the people asked themselves: 'What kind of "masters" are these?' Many of them left their houses and hid in the bush. Gradually, as conditioned responses to such changes allayed their fear, they returned to the villages (cf. Burridge 1960: 12).

Basing their prediction on such Bible references as Luke 21: 25-28,[9] *Kukuaik* leaders had postulated a giant upheaval result-

ing in a new way of life for the Karkar. Later, some of them predicted the bombing of Madang (cf. Lawrence 1964a: 105). When
this occurred they equated the two phenomena as signalling the
punishment of the arrogant Europeans, and the arrival of the expected vehicles of material and social benefits in the persons of
the Japanese. By claiming that the Karkar ancestors lived in
plenty in Tokyo, and promising a new and better way of life in
the future for their descendants, the Japanese quickly secured
political control.

There were exceptions to the general rule that *Kukuaik* followers accepted the Japanese as benefactors. One of these was
Paramount *Luluai* Salum, whose prestigious position depended
on the return of the Australians. Further, he feared that a concentration of Japanese in his strategically important area could
attract Allied bombing raids which would cause damage and loss
of life to the inhabitants. At first he followed a policy of passive
non-co-operation (Patrol Report 23. 1944-45). Then, according to
his sons, an enemy from western Waskia informed the resident
Japanese officer that he was pro-Australian. Matimoto ordered
him to provide food for the troops on penalty of death and re-
prisals to the villagers. To the extent required he complied, but
spent most of the occupation in hiding in the bush. Mileng, the
Lutheran Mission leader, continued as best he could his work of
maintaining the unity and Christian allegiance of the Lutheran
congregation. He visited villages all over the island, administering the sacraments and reassuring the people during their drastic
dysentery epidemic. The Catholic catechist Suguman Matibri and
his brother tried to maintain the small Catholic flock.

Less positive was the behaviour of the *Kukuaik* leader, Kubai
of Boroman, and a small group of men who had worked amicably
as personal servants for Europeans for some years. Kubai retired
to the bush to await events. The others, unwilling to commit
themselves, simply avoided the Japanese until they too could
determine which way the fortunes of war would go. Like many
other New Guineans 'circumstances had made shrewd politicians
of [them] . . . and they were determined to side with the ultimate
winners' (Ryan 1959: 95).

On the other hand, Aitul, Takia's paramount *luluai*, welcomed the Japanese in Madang with gifts. Father Tschauder
suggests that he saw in them an opportunity to achieve the wealth
and prestige so far denied him. Far from benefiting from settler
contact, his village had been subjected to early land alienation
by the Germans, followed by impersonal Company exploitation

from Kavailo Plantation. Aitul himself refused to discuss his wartime experiences with me.

The Takia villagers as a whole liked and respected Maida and, to a lesser extent Sato, their two resident officers who, as noted, safeguarded indigenous life and custom generally, and permitted Christian worship. The Waskia had little rapport with Matimoto, whom, they say, they avoided after he executed the Chinese, Li Hung. To a man, the Karkar despised the ordinary soldiers for their uncouth, unhygienic habits, which, they recalled, were inferior even to those of pigs. But they obeyed them because of their rifles, bayonets, and threats of decapitation.

Thus, with the exception of Salum, village headmen helped the Japanese organize labour and food supplies, neglecting their normal village duties in the process. But, under the command of Aitul, 'who was, as it were, District Officer' (Patrol Report 4. 1944-45), some men, mainly from Takia, set themselves up in positions similar to those of Administration officers. They patrolled the island, bullying and beating people who did not meet their demands for goods and services in a way Maida never permitted his troops. They saw themselves as second in the administering hierarchy of military officers, soldiers, *luluais* and *tultuls*, and indigenous police. Mead (1956: 179) describes how the Japanese in Manus also backed indigenous 'power-seekers' in this way.

The Japanese gave elementary training to approximately 200 men in a school for police at Biu village on the Takia south coast. Although a Patrol Report (4. 1944-45) and Lawrence (1964a: 106) suggest that this scheme had wider political aims, the Biu people and Marup men who attended the school refute this. The Japanese merely gave them a cane as a badge of office and showed them how to supervise the work of digging, building and carrying. They chose some policemen to accompany them when they left Karkar, promising to take them to Tokyo eventually. But when a bomb killed a Takia man accompanying the Japanese retreat to Wewak, his companions dropped behind to bury him and deserted.

As mentioned, between the Japanese evacuation and the arrival of the Australian troops and ANGAU officers, the Karkar suffered severe deprivation through Allied bombardment. Their heaviest loss of life, from dysentery, occurred at this time. Villages from Marangis to Buson were most affected not only with dysentery, but with post-dysenteric arthritis, yaws, and malnutrition. Already short of land through Schmidt's early alienation, their area had been consistently occupied by the Japanese, who made massive demands upon their food supplies. In Waskia alone, the population decreased by 330 between 1940 and 1944 (Patrol Report 4. 1944-45).

The Takia explained that they greeted the first Allied forces with caution for two reasons: fear of the consequences of their co-operation with the Japanese, and the presence among the ANGAU officers of two men who boded ill both for the war-time collaborators and for the pre-war *Kukuaik* leaders. One was W. Middleton, friend of the anti-Japanese Salum and an instigator of the *Kukuaik* enquiry. The other was one of the Administration officers who had investigated the movement. Kubai and Mileng were re-arrested. At their trial, they received sentences of three years' labour on Kulkul Plantation. No further action was taken. In retrospect, the Karkar held little rancour over the sentences, in spite of their devotion to Mileng and their consistent denial of his leadership in *Kukuaik*'s later cargo cult form. The confirmed belief of the Administration and the planters to the contrary made some punishment inevitable, and, in any case, the Lutheran missionaries achieved his release to return to his pastoral duties well before his term expired.

ANGAU's pre-occupation with restoring the European economy and its failure properly to investigate events during the occupation, in particular the activities of Aitul's group, led to deep resentment expressed first in a 'go-slow' movement on Dogowan Plantation. The Administration saw in this a pro-Japanese element, which Marup men working there at that time denied. The reasons they gave for the unrest were as follows: they were angry because Aitul and his henchmen now held high status positions for ANGAU and the Production Control Board, and hence escaped punishment and restitution of plundered goods; they found plantation working conditions intolerable and believed that they received fewer and inferior rations than did ANGAU employees in Madang.[10] But as the late Babob Bangan pointed out, the roots of the trouble lay in the past: even during the 1930s, dissatisfaction over wages, rations and working conditions led to widespread resentment against European employers. Patrol Report 41. 1944-45 gives the official account of the situation: labourers were receiving no wages or loin cloth issues, and it was widely rumoured that the Australian Administration would never pay up. In its dedication to copra production, the P.C.B. provided inadequate quarters, amenities and rations, and made no distinction between those performing heavier or more responsible work, and ordinary labourers. Finally, Karkar was heavily over-recruited.

The sullen, unco-operative approach to work which spread to all Karkar plantations, was only one of a series of 'strikes' for better working conditions and for justice, which occurred in Rabaul, Lae, Madang and Wewak in 1945-46.[11] Some Takia working away from home under contract to ANGAU witnessed these movements, but their influence on the Karkar situation is impossible to discover.

As mentioned, in response to the disturbances among plantation workers, ANGAU officers arrested twelve wartime miscreants, sending Aitul to gaol in Lae, after sacking him as paramount *luluai* of Takia and promoting Salum to this position for the whole of Karkar. They improved plantation labour conditions, renewed their encouragement of village rehabilitation and subjected the people to a programme of anti-Japanese and pro-Australian propaganda (Patrol Report 41. 1944-45). In accordance with traditional conciliatory customs, village leaders brought gifts of food and the 'strike' ended. Yet officials failed to discern the people's real needs and frustrations in this first purely secular mass protest in the history of the island. They aimed merely at restoring a situation where labourers would be obedient and industrious.

For the first twelve years of Australian Administration after 1946, the *kiaps* made their infrequent visits, and once again people feared and avoided them. The *luluai-tultul* system remained the same, inspiring as little co-operation as it had in the past. Without the logic, balance and religious validation of traditional leadership, it was a meaningless imposition. Patrol officers, on the possibly inadequate evidence gathered during their annual census patrols, noted only four efficient *luluais* in 1946-47, and blamed the *luluais'* lack of control for the cargo cult in Kurumtaur in 1952. Patrol Reports refer only briefly to Yali's influence on the island, but the people described to me in detail how his local 'boss boys' took over with no opposition from official headmen in some villages, and ran affairs with military precision.[12] They woke people at dawn to begin the day's activities with drilling and marching, organized gardening and village improvement, and held courts at which they heard charges and handed out sentences. This phase gradually petered out after 1948 when the Administration established a police post at Kinim (Patrol Report 3. 1950; 1) and when the Karkar opposed Yali's attacks on the missions.

G

The Lutheran Mission

As we have seen, the villagers merely tolerated the Administration-sponsored political structure of *kiap*, paramount *luluai*,
luluai and *tultul*. But they actively supported and participated
in the mission congregational hierarchy of missionary, chief
elder, elders, teachers and evangelists. It introduced them to a
system of centralized authority of which they became a part. It
appealed to them because it involved a fairly democratic procedure at village level and a wide range of concerns, both of
which were consistent with traditional social control. It dealt
with these matters within a framework of the people's relationships with the supernatural, an approach neglected by the other
European agents of contact. Mission leadership, validated as it
was by religious sanctions, was compatible with traditional
leadership. Hence clan leaders frequently became elders in the
new structure. The merging of these two roles obscured the
Western distinction between secular and non-secular matters, or
Administration and mission affairs, and enabled these men rather
than the *luluais* to wield considerable power in daily life. This
helped maintain the unity of the patriclans.

The people saw the success of the mission in terms of the superior power of the Christian God. The Marup told how men
were afraid to stand upright before the great fighters, Sob and
Lui, in their heyday, so ruthless and terrifying were they. Yet,
when the two missionaries, George and Eckershoff, visited Marup
soon after establishing their station at Kurum, Sob and Lui, aggressive though they were, felt the power of their god and after
peaceful exchanges, allowed them to leave unharmed. Thus
began a lasting connection with the mission through the village
big men, and what people saw as freedom from the old bonds of
fear.

At regular weekly meetings, mission headmen discussed both
spiritual and secular matters with the villagers, and disciplined
deviants. If their decisions were sometimes harsh, supported, as
people believed, by the stringent conditions of Christianity and
the power of the missionary and his god (cf. Lawrence 1956: 85;
1964a), they were often conditioned by the traditional features
of leadership: the ability to make suggestions acceptable to the
group as a whole and to achieve consensus of opinion through
firmness, skill and sensitivity (cf. Read 1959).

The final point of appeal was the missionaries. In spite of
their paternalism, the villagers found them approachable, concerned and consistent. They appreciated Kunze's distribution of

steel axes in return for food; they loved George and Eckershoff for their devoted efforts at teaching which produced such notable mission leaders as Mileng and Babob of Marup, Yas of Kavailo and Kautil of Kumoria; they named their children after Stahl who frequently stayed in people's houses, sharing their food and smoking local tobacco with them.

Unlike the *kiap*, the missionaries tried to replace and explain what they took away. In place of the old religious system, they offered a new set of deities and a new kind of education which promised important benefits. Mager notes that the people did not distinguish between mission functions and those of the Administration, although as I point out later, they clearly distinguished between the methods used. 'In the light of their former pattern of behaviour and thinking', writes Mager, 'these two functions should be integrated as a unit' (1937: 33; cf. Rowley 1954: 781). And as we have seen, the *Maroltamol* or peace chief, who worked to uphold the 'laws' of the village, was also the clan's ritual expert.

After the Japanese war, both state and mission functions did combine in weekly village councils, at which the *luluai, tultul* and mission leaders conferred before the assembled villagers (Patrol Report 17. 1951-52). They discussed secular matters, such as copra production and the disposal of communally-held money, as well as church, school and general congregational affairs. These meetings opened and closed with prayers.

Perhaps the Karkar's most significant response to the political influence of the Lutheran Mission was to accept the concept of involvement and participation in the Lutheran congregations in the central Madang District as a whole. Evangelists and teachers volunteered for service in mainland areas, sometimes spending many years there with their Karkar wives and children. From the time of Kunze, pupils from remote villages lived and studied together both at Kurum and in Madang. Waskia and Takia adopted the Graged language from the Madang people as a mission lingua franca. After the war, Pidgin replaced Graged to some extent, but by this time inter-congregational bonds were firmly established.

The Planters

Because their own socio-political system remained basically unchanged, the villagers interpreted the European model within its conceptual framework. In terms of actors, they tended to see two total systems: one comprising the missionaries and the other the Administrators and the planters. Their special characteristics

placed the missionaries in a unique category among Europeans.
But the people conceptualized planters and Administration
officers in broad terms, as one. This confusion arose from memories of planters coming with 'police boys' to recruit by force, of
violent efforts to alienate or hold land by Schwartz and Schmidt
respectively, of brutality against a suspected petty thief on a
Company plantation, and of a general system of punishment by
beating or reducing wages. The latter were meagre enough: Kumoria men claimed that earliest wages for contract labour were
at first ten cents a month with keep, then twenty cents and finally
fifty cents. They had experienced plantation work at Dogowan
and Kavailo on Karkar, and away at Sek near Madang, Lae, Rabaul in New Britain, Kavieng in New Ireland and Manus in the
Admiralty Islands. *'Wok nating! Lus nating! Bun istap!'* they
commented.[13] In the absence of the *kiaps*, the planters applied
the law in the same unsympathetic manner, and influenced the
administration of Karkar in their own interests. Only Salum
could boast a special relationship with a planter, and even his
achievements were due to a combination of his European neighbour's power and the influence he gained from his position as
paramount *luluai*.

As a consequence of linking the planters politically with the
Administration, the Karkar interpreted their *de facto* powers as
de jure ones well into the Australian Trusteeship period. Thus,
they themselves helped perpetuate the planters' authoritarian-
ism. Nevertheless, they expanded their world view through
working on European plantations with labourers drawn indiscriminately from many local villages and, increasingly, from
the mainland. This interaction outside the traditional political
unit helped weaken parochialism and, as practical trading ties
diminished, comprised new avenues of communication beyond
the village and its neighbourhood.

EDUCATION[14]

Up to 1952, Administration exhibitions of military strength
taught fear and blind obedience as part of the total socio-political
lesson of racial distinction on Karkar. The missions achieved
almost island-wide literacy in simple reading and writing, the
Lutherans in the Graged language, the Catholics in Pidgin, and
taught people that the Christian deities were supremely powerful. The settlers maintained their superior positions, but made
a positive contribution by providing the only economic educa-

tion of the entire period. Varied as this educational process was, it had one common result: feelings of deprivation and loss of self-respect (cf. Burridge 1960: 24). These in turn created a desire for the power, self-confidence and appurtenances of the white man, in the belief that 'one gets what one wants partly by stylistic correctness' (Rowley 1965: 132).

The Administrations

No Karkar are known to have attended the German Administration's school at Namanula in New Britain or the Australian Mandate Administration's schools. A limited number trained as policemen and medical *tultuls* and worked away from Karkar.

The Administrations achieved so little informal education that people had no comprehension of what central government implied. Even to be a village official required not knowledge, but obedience to the *kiap* in his presence and to traditional and congregational controls in his absence (cf. Rowley 1967: 77). A spokesman among a group of Marup and Kevasob men explained the villagers' situation:

> We understood nothing and they explained nothing. We had no respect for the Government. It would come to the village, and the policemen would kick us about and beat us. The *kiaps* said 'Work! Clean the road! Build latrines!' And we worked. They were strong. We knew nothing, were told nothing, were nothing!

The *Kukuaik* movement was partly a consequence of feelings of racial inferiority and inadequacy, and the belief that Europeans were deliberately concealing the secrets for obtaining wealth and power. As noted, its doctrine and ritual were based on the traditional belief that all knowledge was divinely revealed. In this case, the people appealed for help to the Christian deities. The punishment *Kukuaik* followers received only served to strengthen the conviction that the Administration itself enjoined secrecy about the source of European knowledge. 'After this', one of the abused leaders said, 'we thought the Japanese would be better'. What the Karkar learned from the Japanese occupation must be seen against this background.

Inevitably they made some important discoveries. Not only did they realize that Europeans were not invincible, but, for the first time, they experienced sympathy for certain white men, in particular for the missionaries during their suffering and for two American airmen they saw the Japanese execute at Ameron near Madang. Most memorable of all, the Japanese supported their opinions about European exploitation and racial prejudice and promised them the material wealth and power they had hoped to achieve through *Kukuaik*. Maida's claim to be a Christian seemed to confirm people's suspicions that he was part of the cult prophecy. Because he maintained excellent relations with them throughout the occupation, the cargo cult beliefs he fostered remained even after he left.

ANGAU's prohibition of the pleasant social relations the people quickly established with the Australian forces occupying Karkar seemed further evidence that Administrations were determined to relegate them to an inferior way of life. On the other hand the men who went to Lae and Jacquinot Bay in New Britain were able to form exciting friendships with Australian soldiers, as the Manus had with American troops (cf. Mead 1956: 163-70). Reminiscing about this period, Kabug Bangan of Marup said:

> We talked about the future of New Guinea. They talked about Australia . . . This was the only time I ever sat down with Europeans. They never turned me away. You see, this was a bad time—wartime. So 'master' and native worked together. Before the war the 'masters' were not like this. They used to make us stay a long way from them. Oh, it was a different thing during army time!

Some said that the soldiers claimed the existence of cargo cult in Australia. It is impossible to say whether these tales were told as jokes or whether they were a Karkar fantasy (cf. Hogbin 1951: 298). In any case, people accepted them afterwards as fact, and used them to support claims that the Germans and Australians introduced cargo cults to New Guinea. In this way they validated their own cargoism to Europeans.

Inevitably, some Karkar saw American negroes smartly uniformed and carrying out responsible duties, apparently as wealthy and confident as their white counterparts. It was a short leap to the conclusion that only New Guineans lacked a high standard of living (cf. Hannemann 1948: 13). I heard only one account of a negro explaining that this seeming prosperity only accompanied wartime conditions. He was reported as saying: 'If only negroes had factories, as white Americans have, they too could prosper, just as New Guineans could'.

Meanwhile, the Takia at home reorganized their villages along military camp lines during 1945-47. Although reticent about these activities, some people described how one or two 'boss boys', supporters of Yali, took control in each village. The

beating of a slit gong called people from their beds to parade before these 'boss boys', who gave them the day's work orders which
had to be carried out promptly. As well as the ordinary daily
duties, they had to improve the appearance of the entire village,
aligning and repairing houses, planting neat hedges between
them and clearing back the undergrowth. Special houses were
built and furnished with chairs and tables probably in readiness
for a visit from Yali.[15] While this new mode of living may have
been a plan to obtain goods through a process of imitative
magico-religious ritual, as Hannemann (1948) suggests for the
Madang District, it could also have been related to Yali's instruc-
tions about rehabilitation and improvement of village sites.
Clearly, the Karkar credited Yali with extra-ordinary power, for
they asked the Reverend G. Reitz, the first post-war missionary on
Karkar, whether he had seen the king of New Guinea (Yali), who
was reported to be travelling up the north coast. They thought
there might be something to be gained from the new system,
until they tired of the excessive demands made on their energy
and time, and became disillusioned by Yali's failure to tour
Karkar.

What left the greatest impression from post-war experiences
were the friendships made with Australian soldiers. To describe
but two: Kabug Bangan exchanged letters with an Australian for
some years after he returned to Sydney, and named his daughter
after this man's wife; the Marup councillor cherished memories
of a no-nonsense but egalitarian relationship with the late Roy
Sowerby (then a member of ANGAU), from whom he learnt a
high standard of carpentry. As Schwartz says of the impact of
Americans on Manus, 'the lines that defined the distance between
"master" and "boy" seemed to have faded . . . and life was set
straight' (1962: 225-6).

But life was not set straight any more for the Karkar than
for the Manus (cf. Mead 1956: 168; Schwartz 1962: 226). When
work with ANGAU ended, they both found exploitation and
discrimination firmly re-established, with Administrators and
planters taking up their old positions and themselves relegated to
the distasteful role of 'boys'. Perplexed, some Marup men asked
an officer of the new Provisional Administration why this should
be so. He replied that as there was still so much rehabilitation
to be done on the island, they should think only of this and
should try not to dwell on their relationships with Europeans.
This response shattered their hopes of official recognition of their
new status. In the face of a restored alliance between Administra-

tion and planters, the Karkar turned in desperation to their own methods of self-help with such tremendous energy that it was noted in patrol reports (Patrol Reports 1. 1949-50, 3. 1950-51).

The Missions

To the Karkar, each missionary emerged as an individual, not merely as a representative of a category. His personal contact, concern, and religious validation of what he taught gave rise to affection and acceptance which Administration personnel and planters never received, and encouraged the villagers to draw upon him for their entire intellectual development. The formal aspects of this derived from schools and religious teaching, the informal aspects from the missionaries' influence over secular aspects of life.

Kavailo men believed the first missionaries landing there to be deities (in Takia *tibud*). According to mythology, Kulbob and Manub had left the island in canoes, and now Kunze, arriving from the sea, was presumed to be of a similar nature too, if not Kulbob himself. Later, when more Europeans arrived, the people realized that they could not all be deities, but were possibly spirits of the dead. They showed great interest in the strange material goods being unloaded on the shore (Kriele 1927: 68-9). Kunze (1925) describes their bold curiosity, good humour and frequent thieving. He also reports, and this was a favourite story among the Karkar generally, how the big-men wooed his wife with gifts and love-sorcery. 'We were not clear about Europeans then', the villagers explained. 'We had never seen a white woman. Now we know better.' Through Kunze's painstaking teaching, medical care, and involvement in village affairs, they gradually gained confidence and some young men willingly went to Graged Island to study after the Kavailo station closed in 1895.

The Karkar took readily to work as teachers and evangelists. Even before George and Eckershoff came to the island in 1911, Madoi of Kavailo opened a school in Kunze's old house, another student taught at Kurum, and Sori of Kavailo began a lifetime of teaching in west coast villages in 1910. After the new Lutheran station opened at Kurum, teachers and evangelists spread rapidly along the south and west Takia coasts. Generally people accepted prohibitions on practising infanticide, polygamy, warfare and *barag*, the secret male cult, because they believed the missionaries' god to be so much more powerful than their own deities. Until this time they believed knowledge to have come from Kulbob and they obeyed his 'laws'. Now they thought that perhaps the new god had always given them knowledge and Kulbob only things. The new god gave them his spirit and they tried to obey him. Kunze's description of a mass baptism of 101 people at Kavailo in 1921 suggests that this adaptability was due to the fact that they ceremonially replaced the trappings and ritual of *barag*, as described earlier, with those of Christianity, but retained their traditional belief system:

> People streamed there all day . . . New houses were built to accommodate the visitors . . . and thirty pigs were killed . . . They celebrated 'Mesiab' [Barag] for the last time—though not seriously—to break visibly with the past. Then all the sacred objects were shown publicly before being put in the cult house and burnt with the house (Kriele 1927: 172-4).

Soon after, 100 people celebrated their baptism in a similar way in Bangame in Waskia. Such overt responses led George to write: 'If you were to come to Dampier and visit all the villages and schools . . . your heart would be full of pride and thanks to God, who has achieved this, through his spirit in only a few years' (Kriele 1927: 180-1).

There were setbacks of course. Sori, in 1968 a revered elder living, blind and wasted, in Kavailo, remembered that an outbreak of sickness in a Takia mountain village caused people to blame the new religion and demand the removal of their evangelist. Villagers in Buson, Marangis, and Kuduk opposed him so strongly that he was obliged to wait until the uncompromising older men died before he could make any progress there. Understandably teaching standards were low, and pupils found little use for what they learned. Because of this and of harsh treatment from teachers, many ran away from school. As already mentioned, some Mangar men sought an alternative in the Catholic Mission, and after it was established a number of truants from Lutheran schools found protection there.

The Waskia were slower than the Takia to respond to the Lutheran influence, owing to factions among themselves (Karkar Circuit Report 1954), remoteness from Mission headquarters, problems with their authoritarian Samoan evangelists, and resentment at having to accept Takia teachers and evangelists. Nevertheless the same pattern of responses emerged, even to revolt in some villages against indigenous Lutheran teachers, and approaches to the priest at Tabel for schools and churches. But some northern Waskia violently opposed the Catholics, and under Salum's leadership, tried forcibly to prevent land being marked out for Tabel Mission. Later, Catholic services being held in Bangame were broken up by fighting, in which the priest, Father Tschauder, received a severe blow on the head. Friction between adherents to the two missions grew until pre-occupation with Japanese demands during the war put an end to it.

In spite of the shortcomings of their indigenous teachers, many Lutheran Karkar achieved a degree of literacy in Graged. This gave them access to church literature such as hymn books and parts of the Bible translated into Graged. No total figures on literacy are available, but Mager (1937: 35) reports 54% of village children attending school in 1933, 112 pupils enrolled at the middle school and seminary at Kurum in 1935, and 1,233 adults at catechumenical schools. The three Catholic villages at that time had a central school at Tabel. Schools collapsed during the Japanese occupation and, in their general post-war disillusionment, people made no response to the missionary's urging to rebuild them. Finally, Mileng pursuaded village elders to organize the work, and formal education began again in 1947 (personal communication from the Reverend G. Reitz).

Gaubin Hospital, from its inception in 1948, was an important centre for formal education for its staff-in-training and for informal education in both religious and secular matters for the population at large. The Karkar felt a personal involvement in its affairs: under Tscharke's direction, they had drained the swamp on which it was to be built and constructed the original eighty bed hospital. Nearby Kurum village provided land for staff gardens and permanent access to its fresh-water spring. Despite only token wages, hospital orderlies were respected and deferred to in their villages.

But for some years, fear of modern medical treatment, and the conviction that sorcery caused illness and death prevented many people from voluntarily seeking medical treatment for all but such things as sores and broken bones. According to traditional belief, if a person offended either the spirits of his own or others' ancestors, or if he offended living people, these would cause sickness, through sorcery, which might ultimately lead to death unless the offence were corrected. In particular, malaria, cirrhosis of the liver and bronchial diseases were thought to occur in this way. The occurrence of malaria indicated that the ground was 'not good', and marshy, over-grown areas were especially suspect. When wronged, the spirits beat this earth, causing the disease to rise and attack the offender. The remedy was for relatives of the afflicted person to place branches of the *croton* shrub on the believed source and to perform the relevant *singsing* to placate the spirits. An offender against a living person would have to redress the offence before a cure, either with or without medical aid, was possible. In addition, people made considerable use of traditional remedies: the Marup frequently heated clay from the bank of a stream near the village, wrapped it in a cloth or leaves and applied it to arthritic limbs; they spread gum from a certain tree on running sores and considered the water in which leaves from the *tulip* tree were boiled a splendid tonic for stomach and post-parturition disorders. In some coastal villages, boiling bananas were placed in the hand or at the feet of a convulsive to shock him out of a fit, and a headache or pains elsewhere were treated by chipping the spot with a piece of glass or other sharp object.[16]

In general, the Karkar found the Lutheran custom of dedication and prayer in daily activities compatible with their traditional view of religion as a technical necessity for success. They associated Christianity with the satisfaction of practical needs through the invocation of the Christian deities, performing ritual in the form of prayers and sermons before all important activities such as village meetings, the opening of new schools and churches, and the departure of young people for work on the mainland. While acknowledging the technical skills necessary to construct Gaubin, they ascribed its endurance and success to its dedication to God, and to frequent prayers. This accorded with the traditional intellectual system in which all enterprises occurred within a framework of sacred explanation, sanction and guarantee. Able to absorb Christianity relatively effortlessly into their existing belief system, they never abandoned it at any general level in their desire for European wealth and power, as did some Ngaing and sub-coastal Sengam, at Yali's urging, between 1948 and 1950 (Lawrence 1964a: 187-8). Instead, they incorporated it into a series of religious revivals and cargo cults, described later. These mainly arose from an invidious comparison of their standard of living with that of Europeans on nearby plantations.

The Planters

With rare exceptions the planters did not deliberately try to help the villagers by teaching them skills outside the contract labour situation. Broadly speaking, people responded to them in two ways: first, they copied their example in the hope of obtaining material rewards or overt satisfaction of some sort; and second, where the example, by its very nature, could not be copied, responses were of an intellectual nature. Thus, while they imitated cash crop planting, they could only react with envy to the unattainable European way of life, which they had set as a goal for themselves; with fear to their harsh working conditions; and with feelings of mental and physical inferiority to the settlers' racial prejudice.

Plantation work in itself had very little significance for labourers for five main reasons. To begin with, it occurred outside any religious context; secondly, it entailed working for someone with whom they could not establish a system of reciprocal relationships and hence it had no parallel in traditional village life (cf. Burridge 1960: 20); thirdly, it existed in a sort of vacuum, in that each worker performed only part of the production process, had no understanding of the end product (Lawrence 1964a: 228), and consequently experienced no sense of personal achievement. Further, after the range and sophistication of their material desires increased, many felt little sense of reward in their low wages and harsh conditions. Finally, the Administration's head-tax requirement forced men into plantation labour in a way they hated.

Yet contract work had its uses. Apart from exceptional cases like Salum, Mileng and Yas, voluntary cash crop planting and processing in villages before 1950 resulted mainly from copying unaided the settlers' example. Only rarely, as in the case of Marup's first, primitive, copra drier, did planters give direct help. The few other elementary skills which a minority of workers picked up were insignificant in comparison. Owners of old stands of coconut trees invariably explained to me: 'My father saw how the "masters" planted, and when he finished his "time", he came home and copied them'. But because the learning process was never complete, village planting was haphazard, crop husbandry poor, and production low. Nevertheless, when co-operatives began in 1952, the people had a basic knowledge of the work and a considerable number of mature coconut palms. These provided immediate cash income and the incentive to expand.

As far as social interaction was concerned, a few villagers who had worked for long periods, usually as personal servants for a particular settler, might achieve mild joking relationships with him (personal communication from A. Barnett). This rarely occurred on Company plantations or where owners were not in residence, since changing staff and rigid policies prohibited enduring personal ties. When the Company instigated its policy of employing only mainland labour on its three plantations in the late 1920s, the Karkar were puzzled, then resentful at being kept at a distance in this way.[17] Their antagonism towards Coconut Products Ltd dates from this time.

The people had no doubts as to their place in the new hierarchy: they were strictly workmen for the 'masters'. To them, the planters personified wealth, arrogance, intolerance, power, and remoteness and, in the possession of these alien characteristics, they saw a situation of inexplicable mystery. Like the Tangu and the Manam Islanders, they could not find a means of dissipating the problems white men caused them, nor could they fully account for them (cf. Burridge 1960: 39). As they did in all areas of confusion, they drew upon traditional concepts to explain the European mystique. On the one hand, they expanded their system of categories to include a special one for this group of people whom they no longer regarded as deities, as their forefathers had Kunze, or as spirits of the dead, as they had later European arrivals. As with the Manus, 'when whites ceased to show goodwill, they could no longer see ancestor spirits in them' (Hannemann 1948: 937). On the other hand, they tried to find religious validation for their conclusion in the Bible.

Tentatively the Karkar regarded Europeans as 'another kind of man', because of the obvious physical difference of skin colour (cf. Hannemann 1948: 840). The biblical story of Noah's sons, Shem, Ham and Japheth supported this theory (cf. Hogbin 1951: 242, 248; Lawrence 1964a: 76-7). The next step was to connect white skin with material wealth: during *Kukuaik*, people anticipated that the skin of all believers would turn white after the holocaust, and that cargo would automatically follow. They claimed that Australians believed in even greater physical differences than that of skin colour. According to Takia men, soldiers they met while they were working for ANGAU claimed that Australians at home believed that New Guineans had tails.[18] They asked me anxiously whether Australians still believed this. Aware of European master-race assumptions, and searching in Christian mythology for literal explanations of their material and social disadvantages, they used the Australian stories to clarify some of the unpleasant facts facing them. These could explain why whites neglected even the most formal and basic courtesies of indigenous society, such as occasional visits to villages to sit down, talk and share food; and why physical contact with black-skinned people revolted them.

Devising a special category for Europeans did not, however, reduce envy of their material wealth or diminish the villagers' frustration over unsatisfactory race relations. These feelings were overtly expressed during *Kukuaik*. As it changed from a religious revival to an outright appeal for European goods and power, the idea of terminating the master-servant dichotomy arose. Differences between the descendants of Shem and Ham were now to be corrected: leaders told indentured labourers to return to their villages to avoid remaining for ever 'slaves' of other men, according to Noah's curse on Ham. Later, they explained the suffering that Europeans endured during the war as divine retribution: 'God was angry about the harshness of plantation masters . . . We worked hard, and they beat us and gave us very little for our work. Our situation was terrible. Just as God punished the neglect of Moses' laws, so he punished this by sending the war'. Already consumed by envy, fear and dependence through long contact, after 1946 the people added to this list the disillusionment they felt at being subjected again to social discrimination and exploitation.

Because education, broadly defined, determines the entire intellectual system, I will try to show how the Karkar incorporated what they had learned from the white man into their traditional system of knowledge and how they then applied this expanded body of knowledge towards achieving their material and social goals. My reconstruction of this process is based mainly on those experiences which they considered deeply significant and on problems which they seemed to find seriously disturbing. Some of the events I describe were not intended by the people; others they deliberately engineered in their struggle to place Europeans and themselves in a common conceptual framework.

My main concern here is with the intellectual system as a whole, and with beliefs about the universe and the source of knowledge in particular. To reiterate, they were as follows: the deities, Kulbob and Manub, created the material and immaterial culture, which lesser deities then guarded; spirits of the dead protected individuals and their possessions. To secure the co-operation of these beings, people included them in their view of the everyday world, and communicated with them through ritual in a system of reciprocal quasi-social relationships. They assumed that the deities revealed all knowledge, including ritual, and that sacred knowledge was the only true knowledge.

After contact, the people had to account for Europeans and for their own ambivalent attitudes of antipathy and envy towards them. At first, news of German oppression and land appropriation came to them through trade, mission and indentured labour channels, and from a handful of Graged Islanders who, exiled by the Germans after 1912, chose to live with their Takia trading partners (*Deutsches Kolonialblatt* vol. XXIII (1), 1912: 994-5; Kriele 1927: 191-4). Increasing contact with Europeans on Karkar itself strengthened early antagonism. The villagers accepted Christianity on the assumption that it was the means of becoming like white men. But their efforts to correlate and equate Christian with pagan mythology, even to the extent of seeing it as a technology, failed to produce material results. They were inspired by their literal interpretation of the Bible and the missionaries' prayers and sermons to prepare for the millennium, which they saw first in religious terms, and then as a vehicle for obtaining cargo.

The mass baptism in Kavailo in 1921 may well have been the first expression of Christian fanaticism on Karkar: Rowley (1965: 141) comments that the emotional religious experience was a common characteristic of traditional *rites de passage*, and a universally valuable technique to impress the imagination of participants in religious rituals. Possibly influenced by similar unrest in Madang at this time (Hannemann 1948: 945), Wadau and Kavailo people sponsored the first known Karkar religious revival in 1926. Arising from a deep concern with and preparation for the return of Christ, it involved elements of excess and force, but did not include appeals for European wealth. Yet the Takia, in recalling it, related it to their subsequent cargo activities, as 'the start of this "work" '.[19]

A Wadau woman called Sumal dreamed that she heard voices telling her to gather together all the people. First she went to Kavailo where a mission elder, Nugur, supported her. He and the teacher, Gil, encouraged the Katom and Kavailo to march along the south Takia coast. As they went they cried: 'We are Christ! We are Christ!' and beat people along the way. Biu and neighbouring villagers were congregated at their church in readiness to hear this new talk of God. An old man who witnessed the scene described how the Kavailo marchers beat people with canes and vines, holding some over boxes by the hands and legs as they did so, a method of punishment commonly used by planters. Then they tossed them up in the air in the belief that when they came down they would be strengthened. Confused reports from villagers credit the Lutheran missionary, old Sori, or fear of the aggressive Marup villagers, with turning the crowd back at Kurum. Faint from lack of food and sleep, they returned to Kavailo. What punishment from the Administration followed is not clear, but it was severe enough to prevent Kavailo joining wholeheartedly in the *Kukuaik* movement fifteen years later.

From this time, people tried seriously to syncretize the old and the new beliefs. As, according to tradition, they acknowledged only one intellectual framework, they saw in Christianity not a different religious system, but a European version of their own. They had only to discover the true meaning of the Bible and to relate it to the universe as they knew it. If the Christian god was also their god, as the missionaries said, it should be possible to locate on Karkar the events and physical features described in the Bible. Thus, Gil of Kavailo, searching for a solution to the problem, found a stone in a rugged gully split apart to show its many colours, and believed it to be the stone Moses struck to produce water. He suspected that Noah building the ark was Kulbob constructing his canoe at Kulbob Bay.

This process of correlation continued throughout the 1930s. Painstaking comparisons seemed to reveal only one world view, only one epistemological system and, initially, only one people with the same potential ability, but by the accident of history, with different opportunities for success. Wedges of Christian mythology, inserted into the old belief system, accounted for these differences. For example, the twelve tablets God gave Moses on Mount Sinai became part of a local myth explaining why New Guinean culture was less sophisticated than that of Europeans: when New Guinea lost its 'book' (or tablets) (cf. Burridge 1960: 5)—and some versions of how this happened stated outright that it was stolen by Europeans—it lost the knowledge necessary to build up a superior way of life (cf. Williams 1940: 438). Contradictions and lack of historical sequence seemed irrelevant in the overall picture of coincidences.

The next reported movement was *Kukuaik*.[20] In retrospect, the villagers traced its beginning from the arrival in Madang after 1936 of three strangers, two young men and a girl.[21] They came separately from the north in flimsy canoes. Unlike the Madang people, the Karkar did not relate them to the tradition that Kulbob and Manub would eventually return (cf. Lawrence 1964a: 91). Nakei, a Marup woman then living with her evangelist father at Bunabun on the mainland, and Makel of Mangar, a ships' crew member, claimed actually to have seen them. They, and many villagers who are now familiar with the story, emphasized four strange features: the strangers were short, with strikingly red skin and were neither Japanese, Chinese nor European; they were antagonistic towards Europeans and sympathetic towards the villagers, with whom they stayed overnight; they gave metaphorical warning of the approaching war against Japan; they travelled with little or no food, and when they left, their frail craft shot away into the open ocean as if powered by engines. The Karkar linked them with men of similar appearance manning two flying boats which landed in Kurum harbour during *Kukuaik* and before the Japanese invaded Madang.[22] They took on board a man from Biu village and flew with him to Kavailo Bay. He walked back from there to his home where he died soon after as a result, it is said, of his strange experience. As the times became increasingly disturbed, these incidents formed part of a body of omens of change described by Henkelmann (n.d.) and vividly recalled by the people themselves.[23]

Henkelmann only hints at anti-European attitudes in *Kukuaik*. But a Marup villager said bluntly, 'Long before the war, we were angry with the masters—angry about wages, angry about rations, angry about their behaviour'. In this respect, early anti-European movements in other parts of the Territory almost certainly influenced the Karkar, for at least two former cult leaders referred to the unrest prior to the outbreak of *Kukuaik* as being part of a broader protest movement. They occurred in Rabaul in 1929 (Report to the Council of the League of Nations 1928-9; McCarthy 1959), Northern Bougainville in 1932 (Inselmann 1944: 105), and Madang from about 1933 (Hannemann 1948: 945; Lawrence 1964a: 87-90).

Kukuaik swept Karkar in 1941, at first, as the participants and Hannemann (1948: 946) pointed out, as a means of achieving a 'zealous Christian life' in preparation for the millennium. It began with mass confessions twice a week in specially fenced areas, to strengthen people's faith and cleanse them of sin. Misinterpretation of Henkelmann's Advent sermon on 5 November changed its nature to that of an outright cargo cult. Its doctrine was comparable to that of a cargo movement in the southern Madang District between 1913 and 1933 (Lawrence 1964a: 73-85) and more specifically to the Yam version of the Letub cult in Madang which followed it (Inselmann 1944; Lawrence 1964a: 92-3). The doctrine espoused by the Yam appealed to the Karkar because their Kulbob and Manub myths coincided, whereas other Letub areas reversed the roles of the two deity brothers. It

H

foretold the imminent second coming of Jesus and referred to Christian mythology. Hence *Kukuaik* followers did not overtly oppose the missionaries (although they felt misunderstood by the newly arrived missionary and lay worker on Karkar) and congregation leaders participated with enthusiasm.

Kukuaik doctrine postulated devotion to Christianity in order to achieve the promises of the Bible, which people interpreted literally to mean a comfortable life of ease, not in the hereafter but immediately on earth. Clearly their previous efforts to syncretize the old and new religions had amounted to failure to carry out God's commands and were the cause of their persisting inferior way of life. They burnt all traditional possessions and undertook an intense programme of nightly prayers, public confessions and beautifying cemeteries. After Kubai of Boroman took control, they addressed themselves not only to God and Jesus, but to the spirits of the dead, since from their interpretation of the care white men gave their cemeteries, the spirits would accompany Jesus when he returned with European cargo. The Boroman changed the tune of Hymn No. 8 from the Lutheran hymnal in Graged to a more sprightly one to suit the mood of *Kukuaik*. This hymn then took precedence over all others and people sang it repeatedly:

> We changed the name each time, calling first God, then Jesus and then the spirits. And we pulled the strength of God towards us with our hands and arms. We looked towards the sun or to Kanagioi where the sun would come from. We sang out as if God were a man we could talk to. We sang and waved our arms and kept on singing and singing.

Rhythmic swaying, chanting, 'talking in tongues', seizures and frothing at the mouth became commonplace. People recalled seeing visions of men on horses or motor cycles, but the horses had no hooves and the motor cycles no wheels. Blue, red and white flashes in the sky lit up the whole place and folk prayed wherever and whenever they wished. Kubai appointed 'kings', assisted by 'soldiers', in each village, with himself at the head. People killed their pigs and prepared great feasts. They bought every white shirt and loin cloth and every lamp in the plantation trade stores in readiness for Jesus's arrival. Then, believing that Europeans had received the secret of cargo by sacrificing Jesus, Kubai 'sacrificed' his ailing wife, by placing his hands over her nose and mouth (cf. Schwartz 1962: 270; Lawrence 1964a: 267).[24] He expected her to return by plane with much cargo, as a European woman, and ordered a landing strip to be cleared at Boroman.

Then a rumour began that on a given day the island would turn upside down and new land would replace it. Those who believed in *Kukuaik* would receive a much better way of life with new houses, chairs and tables, and plenty of food without having to work for it. Those who did not follow *Kukuaik* would perish. On this day also, Jesus would appear in judgement. When nothing happened, people told themselves that they had made a mistake and they set another day. Still nothing happened, but they professed not to be alarmed and went on nominating yet other days for the upheaval. Eventually, as described earlier, only the *Totol* arrived with investigating Administration officers. It is said that, as Kubai was apprehended, after a magnificent struggle in which his teeth were smashed and blood streamed down his face, he foretold that a war would come to punish all Europeans. Leaders in other villages also predicted an invasion by planes with bomb attacks. When these events did occur, the villagers saw them as validation of their *Kukuaik* beliefs.

According to the Takia, many of those the *kiaps* arrested were named by the planters, who either employed them or knew of them as important men. Consequently, the real leaders, with the exception of Kubai, often escaped at their expense. Thus one Marup man, employed by a European, was sent to prison in Madang, while Kapom, the real *Kukuaik* leader in Marup who lived and worked in the village, went free. In most cases, the Administration charged employees with breaking their labour contracts rather than with inciting a cargo cult, which would have been difficult to prove under the circumstances of wholesale participation. The aftermath of *Kukuaik*, as with *Letub* on the mainland (cf. Lawrence 1964a: 98), was a militant anti-European sentiment and prophecies of impending punishment for the white men.

The bombing of Madang and the Japanese occupation seemed to fulfil these prophecies. Even after eighteen months, although the Japanese withdrawal and ANGAU's arrival were something of a blow, people continued to validate *Kukuaik* with remarkable tenacity by claiming minor fulfilments of its predictions. For example, when the Australian troops first landed on Karkar and regularly handed out relief rations of rice, biscuits and meat, people believed this to be in some measure a response to Kubai's promises of cargo. Later, when ANGAU recruited men for 'soldiers and policemen', they realized that, in the military train-

ing he had instituted, Kapom, Marup's 'king', had been preparing them for just such a need as this. Further, they contended
that, if Australians also practised cargo cult at home, as they had
been led to believe, then *Kukuaik* was clearly the way to wealth
and power. The Administration had stopped it, not because it
was useless and wasteful, but because its supporters were close
to achieving their goals (cf. Lawrence 1964a: 98, 139). Hence although post-war circumstances inhibited the practice of *Kukuaik*,
its doctrine remained.

Cargo cults after 1946 lacked the religious features that validated *Kukuaik* in the eyes of the villagers. They were minor
events initiated mainly by Yali's former army friends on Karkar
in an environment of widespread but discreet interest in any opportunity for economic development. The Yali movement
seemed to offer an organized means of achieving ambitions built
up during the war. As well, it offered replacements for the
practical leadership and aims of *Kukuaik*. With most Takia
villages organized into immaculate army-style camps under Yali
'boss boys', with the building of 'Yali houses' where these 'boss
boys' met to hold courts and propound Yali's 'laws', Administration authority declined (Patrol Report 3. 1950-51).

From 1948 interest in Yali subsided for four main reasons:
first, apart from a brief visit to a remote Kevasob village in 1946
before the movement really began, Yali never came to Karkar;[25]
second, the people never rejected Christianity and therefore denounced him when he denigrated the missions; third, when the
Administration began to oppose him, they remembered with
fear the consequences of *Kukuaik*; fourth, they were never certain
what the Yali cult was about. In common with most of the seaboard people in the central Madang District, they placed tremendous emphasis on the performance of correct ritual in practical activities. But ritual required mythological validation,
and although groups of Takia men visited Madang and the Rai
Coast for the specific purpose of discovering Yali's doctrine, they
never succeeded.

Economically politically and intellectually, the Karkar
changed little by the 1950s. They maintained, largely unchanged,
their adequate subsistence gardens, but were frustrated in their
efforts to achieve European wealth through their own plantations
and resentful of their continuing inferior status. Secular efforts
having failed, they practised cargo cults, which although superficially varied, had a common basis: the belief in a superhuman
source of knowledge and material goods. In short, they resorted to

an explanation in terms of the traditional epistemology. Yet, in spite of their disillusionment, they were more anxious than ever to achieve a rough equality with Europeans. Hence, they eagerly welcomed the first Administration development scheme in 1952.

4

REACTIONS TO ECONOMIC DEVELOPMENT
PROGRAMMES (1952-68)

THE KARKAR made spectacular progress in the Administration's secular schemes, yet the old values and beliefs still underlay their new economic, political and educational activities, and they integrated the three fields, one with the other. Their expectations of these programmes as means of achieving the European way of life sustained a cargo ideology which existed alongside apparently successful modernization.

The experience of participating in the Karkar Co-operative Societies and the income derived from the development of cash cropping enabled spontaneous village enterprises in the form of stores, road transport, investment of savings in established European-controlled companies, and other minor undertakings.[1] Later, land demarcation aroused considerable concern, and the Papua New Guinea Development Bank's loan scheme lively interest, although neither had a great effect on the actual economy.

CO-OPERATIVE SOCIETIES

Co-operative societies began with promise: the Administration itself recognized that this first official effort to organize economic development immediately alleviated frustration and envy of Europeans (Patrol Report 1. 1956-57). Like traditional trading, co-operative activities involved items not vital to biological survival as long as subsistence gardens continued to flourish. Hence people could place co-operatives in the framework of the traditional socio-economic ethic, practising equivalence in trade to achieve prestige at the cost of a monetary profit.

In 1952, the first co-operatives officer to visit the Karkar found them already producing copra and selling it to European planters at $2 a bag. In accordance with a plan of community ownership instigated by Paramount Luluai Salum, they had bought the *Karkar*, a $12,000 boat suitable for carrying copra, and they had money available for investment. The *Karkar* was running at a loss: it had lost its own anchor and chain and, in return for the loan of one from a mainland planter, it was carrying all this man's copra free to Madang. The co-operatives officer cancelled this unequal bargain and arranged for the Madang Association of Native Societies (MANS) to take over the boat for more efficient management. Each man's investment in it became part of his share capital in the co-operatives. With this, plus their savings from village bank accounts, the Karkar took out shares totalling $40,000 in nine societies, each comprising from three to fourteen villages. Members themselves decided the names and boundaries and elected a director to represent each village, and a chairman in charge of each society. Immediately, the societies paid $6 a bag for copra and the Copra Marketing Board bought this for $8 a bag. After paying a clerk's wages in Madang and accumulating a Reserve Fund, MANS sent vendors a dividend.

Inevitably, there were initial difficulties: according to the co-operatives officer, the original owners did not want to lose the use of the *Karkar* for pleasurable purposes such as fishing and visiting in exchange for promises of more cash if the boat went out of their hands. The Karkar themselves told me that they never understood why it was taken from them. Furthermore, some copra growers tried to cheat MANS by half-filling copra bags with stones and coir with copra only on top. The MANS clerk paid out for this, but the Copra Marketing Board quickly discovered the subterfuge and returned the goods.[2]

Generally, however, there was great enthusiasm over the new scheme. This led to some separation of secular activities from mission influence for the first time, to which village elders contributed by dissociating themselves from official co-operative society positions (although not from involvement in cash cropping). An exception was Yas of Kavailo, a mission leader, who, as mentioned, already owned a reasonably large plantation. He became chairman of MANS in Madang and later, captain of its copra boat.

The history of co-operatives on Karkar was similar in most respects to that on Manus (Schwartz 1966-7: 35-47). Although Bangsik Society on the central west coast failed early, the rest soon did well, and in 1954 MANS replaced the *Karkar* with a larger copra boat, the *Mansip*,[3] to cope with the trade. By 1956 the remaining eight societies with 2,570 members had share capital of $45,000, and two retail trade stores showing a joint turnover of $18,000 in six months. They were buying the bulk of village copra by 1958 when membership increased to nearly 3,000 and share capital to $51,000. Sixteen retail co-operative society stores were operating in 1963.

Towards the end of 1963, the Karkar Co-operative Societies began to decline, a trend reflected for MANS generally in 1964 in the sale of the *Mansip*, which had been running at a loss. The purchase of only 25% of Karkar village copra from March to September 1967 brought a gross copra loss of $939. Stores recorded a loss of $3,549 for 1967. One society, Biadun, showed an improvement in its store trading after the arrival of a well-trained Manus storeman, but its copra turnover continued to fall. With only Bangame recording a credit balance, the societies closed in December 1966 with a total debit balance of $5,408.

The villagers themselves, the co-operatives officers and the settlers shared responsibility, to a greater or lesser extent, for the collapse of the societies. Superficial reasons for failure were as follows.[4] Indigenous clerks lacked adequate education and training and were generally guilty of malpractice; directors and chairmen were apathetic and sometimes dishonest; members rarely honoured trade store debts, were indifferent to mismanagement, and eventually withdrew their support in favour of selling to planters. By establishing over 100 village stores between 1964 and 1967, the people drained trade away from society stores. Careless processing caused owners to lose money when sub-standard copra proved unacceptable in Madang. Producers resented the MANS method of payment by means of a low interim price with a later one based on the world market value. Finally they complained, and Administration reports agree that once established, they received inadequate skilled supervision.

The planters offered attractive alternatives. They sent vehicles to collect green copra and even unopened nuts, for which they made one immediate payment slightly above the MANS interim price. In this way, they gambled on considerable gains if the world markets remained steady or improved, but risked losses if prices should fall. MANS could not take these risks. The unusual drought of 1965 and 1966 increased the villagers' tendency to sell to Europeans for spot cash to buy rice and tinned meat. By this time few people made copra, the number of driers having dropped from 118 in 1962 to twenty-two.

Why the Karkar behaved in apparently self-defeating ways can be explained largely in terms of traditional socio-economic concepts. Relatively ignorant of Western economic procedure, clerks created store surpluses by ordering large quantities of goods for which there was little demand. They sold goods below cost prices and involved members in expensive re-drying or complete rejection of produce, by purchasing sub-standard copra. They gave cash advances for copra, sold store goods on credit, and incurred disproportionately high running expenses. Deliberate mismanagement involved the theft of stock, copra bags and drums, and cheating during copra buying. Dismissal and gaol sentences had no effect on these practices.

The villagers condemned this general pattern of behaviour, yet they accepted individual incidents partly because of their concept of what Morris (1958: 32-3) calls 'terminating economics', in which they viewed money only as a means of exchange and not as a productive medium or as something to be accumulated, and partly because of their social ethic as against individualistic ethic in economic transactions. The Manus referred to such practices as 'spoiling' public funds rather than stealing and considered losses their collective responsibilities (Schwartz 1966-7: 42-3).

Most clerks were local men and, where they were not, people fitted them into a quasi-kinship structure with their society members. Because goods had only a display and distributive value in society, the clerks gave credit and gifts of stock to relatives or friends, and advanced money on copra as part of the formalized generosity required between a man and such relatives as his mother's brothers, to gain prestige, or in return for some service.[5] At times they purchased sub-standard copra through ignorance or carelessness, but they also accepted it for the sake of the transaction itself and the goodwill it implied.

Unfamiliar as they were with the rules for running co-operatives, chairmen and directors had to leave their operation to the clerks, whose dismissal for inefficiency and dishonesty they frequently opposed. Furthermore (and Morris 1958: 37 also makes this point), the education that clerks received was so far above that of the villagers that it placed them beyond the usual sanctions and controls of the community. In the exceptional case of a progressive chairman of Maro Society in Waskia, who tried to prevent traditional socio-economic behaviour threatening economic success in his area, members voted him out of office, replacing him with a much less efficient man. They could act this way because they took for granted the societies' stability. They believed that social relationships and prestige through trading were the *raison d'être* of the co-operatives, whose material goods were a concomitant of living and not something to strive for.

It is difficult to assess to what extent ignorance of the rationale behind the co-operative system forced members to depend on traditional economic assumptions. Certainly they failed to see the relationship of individual effort to returns, and invested their societies with a collectivity reassuring to people ill-equipped to strike out singly even if social sanctions had permitted this. Unaware of copra marketing procedure outside Karkar and the influence of world markets on local prices (cf. Worsley 1957: 35; Brown 1966: 158), they held an unknown controlling body in the organization responsible for their low and irregular returns. This body, they believed, took their profit and sent it away, where or for what purpose they did not know. Confusion of this kind, linked with theories purporting to explain the unequal distribution of wealth between Europeans and New Guineans, led to an explanation of the co-operatives' failure in terms of cargo ideology (cf. Brown 1966: 158). Villagers alleged that, just as the societies began to flourish, this unknown power, which was possibly the Administration or the Australian Government, transferred efficient European supervising officers to other areas to prevent them revealing the secret of true wealth, an idea frequently postulated in connection with popular missionaries (personal communication from the Reverend G. Reitz). They suggested that a deliberate policy to frustrate them prevented the establishment of society copra driers and transport on the island, and disposed first of the *Karkar* and then of the *Mansip*, both of which they considered Karkar and not MANS property. These factors, they believed, rather than their own shortcomings, deprived them of their rightful share of European wealth, and they began to sell their produce again to the planter, whose financial resources seemed limitless and immediate.

Some villagers hoped that their increased transactions with the planters would expand into true social relationships, and that through these they would eventually achieve social and material equality with them and discover the cargo secret. This plan proved disappointing. The gap between Europeans and the Karkar remained, but hope still existed as occasional cargo cult outbreaks and persisting cargoism suggested. Growers maintained such channels of contact with the planters as might later prove useful, while exploring other avenues for economic success: 'We are people', they said 'who like to try everything'. One of these was the proposed new co-operative marketing association mentioned earlier.

Opinions about the co-operatives at the end of 1968 indicated a sentimental attachment to them, although few members now supported them. People in and around Marup frequently referred with great respect to the first Co-operatives Department officers on Karkar as men who brought a measure of purpose and dignity into daily economic life. The societies, although they had not provided the hoped-for material and social equality with Europeans, were still thought to be a good system. They did symbolize in a concrete and communal way an improved Karkar status, thus reflecting the traditional socio-economic ethic of prestige and collectivity. Traditional elements in the social system suffered little change through the introduction of co-operatives. In fact, these elements enabled people not only to tolerate, but to approve of the very factors responsible for their failure. Rowley points out that the dilemma of New Guineans in towns is that traditional social relationships '. . . may become economically impossible while remaining emotionally and socially necessary' (1965: 101). In the case of Karkar such relationships were indeed economically impossible and so people sacrificed economic development through co-operatives in their favour.

Two factors which contributed to the co-operatives' failure, their members' eventual lack of support and unrealistic expectations, also threatened the proposed cocoa marketing association. The sale of cocoa to Europeans was a satisfactory arrangement until 1968, because it protected fledgling growers from fluctuating world prices, village production was low, and fermentaries were expensive. An increased output of 268,650 kilograms of wet bean in 1957 increased transport problems, and official opinion that Europeans were paying too low a price (eleven cents per kg) prompted growers unanimously to support the Administration's plan for a communally-owned fermentary and transport system. At least 1,300 men promised a minimum contribution of $20 towards the initial total outlay of $30,000, on condition that the venture would be supervised by a permanent European manager, for the belief in the white man's mystique persisted. Estimates indicated that over three years, growers would be able to add $32,722 from cocoa, and $18,000 from copra to their cash incomes (Co-operative Activity, Karkar 30.12.1968).

The association's success required the producers' undivided loyalty. Yet during two generations, the Karkar had developed complementary economic ties with the planters which had become an integral part of their lives. Although personal contact with Europeans was still far from ideal, they valued it highly in the hope that they would eventually be able to change it to a relationship in which they could choose to participate and in which they would have an equal voice. The wish to maintain and develop ties with the planters was a complicated matter connected with efforts to achieve status as producers and businessmen, with ideas of manipulating Europeans for possible benefits, and with indebtedness for past cocoa transactions. Not the least consideration was the tradition-oriented pleasure and sense of attainment in spreading trading ties as widely as possible. Important as these factors seemed to the villagers, they were potential threats to the united grower support on which the cocoa marketing scheme depended.[6]

CASH CROPS

The Karkar achieved considerable success in organized cash cropping. As we have seen, their transition from a subsistence to a cash economy began with their own undirected efforts. Further, although official agricultural development plans did not materialize until 1959, the villages responded to the co-operatives officers' more or less unofficial advice to plant coconut trees, by doubling the number of palms between 1955 and 1958.[7] The Marup described how co-operative society directors and sometimes *luluais* and *tultuls*, whose influence as officers in Administration-sponsored concerns people now tended to exaggerate, assumed considerable powers as organizers. They temporarily abandoned traditional work groups based on kinship, mobilizing the entire village to help first one man, then another to get his plantation established. Even old men condemned those failing to participate, since most had some knowledge of the work from European plantation labour. With official encouragement to plant cocoa, the frenzied rush to benefit from the new 'road' to wealth accelerated after 1959, as Table II shows.

As mentioned earlier, land ownership was ideally defined by patrilineal inheritance, but a man might hold permanent rights to land in clans other than his own through adoption, inheritance from his matrikin or gifts from his wife's father or from friends. Commonly, he had temporary rights to plant or rights of usufruct on the land of other clans. In the same flexible manner in which he had planted gardens with a life span of about three years, he continued to plant coconut and cocoa trees with life spans upwards of sixty years. This presented many problems when demarcation committees tried to establish firm clan boundaries a few years later.

By 1964, the only barrier to continued expansion of plantations was a shortage of suitable land. This resulted from a rapid

TABLE II

Cash Crop planting on Karkar: Pre-1961 to 1967*

Coconut Palms			Cocoa Trees
		Up to 1958	56,000
		1958-59	30,000
		1959-60	32,000
Up to 1961	14,072	1960-61	28,000
1961-62	50,322	1961-62	19,000
1962-63	51,797	1962-63	4,000†
1963-64	102,987	1963-64	10,000‡
1964-65	79,387	1964-65	15,000
1965-66	19,122	1965-66	10,000
1966-67	7,017	1966-67	14,000
TOTAL	324,704	TOTAL	218,000

* Figures from D.A.S.F. Reports 1961-67 and from the D.A.S.F. officer on Karkar.
† The drop in 1962-63 was probably due to a D.A.S.F. officer living on Karkar for only two to three months (personal communication D.A.S.F. officer, Karkar).
‡ D.A.S.F. figures give 56,000 cocoa trees planted in 1963-64. The Karkar D.A.S.F. officer estimated that it should be only 10,000 trees, which fits current totals.

population increase since the end of the Pacific war and from the fact that cash crops, unlike subsistence gardens, permanently monopolized land. Litigation and some unacceptable decisions of the demarcation committees persuaded men that they must plant their land with cash crops as a means of securing it. On Karkar, dissension rarely occurred over boundaries as such, but rather over areas the rights to which could not be validated through patrilineal inheritance. Thus, when Babu clan in Marup claimed a certain block of land, Labug clan hastened to protect what it considered its rights by planting coconuts there, only to have them torn out by Babu members.

As had happened among the Orokaiva (Morawetz 1967: 20), some men feared that land left as bush might be taken over by New Guineans from less well-endowed mainland areas. In 1967, Councillor Kabug told the assembled Marup villagers that land was theirs only if they used it. 'If you do not plant all your land', he said, 'you will find a Chimbu or Sepik sitting on it'.[8] Although Kabug preached complete land use through cash cropping as evidence of fitness for self-government, most people planted for the immediate reasons of preparing for a rumoured Local Government Council income- and land-tax, to cope with the increas-

ing cash demands of daily life, to improve their general standard of living and to gain prestige.

On the whole, organization of labour for cash cropping reflected the traditional pattern. The directors' and *luluais'* mo-
bilization of the entire village as a work force was only a temporary measure which, they admitted in Marup, was aimed at
establishing plantations for themselves (cf. Finney 1969: 30-1).
Soon customary work groups of lineage and clan members augmented by matrikin and affines re-appeared and sometimes,
public spirited villagers co-operated as a group to help the
councillor, the *komiti*, the pastor or pastor's assistant, and the
truck driver.

Since traditional and modern leadership on Karkar tended to
coincide, the ability of traditional big-men to command more
labour than could ordinary villagers was difficult to establish (cf.
Finney 1968: 398). In any case, the extensive duties of many
modern leaders demanded more assistance than their lineages
and clans could provide, and their prestige depended upon the
consistent flow of labour they could organize. The councillor and
komiti had obvious advantages in this respect, since it was their
formal duty to allocate Administration and mission work to
villagers. But as disgruntled villagers were in a position to replace
them in future elections, they practised discretion. Prevented by
the demands of their positions from contributing their own
labour, they organized reciprocity of services, mainly through
their lineage members, who benefited by their leaders' prestige
and received material rewards from them whenever possible. All
communal work concluded with a generous meal and gifts of
tobacco and betel nut in the traditional way.

Most modern leaders were successful planters, but not all
successful planters were leaders in any but the economic field. An
individual who was simply a successful businessman received no
special labour benefits. One such, Wabei of Mangar, paid cash
for labour, apart from arrangements made with his lineage members in the ordinary way. He also hired as workers men whose
contracts with the settlers had expired, but who wished to remain
on Karkar. Probably three or four Waskia employed mainland
men in this way at very low wages. But because they did not provide approved housing in accordance with Labour Department
regulations, they were unwilling to give information about this
practice. Only Pastor Benbet Mileng (the son of the late mission
teacher and leader, Mileng) and the Salum family[9] employed
mainland labourers on more-or-less officially approved lines. The

former employed about five, the number varying according to the regularity of wage-payment. The latter employed fifty labourers in all in 1968, but these included relatives, local Kaul villagers, men from the mainland at Bogia and from neighbouring Manam Island.

Like the organization of work groups, the division of labour in cash cropping followed the traditional pattern. Men performed the heavy work, while light repetitive tasks fell to the women. Increasingly, men cleared, fenced and planted cash crops on virgin soil. They now planted large subsistence gardens so that they would be suitable for cash crops as soon as their produce was exhausted. They cut the long grass between trees, pruned cocoa trees, cut copra and attended to the few village driers. They carried bags of copra to the road and received the payment for them. Women cleared and burnt the small growth on new land, helped with planting coconut and cocoa seedlings, and gathered coconuts ready for husking, splitting and cutting into copra by the men. Apart from pruning, they performed all work connected with cocoa. Once a fortnight or once a week, depending on the season, they harvested and broke the ripe pods, secured the wet beans in bags or baskets, and carried them to central points in the village, along the main road, or at the European plantations themselves for sale. They used the income for their own and their children's needs, handing any reasonable balance over to their husbands. According to the Marup, this system evolved when copra production far outstripped cocoa, whose meagre returns made men disinclined to concern themselves with it. As cocoa incomes increase, this pattern might be expected to change. The likelihood of this happening was indicated by Wabei of Mangar, a big cocoa producer, who always accompanied his wet bean to the European buyer and received the payment himself.

Women continued to do the routine daily work in the food gardens. Generally, people still depended for food on their own produce, but a few villages, such as Kaul in Waskia, with a long history of cash cropping, increasingly relied on rice and tinned fish or meat from the trade store.

Although Karkar Circuit Reports (1955, 1961) charge the villagers with increasing secularity at the expense of their loyalty to Christianity, most people denied this. Their prayers and sermons indicated a general belief in the ability of the Christian god to grant them success in cash cropping and Pastor Benbet Mileng echoed the general opinion about working on village plantations on Sundays, a day formerly devoted to church-going, when he said: 'If a man goes to church, rests a little, then goes to work on a Sunday, it's all right, provided he believes truly in God'.

Of course, practical considerations caused attitudes towards work and religion to vary. For example, Sei, a former councillor of Marup, had little land, an adult family employed in wage work, and a daughter married to the European owner of Biabi from whom he obtained occasional luxuries. He maintained that to work on Sundays was against the 'laws' of the mission and the welfare of the human body. On the other hand, the present councillor, Kabug, with a relatively large plantation and land still to be planted, a family of young children and heavy demands on his hospitality as councillor and vice-president of the Karkar Council and leader of Balug clan, advised people not to hide behind the 'law' of the church. 'There is not time for this now', he said. 'I go to church, come home, change my clothes, get my axe and knife, and go off to work on my cash crops'.

Clearly cash cropping left less time for congregational duties, to which people formerly devoted one day a week. Henceforth they combined this with compulsory weekly work for the Administration. Cash crops provided many who were not enthusiastic mission supporters with a new interest, and extended the energies of the rest to cope with both activities. In the early stages, it suggested to most a secular means of achieving the white man's way of life.

From about 1960 cargo ideology and practices became noticeably widespread on the island (Karkar Circuit Reports 1960-64). They seem to have been given impetus by the presence of a team of scientists representing America in the celebration of the Geophysical Year in 1962. This group carried out research on Mt Kanagioi, where an elaborate station was established. People from Kurum, Mangar, Liloi, Boroman and Gamog carried the extensive equipment and food supplies up there. In 1967-68 they still talked about the great quantity and richness of these goods and conjectured about the real reasons for the visit. According to some Gaubin staff, rumours about strange ships, submarines and armies were rife. It became common knowledge that a cleared area near Boroman was being used for nightly meetings. Later, some Gaubin orderlies met a group of Liloi men marching from their village to Boroman with make-believe wooden rifles over their shoulders. Rumours of armies persisted.

During the 1960s, in two Takia areas centred on Kumoria and Kevasob, groups of people, anxious for immediate and greater wealth than their largely immature plantations promised, performed ritual for material goods. The Kumoria cult, including in its scope the villages of Daup, Patilo, Did, Dumad, Kurum and Boroman, reached a climax in 1964 before the Administration intervened. Its leader, Mileng Gubug, was a partly-trained former student of Ameron Lutheran Bible School. Short and slight of stature, he seemed too delicate to undertake physical work, depending on others for subsistence and refraining from cash cropping. He had large piercing eyes set in a pallid face, and an intense, nervous manner, which his followers believed signified spiritual strength. A striking thing about him was his speech. He never troubled to form words properly, either in his own language, Pidgin or English (of which he spoke a little). He blurred one word into the next at a tremendous speed so that it was difficult to follow what he had to say. A voluble man, he was obsessed with Bible stories, people praying on mountains, close interaction between New Guineans and Europeans, and modern European household goods. He repeated to me in detail conversations he claimed to have held with God when, he believed, he had died after being ill in Yagaum Lutheran Hospital in Madang: God listed all his sins on a large blackboard, then charged him to carry out special work for him. After a recovery he described as miraculous, he decided to devote the rest of his life to this 'work'.[10]

Mileng held prayer meetings in the bush, at which he encouraged people to confess their sins, and promised them material rewards if they believed in him as the emissary of God. In 1963-64, to fulfil these promises, he somehow got possession of many valuable accoutrements from the Catholic Church at Tabel, causing them to appear on an altar at his bush meeting place. Afterwards he gave some of them into the keeping of his main supporters, many of them leaders from his own and surrounding villages. When the Catholic priest reported the loss, an Administration officer investigated rumours about unusual events at Kumoria. He charged Mileng and some twenty-five other men, sentenced Mileng to six weeks imprisonment and retrieved most of the valuables. Mileng consistently denied that he had stolen them, and to this day, countless villagers on Karkar believe that, because of their great number and value, these goods could not possibly have been the property of one local church but must have appeared by extra-human means.

In 1967 Mileng inspired another cult, which the Kumoria villagers claimed became an embarrassment, since it brought no

J

material results and subjected them to ridicule from local Europeans. To escape this situation, Mileng took a second wife in Boroman, where he went to live with his affines. Boroman, formerly the centre of *Kukuaik*, welcomed him, providing all his needs and responding to his undoubted charisma as a cult leader. This time, the movement kept within the law and continued unchecked in a mild form.

In 1968 Mileng sent a message to me in Marup asking that I come to visit him. His manner was mysterious and his appearance more fragile than ever. He showed me a cheap medal he wore around his neck, suggesting that it came directly from a sacred place. He asked me to send him pictures of modern European household appliances and furniture on my return to Australia. During our conversation he constantly implied that he and I shared some special knowledge, and that he really had no need to explain his ideas to me, since I already understood them. He insisted on accompanying me back on the walk from Boroman to the coastal road, giving me a gift of galip nuts as we parted. When I left Karkar, he appeared at the jetty with more galip nuts which he handed over with many meaningful looks and nods. Without doubt he had fitted me into his scheme of things.[11]

The Kevasob cult, although less dynamic than the Kumoria one, was equally persistent. Its leader, Ulel, formerly of Marup, was in his mid-fifties and had worked for many years on plantations near Rabaul. Fanatically religious, he claimed, like Mileng, to have received divine sanction from God for his 'work'. After an emotional disorder which, he said, followed his wife's desertion to another man, he had suffered the loss of his voice. His hoarse whisper and frequent, nervous laugh distinguished him from other men. He too did not plant cash crops. He regularly sought me out to discuss the true meaning of Bible stories and to question me about the future of New Guineans and Europeans. During our meetings he related many long and complex stories with obvious cargo cult significance.

Kevasob people told me that in 1961, Ulel, with the help of two Kevasob men, organized cargo activities, which occasionally reached a climax, but never entirely subsided. He marked every known burial place on Kevasob land, including the graves of children who had died or of men killed long ago in feuds. Here people cleared the bush and planted flowers and shrubs. In the village itself a beautification programme began similar to that undertaken in response to Yali's recommendations fifteen years before. The Kevasob tore down old houses, replacing them with neat rows of new ones built about a central grassy square. They surrounded them with fences of colourful shrubs and flowers, which also lined the road approaching the village. They banished the pigs to enclosures in the bush and, in all, made of Kevasob the most attractive village on Karkar. Every night, they met to pray and confess their sins. The programme continued for some years, with the leaders exhorting people to strive, not for current limited prosperity, but for real rewards in the future, through the goodwill of God, Jesus, and ancestor spirits.

Eventually, some villagers abandoned this considerable labour in favour of extending their plantations. Ulel, publicly reprimanding them, said that their withdrawal would displease God, and hence would endanger the success of the plan. In 1968, he pointed out to me with some satisfaction that, in spite of their preference for business, these men had not achieved true wealth. The movement continued to attract people, even those who no longer participated in it admitting that it might still prove efficacious. In most Karkar villages, however, cargo ideology did not lead to cargo cult and people used their cash incomes to acquire symbols of European prestige in the ways described below.

SPONTANEOUS VILLAGE ENTERPRISES

Village stores, transport and copra trading enterprises, and investment in Territory and Australian companies evolved spontaneously as secondary responses to Administration economic development schemes, roughly in accordance with Epstein's scheme of development for small scale societies (1970: 17). Most popular were stores maintained by income from cash crops. Like their co-operative society models, they operated on traditional socio-economic concepts emphasizing the accumulation of prestige. They were themselves visible symbols of prestige as well as vehicles for display and distribution. In Finney's terms, they were 'conspicuous investment' (1968: 395), but investment in prestige. In a sense, they may also be labelled conspicuous consumption, since their actual construction was a major consideration, regardless of their function.

The first trade store opened in 1964 in Marup village and more than a hundred stores and nine bakeries operated on Karkar by 1968 (cf. Schwartz 1966-7: 40-1). Owing to confusion over licensing regulations, only sixty-seven were registered by February of that year (Traders' Licences, February 1967-8).

As described, the Karkar involved the three European private planters in their mania for trade stores, gaining a superficial knowledge of European trading concepts from them. Because each settler emphasized different aspects of his economic arrangements with the villagers, results varied. One of them quite unwittingly discouraged among the people the concept of making a profit in business by insisting that those who were in debt to him for their store building materials and stock send all their cash crops to him in lieu of cash payments. By this means cash crops and not store profits were clearly supporting the new ventures. Although not actively encouraging this practice, another planter did not stop it. He did, however, stress the necessity of selling goods for more than the cost price and got his clerk to write the selling price of each commodity alongside its cost price on invoices. By refusing to accept further orders until previous assignments were almost paid for, he prevented store owners from incurring large debts. A third planter, by meticulous supervision of store transactions, forced storekeepers to compartmentalize their incomes and in some cases to practise a profit-making policy.

All stores in the first group collapsed. Two in the second thrived, while four probably made small profits. Only one actually failed under the third system, most just survived and a few built up adequate stock and bank accounts of between $150 and $200.

Ambitious men quickly realized that their cash crops provided a useful tool for obtaining assistance in new business ventures, first with their European neighbours, and later, as debts with them occurred, with other Europeans further away. A planter in Takia referred to this sort of economic manipulation when a successful Waskia entrepreneur drove into his yard for the first time: 'He's either fallen out with Kulili, or he wants something from me they can't give him'.

Most store organizers occupied positions of some status in modern Karkar society as councillors, elders, pastors, teachers or co-operatives clerks. Frequently they were clan leaders as well. As Finney points out (1968: 336), New Guinea entrepreneurs excel at financing business ventures with other people's money. The Karkar financed their stores by borrowing, lending and repaying as they had done before with pig exchanges and trading. As a rule the patrikin provided money from cash crops for building materials and stock, labour for constructing and staffing the store, and food for the elaborate opening feast with its accompanying religious service. A small minority of stores operated like miniature co-operatives on a formal share capital basis, with members drawn from the lineage, clan, or in the case of Keng village in Waskia, from the entire settlement. Only foreigners, or people in exceptional circumstances like Pastor Benbet Mileng of Tabong Plantation (Map III), financed their stores themselves. But as in the old exchanges and trade, the return was not always in kind: the store organizer sometimes repaid cash contributions with services of some sort, and conversely, he repaid people for their labour with goods from his store. One Marup man repaid men clearing his land with store goods. Not surprisingly, his store later closed down in debt. Such practices did not help balance the books, where there were any.

Knowing what Europeans expected of them, most storekeepers claimed that they followed Western trading practices, including making a profit. Apart from two storekeepers who were also teachers, and those supervised by one of the planters, they kept no adequate records of business transactions and therefore could not check their financial position as they went along. In fact, Western economic principles directly opposed their idea of a store's function as a symbol of success and means of earning prestige through providing a service to people. Consequently, storekeepers gave credit, sold goods below cost price, gave handouts to kin and friends and took stock for their own use. Under these conditions they could not make a profit and frequently incurred debts to Europeans. Table III summarizes the situation in Marup in 1968. Figures would have given a more precise picture of trading but none were available.

Four out of the eight store organizers claimed a profit, two claimed that they broke even, and two were in an obvious state of financial collapse. Six claimed not to be in debt and all denied giving credit. In fact, five were in debt to expatriates or to the Lutheran Mission Supply House in Madang, and they all gave credit. Only one (G in Table III), kept a store bank account separate from other income, so that profit or loss among the rest was impossible to check. Even this one, being a cheque account, provided no readily available record, and the owners did not understand or retain the monthly statements. They merely paid accounts promptly and, although they made no claims of making a profit, probably sold goods for roughly what they paid for them.

Marup store owners, lacking a profit motive, explained the logic of bolstering stores with cash crop income on the basis that stores had no means of support and therefore required some out-

TABLE III

Debt, Profit and History of Stores in Marup

Positions of store organizers	Claims of profit	Claims of debt*	Real debt situation	Stores December 1966-68
A (church leader, clan leader)	yes	no	debt	rebuilt but never re-opened
B (truck driver, clan leader, church councillor)	no	no	no debt	remains
C (councillor, clan leader)	no	yes	debt	closed, re-opened under new management
D (former co-op. clerk)	yes	no	debt	closed
E (leading elder, clan leader)	yes	no	debt	moved and rebuilt
F (pastor's assistant, non-Marup)	yes	no	no debt	remains
G (includes teacher, ex-councillor, mission elder, saw-mill manager)	no	no	no debt	remains
H (educated future clan leader not resident in Marup)	no	no	debt	closed, re-opened and closed

* to settlers or Lutheran Mission supply stores.

side finance. 'A store has no *Papa*', a Marup organizer said. 'It has no coconuts or cocoa, so if it is short of cash, they can help it.' As noted, some planters perpetuated this idea by accepting cash crops in return for stock for stores. Usually this was the only way to meet debts and it created a false sense of complacency about trading ventures.

As with co-operative society stores, people refused to lay charges against their debtors on two grounds: first, that they themselves gave the credit which led to the debts, and second, to demand payment from relatives and friends would bring shame. Nor would they bring such matters before informal village courts. An educated and successful trader from Koropak in Waskia worked out a compromise. Forced by the very nature of society to give handouts to certain relatives and friends, he balanced his losses with money from his own pocket.

People's enthusiasm for stores as a means of extending and cementing their social ties and achieving prestige, led to too many stores and to inefficient management. Villagers did not recognize this. When an experienced storeman from the Lutheran Supply House in Madang suggested that the eight Marup stores amalgamate, clan and lineage sectionalism, plus the above factors, led to an outright veto. The real problem of mismanagement was never mentioned. Instead, people blamed a shortage of capital with which to buy adequate stock, agreeing that when cash crop incomes increased, this difficulty would disappear: if, like the settlers, they had plenty of money to begin with, their stores would run well.

In the meantime, all successful primary producers nursed the ambition to open a store. Their overt reasons for this were to 'give work to cocoa and copra' and to 'help relatives'. By the former, they meant putting income from cash crops to work to establish and maintain stores. This was Morris's 'terminating economics' (1958: 32) referred to earlier, in which villagers envisaged income not as a productive medium, but as a means of buying and doing what Europeans bought and did. In fact, as Finney (1969: 48 fn. 2) suggests for Goroka businessmen, it is doubtful if the Karkar understood the term 'profit' (in Pidgin *winmani*), even though they frequently used it. Through 'helping relatives', in other words through creating an extensive network of credit and gift-giving, they achieved prestige. Storekeepers used the credit they built up in this way to help them maintain their positions as big-men, as their ancestors had done through exchanges and trade.

Another important and covert reason for entering the trade store business was that it provided opportunities for more intimate interaction with Europeans than did the sale of cash crops.

The Karkar saw selling to and buying from Europeans as part of a long term exchange relationship influencing social life in many spheres and not in terms of a single transaction 'made and completed with the giving and receiving of goods, services or money' (Brown 1970: 99). They saw their new relationship with Europeans as between *tizan*, their former inherited and lifelong trading partners. This accounts for the frequent comment about planters: 'They help me with cargo for my store, and I help them with copra and cocoa'. The satisfaction of being able to conduct business with Europeans on a presumed roughly equal footing, and the absence of an adequate system of book-keeping caused people to see these transactions purely in terms of an equivalent exchange of goods and services.

It would be a mistake to presume that store-keepers were not bewildered by the constant problems and frequent failures of village stores. Table III shows the changes in the history of Marup stores over a period of two years. While their integration into the existing tradition-oriented socio-economic system obscured their specific performance and the need to improve management, an increasing number of storekeepers realized that their stores were not flourishing like those of the settlers: Europeans criticized the way they operated, debts remained, the kind and amount of stock kept was inferior to that in expatriates' stores,[12] and expenses of re-stocking were difficult to meet.

Many explained their quandary in terms of the old suspicion that Europeans deliberately concealed important information about trading. That they had been forced to enter a previously exclusively European field on their own initiative substantiated this idea. 'Australians came and taught us business in words only', commented the Marup councillor. His brother's son claimed that he had made no true Australian friends during seven years as a storeman at the Lutheran Mission Supply House in Madang because Europeans had explained how to start a store, but had deliberately failed to teach him how to maintain it as they did their own. One store owner revealed feelings of inadequacy by Western norms, when I called at his store for a casual chat. Unlocking a drawer behind the counter, he scooped up a large handful of twenty cent pieces, which he presented to me. When I protested, he told me in distress that things would go badly for him if I refused to accept the money. Clearly this was an investment in good fortune for his business. It is conjectural whether he hoped to obtain the secret knowledge of success from me as a European who, *ipso facto*, must have it, or whether his action was inspired by a growing conviction among the Takia that I was a benign spirit of the dead and therefore had access to the cargo itself.[13]

In short, the co-operatives, which were the main stimulus for village trade stores, were an inadequate means of economic education (cf. Morris 1958), providing only the outward form of Western trading without its underlying concepts. The anomaly of a European economic structure based on the traditional socio-economic ethic led to bewilderment and suspicion of Europeans. Yet, unlike the co-operative stores, village stores often survived with little or no profit on the proceeds of cash crops. In other words, traditional social values undermined stores from the European point of view of capital expansion, at the same time as they maintained them as symbols of prestige. The same traditions still operated when village planters extended their horizons beyond the trade stores movement to vehicles.

Except for the *Samiri*, a copra boat owned by the Salum family, and managed for them by the Middletons, the Karkar confined themselves to road transport businesses. As cash crops matured, bringing in higher cash incomes, the people began to buy utility trucks and tractors with trailers to carry both goods and passengers. These enterprises bore many features in common with trade stores: the special status of organizers, purchasing arrangements through settlers, the communal nature of financial contributions, and dependence on produce income for their support. Consequently, they too were mainly non-profit making prestige symbols, a result of economic development rather than economic ventures in themselves.

Of the fifty-eight vehicles (including motor cycles) registered on Karkar in 1968, sixteen were owned by villagers who probably owned a further three utility trucks whose conditions of purchase required their registration in Madang.[14] Neighbouring Europeans arranged the purchases on a reasonable deposit and monthly instalments. Although sponsoring the buyers, they avoided financial involvement themselves. Nevertheless owners presumed heavily on the assistance of the Kulili and Dogowan planters for registration, insurance, repairs and fuel supplies. At times planters even took over full management of trucks to help reduce debts and pay instalments. As the number of vehicles increased, such supervision became impossible, much to the indignation of some villagers. As well, constant pressure for payment of instalments caused considerable friction, yet buyers and advisers remained bound to each other, albeit sometimes unwillingly, the former because they needed assistance, and the latter because the political climate demanded their co-operation.

Apart from three relatively successful transport businesses in Waskia, trucks were financial liabilities. Through the inexperience and carelessness of most drivers, mechanical and body repairs were constantly needed. Of the nine village trucks in 1968, two were smashed beyond repair soon after purchase, two remained almost continuously immobile because of the shortage of drivers, and the rest were regularly out of action undergoing repairs in plantation workshops.

As Jackman (1967: 10) and To Robert (1967: 33) both comment, the use of funds belonging to the kin or local group may impose intolerable strains, demands and obligations on business organizers. The possibility of Development Bank loans after 1968 suggested future changes in the method of purchase, and a probable increase in the number of transport enterprises.[15] In the meantime, people placed vehicles high on their list of ambitions once plantations reached full production.

A minority of adventurous men seized other opportunities to enter the European economic field. They established small kin-based companies, such as a cement brickworks financed by a lineage in Marangis village, and a short-lived restaurant on the south-west coast (cf. Epstein 1968: 34; Finney 1969: 10, 20). As with the Manus (Schwartz 1966-7: 39), six clan- or lineage-owned companies, registered with the Copra Marketing Board, produced cash crops communally, and marketed their own and occasionally other villagers' copra. Those enterprises that survived did so through traditional reciprocity and with little or no profit.

Formal investment in large established companies appealed strongly, but because most people, fearing European disapproval, were secretive about actual transactions, I could not get comprehensive figures. Of main interest were Namasu and certain enterprises in Australia. Namasu, created from Lutheran Mission trading interests as an independent company under European management, had a majority of New Guinean shareholders and paid a high interest rate of 10% (cf. Fairbairn 1967: 77-88). Yet, in 1968, the four Marup investors professed disappointment at their returns, and lack of confidence in the company because it had no stores or driers, in other words, visible symbols, on Karkar. Furthermore, they felt that Namasu, dealing only in copra, catered inadequately for their needs.

In May 1966, after hearing of the proposed closure of the co-operatives, Namasu employees from Madang arrived to gauge the likelihood of success of a proposed wholesale store in Takia and improved produce marketing facilities. Local opinions varied. On the one hand, Sei of Marup admitted: 'We get excited over all forms of business, and go from one to the other to get the best deal. There may be something in favour of Namasu's claim that it belongs to us New Guineans and not the "masters". On the other hand, Councillor Kabug found this an argument against Namasu: 'It's too much New Guinea', he said, 'I want to invest in Australian companies'.

The common motivation for investing in Australian companies was the belief that Europeans still concealed important knowledge from New Guineans, thereby preventing local businesses from being really successful. The villagers gained their information about investment overseas from advertisements in papers and magazines, and from educated young people returning home on leave from the major towns. Furthermore, an agent in Rabaul for Australian Fixed Trust catered especially for Papua New Guineans by advertising and sending out information in Pidgin on request.

In 1969 four Marup men admitted to having investments in Australian companies. Nine others asked me for information and advice. Only one had approached a European previously, all other investments being made in direct response to advertisements. The transactions of one of these men, probably the most active investor in Marup, were as follows:

1960	Territory Premium Securities (advised by Administration officer)	$120
1967	Permanent Building Society Limited (Sydney)	$100
1967	Bank of New South Wales Cambridge Investment Society	$100
1968	Bank of New South Wales Cambridge Investment Society (on behalf of his lineage store shareholders)	$100
1968	Australian Fixed Trust (Brisbane)	$100

Four major problems faced investors: their unrealistic expectations of high profits and substantial loans, their concept of personal reciprocity rather than impersonal capital investment, and ignorance of simple economic terms and of the significance of Western advertising. Hence the Marup man referred to above believed that after a year's investment with one company he would receive $100 and that because he 'helped' the company now, it would automatically 'help' him with a loan later. Nama-su's favourable 10% interest rate compared to the usual 5 or 6% of Australian companies was meaningless to the villagers. Unable to interpret interest rates, they accepted advertising as outright promises rather than as a series of short cut images. Thus an advertisement suggesting that the investor could achieve his dearest wish, be it a luxurious house, yacht or car, if he bought shares in a certain company, convinced a Mangar mission teacher that after a year he could take his choice of any of these in return for the $26 he had invested. Such misconceptions, in the face of local failure in co-operatives, boats, stores and trucks, supported expectations of rich rewards from Australian economic enterprises.

LAND DEMARCATION AND THE PAPUA NEW GUINEA DEVELOPMENT BANK LOAN SCHEME

The most recent official economic innovations on Karkar were land demarcation and the Papua New Guinea Development Bank plan for financing indigenous enterprise. In his study of land tenure conversion in the Orokaiva village of Ombi-Tara, Morawetz notes that '. . . any alteration in the tenure system is bound to have far-reaching social implications' (1967: 23). Yet he found that the formalities of individual titles' registration had little effect on valued customs. Demarcation on Karkar indicated a similar outcome, although occurring under different conditions from the Ombi-Tara, where land is plentiful. It re-affirmed the formal groups of the traditional kinship structure but weakened cross-linking relationships through land, confirming Karkar as a patrilineal society dependent on land ownership.

Demarcation took place in a tense situation of already existing litigation over land (Patrol Reports 1956-62) and widespread land shortage. To secure the land to which they had rights, and frequently in the hope of acquiring more land, people readily accepted the idea of defining permanent village and clan boundaries. Of the choices of registered title that demarcation offered, the Takia and Waskia decided on registration of land under communal title: clan leaders, in conjunction with leaders of neighbouring villages, were to decide first on village boundaries, and second on clan boundaries within each village. But in the absence of official allowance for land acquired outside the patri-clan, demarcation committees tried to force all land into neat clan boundaries, even where the original clan acknowledged its alienation (cf. Reay 1969a: 17).[16] On learning of this, the Land Titles Commissioner in Madang held public meetings on Karkar in June 1968 at which the Takia decided that land given to a daughter on her marriage (and henceforth controlled by her husband), land gifts in return for some service, and land bought for money should be registered under individual title if the current owners wished. The Waskia favoured individual title only for land bought for money. Both groups agreed on the registration under communal clan title of all land outside these special categories.

The two demarcation committees began work on the western borders of Waskia and Takia during 1966. By Christmas, the chairman for Waskia, Loan of Kurum, had worked his way from Buson to Mater and Keng. Stahl Salum, the chairman for Takia, delayed by a stream of bitter arguments, had moved only from Buson southwards to Mangar 1 and Marup. When the programme ceased at the end of 1968, the boundaries of the east coast Karkar villages remained unauthorized by the demarcation committees and official surveying and recording of boundaries extended only from Keng in Waskia to Kurum in Takia.[17]

In 1966 three main categories of land problems already existed: planting cash crops on another man's land with or without his permission, land gifts out of the patriclan, and land seized or lent as an outcome of warfare. In the first case, the owner frequently claimed the land back when cash crops matured but the planter refused to vacate it on the grounds that he himself had planted and husbanded the trees. In the second case, kin involvement was often an ameliorating factor in a dispute: 'They won't hurt me', Benbet Mileng said of his mother's landless kin living in Kurum, 'I'm their child'. Yet sometimes even lineage members gave way to violence during long and bitter feuds. In the rare instances where relatives were not involved the possibility of a peaceful solution was slight.

In the case of land changing hands as a prize of warfare, Marup was in the thick of violent arguments, the very land its houses occupied being properly the property of Wakon, which had taken it from the vanquished Medan people. Above all, landless descendants of war refugees, for long denied the opportunity of retaliation against their victors, now saw in demarcation a last chance to regain their land.

Demarcation had good and bad effects. Its achievements can be assessed according to Western or traditional Karkar values. The first concern the beginning of individualism at the expense of the social ethic on Karkar. One example of economic gain over social loss was the frequent establishment of land contiguity that was necessary for efficient and economical planting, albeit at the cost of the fragmentation which formerly reinforced inter-clan links. The method used was to exchange or, if necessary, to buy land, a relatively simple process when close kin were involved, but otherwise requiring prolonged and complicated negotiations. Once completed, demarcation provided channels for formal registration of future land transactions and hence their inviolability. This encouraged the beginning of some spontaneous resettlement from the crowded west coast to the east: two Marup men bought land at Yagadun. It is worth noting that these purchases did not occur outside an existing social context: Bilei of Marup had worked for seventeen years as foreman of labour on the Catholic plantation of Taab on the east coast and rarely returned to his own village; Kalei Babob had been mission teacher at the east coast Lutheran school at Anul. Others were considering this alternative to land shortage, although owners in that sparsely populated area were by no means anxious to sell.

Further, demarcation provided a suitable vehicle for introducing information about income tax and bank loans. Some villagers favoured the Council tax being replaced by a Council income tax as a means of bringing in more money to pay for better public amenities, including the employment of labourers to perform onerous weekly Council work. Most feared it as an individual burden, preferring taxation on a lineage or clan basis in accordance with the communal land registration they had chosen.

One of the most exciting aspects of demarcation, people felt, was that it satisfied a Development Bank loan requirement of a registered title to land. Even after the wider programme ceased, a few ambitious men like Sibon, president of the Local Government Council, had their land surveyed and titles registered in readiness for loan applications. Finally, the repeated and lengthy negotiations, and the intimate involvement of the people prevented that vacuum of ignorance and confusion so often attendant on modern development schemes. While chairmen sometimes exceeded their powers by making arbitrary or biased decisions (cf. Hide 1971), they patiently explained the concepts and advantages of registration in such a way that most people accepted it as logical and useful.

The villagers experienced considerable satisfaction of a traditional nature as a result of demarcation. For example, they saw officials acknowledging their customs for the first time, particularly the existence and integrity of the clan as a social unit in the modern situation. During demarcation, the kindred as a whole continued to perform its traditional role as a mediating body in all serious disputes some attending in groups from all the surrounding villages. It frequently managed to contain threatened violence within the kin-dominated system of social control.

In all, it was a time of excitement, activity, reminiscence, socializing and feuding. Claims over land called for recitations of genealogies and legends to support or undo claims. There were tales of war and conquest, of giving hospitality to outcasts and succour to the defeated; of sorcery and exchanges of valued clay pots, pigs, bracelets and dogs' teeth. Villagers fortunate enough to have old men as repositories for this information sometimes won land simply because their opponents had no counterparts. 'Old men are our books', they said, 'and we must listen to them'.

If demarcation had its advantages, it also had its apparently ill effects due to the complex nature of existing land-use arrangements, official ignorance of customary tenure and traditional beliefs, and the people's own misinterpretations. To begin with, the ferocity of land disputes increased as people devoted all their energies to what they believed to be a last opportunity for litigation. Thus the Dumad people expected the Commission to oust descendants of Kagil war refugees currently occupying some of their land and to reinstate the Dumad on their traditional territory now comprising Dogowan Plantation.[18] They explained that formerly they had considered the sale of land to Europeans to be final, but now realized that they could regain these areas. Other disputes derived from the new rigidity placed on a land tenure system, whose traditional keynote was flexibility (cf. Reay 1969a). Demarcation imposed this rigidity in retrospect, by forcing firm Western interpretations of buying, giving and lending upon a fluid, socially and politically convenient system of land acquisition. Shifting subsistence agriculture did not require strict categorization of rights to use land and now anxiety over the new concepts about land caused serious conflict.

The new boundary definition highlighted land shortages over much of Karkar, arousing fears for the future and panic to plant quickly to secure land. People expressed their anxiety in a sudden interest in birth control measures,[19] consideration of migration to the less populous east coast, and unprecedently fierce quarrels between close kin.

Because the Land Titles Commission initially made no provision for newly evolving or newly evolved clans, or, as we have seen, for non-patrilineal methods of acquiring land, the Karkar concluded that all land inside an established clan's boundaries was to be registered under that clan's name. Efforts to enforce this interpretation caused anger and despair to members of new clans struggling for acknowledgement, and to individuals with legitimate permanent rights to land outside their patriclans. The Commission became aware of this problem only in 1968 when it requested such boundaries to be reappraised in the interests of accuracy rather than neatness.

Finally, justice was not always done: the dynamic, prestigious claimant who could persuade the chairman that he knew most about the history of the land in question was most likely to win. In a situation where the chairman assumed powers which seemed to the people to have official European sanction, such findings carried considerable weight, although they were not legally final. As the Land Titles Commission officers said, some kind of decision had to be made before an appeal could be lodged against it. But there were two negative aspects of this procedure: the psychological advantage both at a personal level and in court, in having a decision already made in one's favour, and the fact that many villagers might not understand the system of appeal or might lack the courage to confront senior European officials. The latter happened after the Japanese war when, as Sack (1971: 15) points out for New Guinea generally, some people accepted land alienation to Europeans as a fact, although not necessarily as being just.

On Karkar, however, some individuals refused to accept decisions made over disputed land. A spate of post-adjudication quarrels broke out, during which dissatisfied claimants secretly moved cement boundary markers in their own favour or even tore them from the ground in open defiance of a system which, they felt, could so abuse their rights. Medan people and the villagers from Bafor applied to the Commission to have the entire process, including surveying, re-done. Many who considered themselves unjustly impoverished by demarcation threatened to regain their land with violence if necessary in the future. However, the suspension of the mass programme, with surveying and registration going ahead only in response to specific requests, provided a breathing space for people to resort to traditional measures for equalizing land rights or settling disputes without the loss of face suffered during demarcation negotiations.[20]

In order to achieve its aim of securing for the individual complete control over his land and its produce and of reducing the prevalence of disputes, the Land Titles Commission would have had to prise the land away from its traditional social, religious and political associations. But to place it in a strictly secular economic category would have destroyed that interdependence of men with their land described by Salisbury (1962, 1970), Brookfield and Brown (1963), Hogbin (1967a, b) and others. This is a difficult process, for to touch the land of the New Guinean is to touch the very core of his life. Just as the Karkar perpetuated customary institutions in cash cropping, it seemed likely that they would retain and even emphasize patri-filiation and clan guardianship in the case of land tenure, but at the expense of their wider kindred ties. It is too early yet to test Rowley's (1965: 125) contention that New Guinea is neither physically nor socially suited to a system of permanent land titles and to gauge their usefulness against bank loans for development. Indications on Karkar are that this kind of land tenure, where it does exist, will succumb, as it has among the Ombi-Tara (Morawetz 1967: 35-6), to traditional practices beneath its sophisticated surface.[21]

Loans offered by the Papua New Guinea Development Bank were closely connected with land titles. They created enormous interest and prompted most special requests for individual or small-group title. The villagers' main dilemma seemed to be in getting the Bank to accept group rather than individual registered title, but after much negotiation, it had agreed to accept a lineage registered title from Sibon of Wadau. By June 1968, six Karkar men had applied for loans, but as investigations were not completed, none had as yet been granted.

In the new economic ventures generally, the rare, successful entrepreneur had special difficulties, for he ran the risk of being accused of deliberately withholding crucial knowledge, of having sorcery performed against him, or of suffering public disapproval (cf. Finney 1969: 32; Kent Wilson 1969: 35). Nothing but fear of sorcery prevented a Kumoria man from building himself a European-style house from the proceeds of his successful trade store. And a young mission school head teacher, who owned a thriving store, told me in some embarrassment of his situation. With savings from his store in Waskia, he bought a utility truck. His new venture went so well that soon rumour had it that he was getting goods and money from the ancestors the way Europeans were reputed to do. Then a Kaul man accused him, not of earning his money, but of actually manufacturing it. Waskia villagers called a meeting at which they asked him to disclose his secret. 'So I told them: "Look at this money!" and I took some money from my pocket and held it out towards them. "It is not mine. It was in

K

your hands before. Then you brought it to my store and gave it to me for rice, fish and meat. And now it is in my hands. This is how I got it." And some believed me and some didn't', he sighed.

In conclusion, it can be said that the Administration's economic development programmes resulted in a series of officially unplanned intellectual and practical responses, and fostered social as well as economic ambitions. The people used cash crops, which occupied a place comparable with traditional prestigious trading items, in economic arrangements with Europeans to obtain symbols of prestige in the current idiom. That idiom was European. They placed these symbols, in the form of trade stores and trucks, in their old socio-economic framework, valuing them for their social and service benefits, and making up the inevitable deficits with income from copra and cocoa. Paradoxically, the kindred both supported and undermined the modern economy. It provided labour and capital contributions, but thereby permitted the use of money only as a medium of exchange rather than as a store of capital. Its possible alternative, loans from the Papua New Guinea Development Bank, still did not overcome traditional kin loyalties.

With Administration assistance stopping short at cash crops and co-operative societies, the villagers relied heavily on the planters for assistance in other economic fields. To make this reliance more palatable, they tried to develop a reciprocal relationship, instead of one of dependence. They carried the same concept over into investment in Australian companies, believing that, in return for money invested, they would receive generous returns. Clearly, traditional concepts of kinship, prestige as the only socially acceptable form of profit, and unrealistic economic and social expectations jeopardized modern economic success. Yet in their recent experiments connected with marketing and applications for loans, people still set up joint enterprises on a kinship basis as a serious effort to maintain the old values and institutions in a new economic environment. Their deliberate adoption of this course from among a number of alternatives suggests a step towards an indigenous modern system, based on a substantial existing structure, rather than acceptance of a system derived from Western society and superimposed uncomfortably on the old.[22]

5

REACTIONS TO POLITICAL DEVELOPMENT
PROGRAMMES (1952-68)

Faced with a technologically sophisticated European material culture, many New Guineans devise their own rational methods of satisfying their needs. Others, especially those living in traditional circumstances, may, according to Rowley (1965: 186), try to achieve their wishes through the practice of cargo cult, or they may willingly accept official development schemes. Even when the last is the case, Brown (1966: 160-1) warns that the strains and impatience of inevitably slow progress may well result in alternating cargo cult and secular activities. Both Rowley's and Brown's points of view were relevant on Karkar. The people saw political development as the logical consequence of economic development, perhaps because in the past men achieved or maintained political status largely through economic manipulation. Yet feelings of dissatisfaction and deprivation persisted in spite of successful cash cropping, and official political development schemes fell short of expectations. It is true that these schemes had brought to an end the system of direct rule through Administration patrol officers and induced amenable, if self-interested gestures from planters. But they failed to bring the power, ability and self-confidence of white men, which, it appeared, enabled them to obtain and keep the things they wanted. Consequently, people continued to regard the means of acquiring material goods (and hence status), as divorced from secular effort.

LOCAL POLITICS

At the local level, political and social control derived from three sources: the traditional political structure, the mission or ELCONG structure, and the imposed Australian political structure. Lineages and clans maintained their significance under their ascribed leaders, while a shared name and territory, and extensive affinal and cognatic ties perpetuated village solidarity. In 1956 the Lutheran congregational structure composed initially of elders, evangelists, teachers and missionary, became the modern segmented hierarchy of ELCONG referred to earlier. My comments here are restricted to Lutheran areas since, as noted, there was no delegation of authority among the small Catholic minority. Elected councillors replaced *luluais* and *tultuls* in 1958. The villagers blended these three systems into one general system of control, their ideal of a successful leader being one who followed the advice they claimed to have received from the officer introducing local government on Karkar (but in ways not forseen by him): that three kinds of 'law' must prevail—those of the village, the church and the Administration.

Under the *luluais* and *tultuls* after the war, the old coercion persisted. 'We knew nothing! Only what the Administration told us: to clean roads and the village, and to build toilets', Mangar villagers recalled. 'We learned nothing more than that, and were abused if we didn't do what we were told.' Much as they despised this system, they were apprehensive of the inception of Local Government Councils at first, because cohesion at the language group level had no counterpart in the traditional fragmented political system. Further, as Lawrence (1964a: 270) notes for the Southern Madang District, people wanted a generalized social system like their traditional structure, rather than separate specialized systems within the state as a whole. Therefore they were reassured by their interpretation of the organizing officer's advice as encouragement to incorporate Administration, mission and traditional concepts of control into one system, and by his request to former village officials and congregation elders to help the new councillors in their work. The Councils, it seemed, would be, in a sense, an amalgamation and extension of a familiar system. This was an opposite view to that held by the Kuma in the Highlands. 'They believed that Councils, being entirely new institutions, must be run by "new" men' (Reay 1964: 251).

Interest was high in the first elections in 1958 with 93% of Waskia and 94% of Takia electors voting. A few more women than men voted. Former village headmen figured strongly in the new political medium. Of the fifty-four candidates for Waskia's twenty-five seats, twenty-four had been *luluais* and *tultuls*, of whom ten succeeded. Twenty former headmen appeared among the fifty-three candidates for Takia's twenty-six seats, ten being elected. Successful candidates were invariably middle-aged men with large families who had worked at some time for Europeans. As the breakdown of councillors show (Table IV), the great majority were Administration officials of some sort.

TABLE IV

*Backgrounds of Councillors elected to the First Local
Government Councils (1958)*

		Government officials	Mission workers	Villagers
WASKIA	*luluais* ⎱ *tultuls* ⎰	10	3	2
	medical *tultuls*	7		
	medical officer	1		
	co-operatives directors	2		
	TOTAL:	20	3	2
TAKIA	*luluais* ⎱ *tultuls* ⎰	11	4	4
	medical *tultuls*	1		
	medical officer	1		
	co-operatives directors	3		
	Agriculture Department assistant	1		
	policeman	1		
	TOTAL:	18	4	4

Electors replaced few councillors after the first term, but by
1961 self-confidence inspired more candidates to nominate and
the replacement figure rose sharply. After the amalgamation of
the two Councils in 1963, it dropped slightly and has since remained fairly constant.

Four councillors from each language group have retained their
seats since 1957, including the president and vice-president since
amalgamation, Sibon of Wadau and Jongale of Tugutugu. In
1966 a total of seventy-two candidates contested the twenty-eight
seats. Five wards were closely contested, the rest having clear-cut
winners. Three councillors were elected unopposed. From 1957
to 1966 the turnout of voters dropped from over 93% to 56%.
Official opinion was that people simply would not make the
effort to vote.

Although settlers reported local antagonism towards the two
Councils amalgamating, this was no longer apparent by 1967.
By then councillors from Takia and Waskia were on excellent

terms (cf. Parker 1966: 262), mixing freely during and after meetings, joking, smoking and eating betel nut together. Admittedly they tended to stress the needs of their own villages, yet they made real efforts to consider the welfare of Karkar as a whole. As between the two language groups, they were sensitive to potential problems. With money available for the first of the mountain roads in 1968, they agreed to allocate it to Kaul village in Waskia, while emphasizing that the complex of Takia villages around Marup would benefit next. A nice example of awareness of the need for ethnic balance occurred when councillors chose a Takia, a Waskia and a Bagabag Islander for the crew of the new Council boat, which they named the *Watabag* from the first few letters of each area.

Amalgamation did deal a blow to the ordinary Takia villagers' interest in local government. Previously, some people, including *komiti* men, had attended their local Council Chambers at times, but it was virtually impossible to travel the long distance to Bakul from the south and east coasts, especially on such occasions as the arrival of the United Nations Visiting Mission, when all available transport was engaged in ferrying councillors and official guests to the Council Chambers. Consequently people had to rely entirely on their councillors' reports.

Council achievements for 1965 received high praise in the Administration's Review of Operations (31.6.1965) and in a Local Government Council Inspection Report (5.6.1965). Councillors originated almost all policy and carried out their village duties responsibly and efficiently. The Council effectively provided Administration school buildings and controlled indigenous plantations as well as influencing village works programmes towards more reasonable and useful projects than before, such as wells, houses, latrines and community centres. It extended its activities in road-building and in what the reports describe as the 'perfect' maintenance and operation of transport. Nevertheless, both documents commented unfavourably on the shortage of skilled workers for works programmes, on errors, cash deficiencies and unpaid accounts discovered in the financial records. They noted the reluctance of councillors to deal with European firms on Council business in connection with buying goods and services because of feelings of inadequacy in what seemed a complex, hitherto exclusively European field.

In spite of these difficulties, 1967-68 brought further expansion: the Council employed sixty full-time and part-time workers; its total revenue for the year ending in June 1968 was $59,000, including $21,000 grants-in-aid and subsidies for major works, and Council tax of $9 for adult males. Councillors' involvement and self-confidence had increased to the extent that they began to press for measures opposed by Administration departments. For example, they would not accept a Police Department refusal to impose a 30 m.p.h. (48 kilometres) speed limit in certain areas because Karkar was outside the Madang town limit. Arguing that life on the island was as valuable as it was elsewhere, they applied again for special limits, which were still under consideration in 1968.

In fact, the Council's standard of achievements generally had dropped since 1965. Poor school facilities, insufficient village labour for schools' maintenance, and widespread truancy caused some teachers to threaten officially to register their lack of confidence in the Council. Health Committee members complained that the villagers ignored their hygiene recommendations. Consequently, pigs strayed through residential areas and many houses were sub-standard and without latrines. Shortages of medical supplies restricted aid post orderlies in their work. The suspension of the Council clerk in 1966 pending charges of stealing left the Samarai works manager and the European Administration officer-in-charge no choice but to do his work. This left gaps in supervision elsewhere: by 1968 vehicles were in such disrepair that councillors planned to offer for tender most Council transport; the *Watabag*, bought with the aid of an $11,000 loan, was running without a regular timetable and therefore at a loss; and expensive road working equipment constantly broke down and lay idle for weeks at a time.

Much of the work that Councils do is on an agency/contract basis and the work is financed on condition that the contract is honoured. At length in March 1968, a specialist adviser to local government councils criticized the Council for breaking the conditions of its grants-in-aid. He objected to the costly employment of an unskilled grader driver, to the Council's failure to have equipment regularly inspected by a qualified mechanic as agreed to by contract, and to its use of Government-owned tractors for work other than that financed by the Public Works Department. In short, the Council was receiving money from the Administration for work which was not being done.

These problems derived from three main sources: the shortage of skilled labour, the general characteristics of the councillors, and the shortcomings inherent in the local government system. Lack of suitably trained workers created waste in a way that was particularly noticeable in a relatively wealthy Council area like Karkar. The re-direction of the officer-in-charge and the works supervisor to clerk's duties was uneconomical, while the employ- ment of irresponsible, unskilled workers under inadequate super- vision incurred heavy expenses in terms of damaged vehicles, de- terioration of on-going programmes and possible cancellation of subsidies. This situation placed serious strains on other em- ployees and on the councillors themselves. To overcome some of these problems, councillors formed a Roads Committee in 1968 and placed one of their number in charge of the *Watabag*. Al- ready burdened with numerous Council and private affairs, and with no clear idea of what this new undertaking entailed (cf. Hastings 1969: 164), these men were not enthusiastic about their additional responsibilities.

The second problem area concerned the councillors' limita- tions. As in most councils, a minority bore the bulk of the re- sponsibility (Local Government Council Reports 1965, 1966, 1968). Yet even these men had to battle against their ignorance of the medium in which they worked. The electors' traditionally oriented view of the ideal characteristics of councillors auto- matically disqualified young, educated men, most of whom worked on the mainland in any case, and who saw prestige in terms of the European way of life in general rather than in local political achievement.[1] As Reay (1964: 225) observes, the Ad- ministration taught people nothing of the kind of characteristics democratic representatives should have. Karkar electors de- manded

> . . . men with different sorts of qualities than mere European education. Men who would follow the Europeans, the mission and the government, and who knew the way of the village. They must be mature men with families . . . people like us.

With only elementary mission or no education, councillors found financial estimates, complicated by grants-in-aid and sub- sidies, completely beyond their comprehension. Some Administra- tion critics saw their neglect of terms of contract as sheer mis- management, but they themselves regarded the money in ques- tion as another source of revenue. They were unaware that its continuance depended on obligations being met and were angered by the threat to withdraw the contracts as being an insult to their progressive Council.

The councillors' misguided enthusiasm for new ventures was a further hazard to financial soundness and to the works pro- gramme. They considered each new undertaking as an indication of increasing prestige and a means of earning further Administration praise, and envy from nearby mainland councils. By continuing to accept subsidies and loans without appreciating the accompanying heavy burden of responsibility, they failed to consolidate many of their initial undertakings.

Although local government was intended by the Government to act as a training school for participation in self-government, it was an inadequate medium of education. Supervising officers, and later advising officers were placed in the invidious position of having to encourage councillors to take responsibility, make decisions and get results, and at the same time having to oppose their wishes to make rules to enforce action (Salisbury 1964: 234). Democratic procedure under these circumstances was almost impossible. Again, advising officers were to interfere in the running of councils as little as possible, an unrealistic proposition when councillors depended on traditional values and beliefs to wrestle with complex Western institutions. Finally, the councillors had to participate much more in implementing actual programmes than their Australian counterparts, but the only training available on Karkar for committee work had been a school held for one week in 1965 for the Health Committee. Some councillors had received some general council education at local government training schools at Danben near Madang. Their reports indicated that even these stressed expansion of council undertakings rather than consolidation of what had already been initiated.

The following is a verbatim report (translated from Pidgin) of an exchange concerning Council tax evaders, between councillors and their advising officer in May 1968. It illustrates some of the difficulties described above:

Vice-President Jongale (deputizing for President Sibon in the chair):
> Notices have been sent to people who have not paid the annual Council tax, but they were not worried and did not pay up.

Galat: We can't let them get away with this. Put pressure on them!

Kabug: Councillors must find out these tax offenders and send them to the Council office.

Jamal: They only run away—and anyway, some councillors haven't paid yet!

Bakin: Tax them and imprison them.

Timothy (Council Clerk):
> Some men have been charged at court, and fined or imprisoned. And still they haven't paid.

Bakin: Bring them to court again!

Jongale: The *kiap* must do something about this: he must im-
           prison them and leave them there.
Kiap: But then this man thinks he has paid his tax debt by
           being in prison. Prison doesn't help him find the money.
Galat: If this happens, the police must come to his village and
           take his pig or his coconuts and get the money from
           selling these.
Jongale: Make these defaulters come to the *kiap*'s office at Miak
           next Wednesday for punishment.
Kiap: But Miak is too far for them to come from the other side
           of the island!
Bakin: The law says that the Council has power. Now when will
           the Council's power come up?
Jamal: The *kiap* must take over this work. We try all kinds of
           work and nobody listens to us. The *kiap* must do this so
           that Karkar progresses.
Kiap: Do you want to get rid of the Council and put the *luluai*
           and *tultul* regime back again, and have the *kiap* ordering
           everyone about again? No. *You* do the work and if you
           can't manage it, put in new councillors.
Jamal: Well, the *kiap* will have to talk strongly to people.
Mulul: We'll try again. If not, the *kiap* will help us. He's right.
           We ourselves are the Council.
Kabug: Yes, we decide what the Council will do and we don't
           work hard enough at it. We must bring evaders to court
           and charge them over this.
Bakin: This Council hasn't got a prison itself—we ourselves
           have no power. Who can show me what to do?
Kabug: True, the magistrate only comes once a month from Ma-
           dang, but the *kiap* must hear cases in the meantime.
Jongale: We are wasting too much time on this matter.

Although councillors increased their sophistication in debat-
ing and formulating policy, the *élite* among them realized their
deficiencies. Vice-President Jongale implied this when he made
the following comment on the need for a skilled, honest clerk: 'If
councillors cannot be educated in European ways, then we must
be able to buy this [European] education'. Figuratively speaking,
they 'bought' education by agreeing to a multi-racial Council, in
which Europeans were to provide the knowledge indigenous
members lacked.

Salisbury (1964) describes the unfavourable reactions of the
Tolai, and Reay (1964) of the Tolai and Kuma, to local government councils. The Tolai big-men considered the administrative
role of the councillors to be beneath them, and, according to
Reay, some villagers near Rabaul wished to return to traditional

methods of political control. The Kuma wanted direct rule through indigenous officials restored. On Karkar, in spite of some problems and disillusionment, people prized the new system as an important step towards restoring their dignity and social integrity. As Cochrane (1970: 93-4) writes of Malaita, the new institution allowed people to elect their own big-men to positions of high status in the imposed system of government and represented European recognition of them, if not as equals, at least as men able to conduct their own local affairs.

Apart from voting, the sum of the ordinary Karkar villager's involvement in the new local politics was little more than awareness and appreciation of his new improved status. But the councillors' complex and demanding duties meant that they had in fact, if not in theory, to be modern versions of traditional big men, using the old methods of persuasion through oratory, personality and prestige to get people to co-operate in new schemes such as land demarcation and national elections, and to enable them to cope with subsequent problems. They mediated in quarrels over pigs, sorcery, stealing and women. They disseminated news, organized labour and, although not legally responsible for order in their villages, were held by the people to be ultimately answerable for village harmony and prosperity.

Councillors considered themselves hard-working men, spending most of their time, especially if they were committee members, on Council duties. By work, they meant everything that impinged on their role as councillors, including their efforts to build and maintain prestige. They were not referring to religious ritual as would have been the case with traditional big-men before contact. Many felt keenly the anomaly of having, with virtually no official supporting power, to organize people. Some suffered considerable anxiety about their lack of achievement. In particular, members of the three patrolling Committees of Agriculture, Education and Health complained that the villagers ignored their injunctions and threats of court charges.

Clearly, although official plans were for councillors to be local politicians, they became civil servants as well, successful councillors depending largely, as did traditional leaders, on personal qualities to keep control. These qualities included technical skills, organizing ability and showmanship through rhetoric, generosity, and displays of wealth and 'power'. Above all, these men had to be able to manipulate enough people to assist them in their gardens and plantations. Without this the whole generalized system broke down: they could not maintain status because they lacked the necessary material goods for display and hospitality; if they attended to the time-consuming business of agriculture themselves, their work as councillors suffered both in and out of the village, and consequently they lost prestige in their official, modern capacity, and hence the villagers' co-operation.

Councillors relied on achievement rather than vote-catching just as big men did in the past. In 1966, with one exception, they did nothing unusual at election time (cf. Reay 1964: 255) but depended on impressions made during office. A general dislike of outright self-aggrandizement drove ambitious men to impress electors in other ways. They involved themselves constantly and fully in local affairs, did their utmost to meet the needs of their villages, and relentlessly pursued prestige. 'We are not like Europeans, who would stand up and cry "Vote for me! Vote for me!" ' said Vice-President Jongale, explaining the approved behaviour at election time. 'Although I would like to be re-elected, I will only let it be known that I am standing again. Then I'll wait. People will vote, and the *kiap* will tell me whether I have won or not.'

Generally, electors saw their Council as a symbol of their sophistication and superiority over other New Guineans, both with and without councils, frequently crediting its success to their devotion to Christianity, which they considered a necessary adjunct to modern development.[2] They knew the history and concerns of the Council. Coastal dwellers were largely uncritical of its works since they benefited most from roads, aid posts, schools and water supplies, but mountain people were outspoken about Council neglect of their needs and the consequent heavy labour this entailed in road repairs and transporting cash crops. Nevertheless, even they felt that the institution was an important socio-political step forward for two main reasons: first, like other Karkar villagers, they felt that they gained in status by participating in their own government through electing representatives and deciding on their annual tax; second, they considered the replacement of direct rule through *kiaps* and police patrols by Council administration an important contribution towards removing the racial imbalance between themselves and Europeans.

Electors rarely openly criticized a councillor of their own village. To do so would have been a betrayal of village solidarity and would have unwisely risked incurring his dislike. Where several villages comprised one ward, inhabitants of villages other than that of the councillor invariably complained of neglect. One such village, Kevasob, included in a ward with Liloi and Wakon with whom it had few traditional ties, actually made overtures to the Marup councillor to represent them. While an exceptionally competent *komiti* could have bridged the gap between a councillor and villages in his ward other than his own, people preferred to have Council information brought to them first hand. In any case, the *komiti* system rarely worked effectively: it was a position requiring much time and effort yet it lacked real prestige and excitement.

Asked to comment on the quality of councillors generally, people were non-committal: 'Some are strong and work hard and some only eat betel nut and don't think of work'. They admired the eight councillors who had held office since the inception of local government, and had special respect for President Sibon and Vice-President Jongale for their long and successful tenure of special positions, although neither of these men practised the despotism, flamboyance and nepotism claimed by Salisbury (1964: 235) for the Tolai and to a lesser extent by Cochrane (1970: 94-101) for the Malaita people. Although few villagers envied the councillors their busy lives away from their private business affairs, they delighted in discussing local politics and were anxious to learn more about them.

In 1966, councillors rejected an Administration suggestion for a multi-racial Council for a reason similar to that put forward by members of the Mataungan Association three years later in Rabaul: that Europeans would dominate meetings and prevent the people from directing their own political affairs (cf. Epstein 1969-70: 11; Gunther 1970: 29). At the end of 1967, hopeful that carefully selected European members might counterbalance their own educational inadequacies (which was not a Tolai problem to the same degree), they modified their stand. They decided unanimously that Tscharke of Gaubin, a man competent in many fields and sensitive to the underlying currents of Karkar life after twenty years' residence, and Lloyd of Dogowan, a successful, hard-headed businessman, could best meet their needs.[3] Electors agreed with their councillors that there should be enough white men to teach but not to control, and that they would be a means of removing the long-felt frustration of one form of taxation, one law and one kind of knowledge for Europeans and another for indigenes (cf. Rowley 1965: 180). They also mistakenly believed that European tax would considerably increase Council revenue, whereas each male European, like themselves was required to pay only $9 annually.

Although the Karkar unanimously decided on Tscharke and

Lloyd as desirable members in what was virtually an island-wide co-optation, the ingrained master-servant relationship made them suspect that they might be forced to vote for white men they did not want and there was general relief when John Middleton quashed a rumour that his Kulili manager was opposing popular Vice-President Jongale. Other than the two already mentioned, only one European nominated: the head teacher of the Adminis-tration school at Dangsai. He decided to stand at the last minute, when electors had already reached a consensus of opinion on a desirable candidate. Both Tscharke and Lloyd were elected as planned to represent the villages of Kurum and Did respec-tively. Of the voters in the two wards concerned, Kurum people, who had long been anxious to have Tscharke represent them, arranged for just over half of their votes to go to him while the rest went to their former councillor, Galat, in order to save him the embarrassment of a sound defeat. The other ward, Did, may not have been so unanimous or so carefully organized be-cause Lloyd did some thorough European-style campaigning there and had a resounding, if less subtle victory. In any case, people assured me that the results were a foregone conclusion.[4]

Councillor Kabug Bilag

Kabug Bilag was a successful leader because he had the kind of insight into the conflicting requirements of leadership de-scribed by Read (1959: 434) for traditional big-men, and because most people believed he had authority from an external source. In fact, he based his control largely on bluff, acting as if he had fixed authority, and drawing as well on the residue of his former status as a *tultul* and his prestige and traditional manipulative skills as a clan leader.

Instances of despots drawing on claimed external authority from the Australian Administration to maintain their positions, as described by Hogbin (1951) and Brown (1963) and discussed by Salisbury (1964), should not be construed as a general rule. Indeed, Salisbury contends that, traditionally, a form of serial despotism, in which leaders possessed power but not authority, was more often the case than was the ideal of democratic equality, and that in very recent times, closer contact with the Administra-tion has enabled villagers to curb in their leaders the sort of ex-ploitation some *luluais* once practised. Strathern (1966) questions Salisbury's claim that, in some traditional societies, non-heredit-ary leaders were permitted to be autonomous when no apparent means existed of controlling those they wished to dominate.

While admitting that big men in Hagen may formerly have treated certain supporters despotically, he shows that today councillors are mainly young men, the real leaders being older men, who continue to direct the wealth of others by persuasion and negotiation. The general prevalence of wealth now gives the big man greater scope for his skills and other men the choice of supporting him. In Marup, Councillor Kabug also operated within a relatively wealthy society, but his main efforts were directed towards implementing official policy and he used his varied store of influence, real or imaginary, towards this end, somewhat like the Siane bureaucratic councillor (Salisbury 1964: 232), rather than towards building himself up into a despot for personal reasons.

The Marup councillor was insatiably curious about the world outside Karkar and particularly about life in Australia. He enjoyed recounting myths and old and current customs, and when uncertain he consulted, on his own initiative, old men known to be experts in these fields. On wet days when outside work was impossible and he was free of Council duties, he frequently sat on my verandah for up to five hours. Then he would discuss his problems as councillor, trade store and truck organizer, and father of a large family for whose future he was both ambitious and anxious in the changing economic environment. His moods were not always predictable for he had a dry wit, fiery temper and liking for European alcohol. But the energy and persistence with which he devoted himself to local affairs and his success in these matters could arouse only admiration. He was one of my most spontaneous and reliable sources of information.

He gave his history as follows. The only son of Bilag, the pre-war *tultul* in Marup 1, he attended the village mission school for more years than he could remember, before going on to the central mission school at Kurum for two years. During this time he learned such things as reading and writing but no useful tradesman's skills. He returned to the village briefly before signing a contract for three years' labour on Dogowan Plantation. He received the equivalent of thirty cents a month, food and tobacco during the first two years. Then the Japanese arrived. Like the majority of villagers, he carried goods and worked as a labourer for them when required on Karkar and in Madang. Afterwards, recruited by ANGAU, he served in New Britain and Lae, establishing friendly relations with a number of American and Australian soldiers and meeting some American Negroes.

The carpentry he learned at this time enabled him to build for himself one of the largest and most solid houses in Marup.

On Kabug's return home from ANGAU service, he found the village in mourning for his father. Consequently, he inherited leadership of Balug, his father's adoptive clan, at the same time maintaining strong ties with the lineage of his father's birth in Lul clan. When the leader of this Lul lineage died, leaving only young sons, he took his place. Direct links through his mother with a second lineage in Lul, and marriage with a woman (the daughter of the hereditary clan leader) in the third, placed him in an influential position vis-à-vis this large clan. Further influence came his way when, on the retirement of the *tultul* following his father, Kabug himself was appointed and held the position until local government began six years later.

By 1968, Kabug Bilag had been councillor of Marup 1 and 2 for eight years. He was a member of the Executive and Finance Committees and a vice-president of the Multi-Racial Council. He was forty-seven years old and lived with his wife, seven children and his daughter-in-law and grandchild in the centre of Marup 1. His father's elderly brother of Lul clan, this man's wife and their daughter shared his house. Situated on its left was the shed housing the village truck and near this, Kabug's two-roomed bakery. Opposite the house was his small trade store. He called public meetings in the broad shady clearing surrounded by these buildings. Young female relatives swept the hard earth clean and the villagers sat on the steps of the store and bakery, on the gnarled roots of the tree in the centre, and on broad sheaths that fell from the *limbung* tree. The councillor addressed them from the steps of his house, moving out into the centre of the clearing when he wished to stress a point or to allocate labour.

He believed sincerely in the Local Government Council. He admitted that it was hard work for the councillor, but good work. It encouraged people to be industrious, make money and pay taxes which would come back to them in various forms to improve their way of life. The Council meant that Europeans no longer ordered one about as if one were a pig or a dog as they had during the time of the *luluai* and *tultul*—it was as if they now said: 'All right! Stand up on your own now! You're a man indeed!'

Kabug's views on the necessary qualities and duties of a councillor were clear: he must be hard, smart, industrious and able to speak out (in transliterated Pidgin *fire up*); he must faithfully report everything of importance that occurred in the Council

Chambers and constantly emphasize that only hard work would achieve a better standard of living and independence in New Guinea; he must ensure that his electors' needs reached the Executive Committee on its annual patrol, delegate Administration work, and settle disputes; he was responsible for receiving official visitors and organizing major village events outside the province of church leaders. 'Being a councillor is hard work', Kabug concluded. 'If people think I sleep, they will sleep. If they think I am alert and constantly keeping an eye on things they will respect me and co-operate with me.'

The Karkar considered Kabug a successful councillor and the Administration officer-in-charge placed him among the four most effective members. Kabug's task was a difficult and complex one.

The Council met on the third Wednesday and its committees on the first Wednesday of each month. Kabug informed his electors of events at the following customary Monday morning meeting, a feature of all Karkar villages. In Marup 1 these meetings began outside Kabug's house with the pastor conducting a short religious service, announcing church news and perhaps giving some moral exhortation. Although not an active congregation member, Kabug always allowed church leaders precedence in this way. An impressive orator, on the whole he reported accurately, only embellishing the facts to hold his listeners' attention and to activate them. First, he listed communal work to be done, gave out news, emphasizing relevant matters arising from the previous Council or Council committee meeting, reminded people that their contributions were due towards the debt on the Marup truck which he managed, and, if necessary, held an informal court. Afterwards, he delegated work to be done in the village, on the roads, and at the schools. In Marup 2, his *komiti* organized working parties and supervised the work, but in Marup 1, the *komiti* having resigned in 1967, the councillor himself did the job. The meeting concluded in Marup 1, he would then walk up to the Marup 2 meeting to tell people about Council affairs affecting them, to hand on any other news and to mediate, if requested, in any disputes.

Urgent public matters merited a special day or night meeting, which Kabug announced on the big slitgong outside his house. If they concerned only a limited number of people, he visited their houses or privately requested them to come to his. In accordance with his belief that a leader jeopardized his position by remaining silent and allowing his presence to be unfelt for too long, he

L

took advantage of every gathering, whatever its nature, to speak about matters for which he, as councillor, was responsible. In particular, he took his role of economic and political educator seriously, frequently introducing themes of economic development and nationalism, and inevitably imposing his own point of view. This was particularly apparent before the 1968 House of Assembly elections, when, like other councillors, he practised political partisanship during his education programme, favouring Middleton of Kulili Plantation for the Open Electorate and Garrett of Madang for the Regional. He argued that being wealthy, knowledgeable, self-confident, and therefore powerful, these two men could represent the Karkar more adequately and achieve more for them in the complex arena of national politics than could a local man. He achieved a consensus of opinion in accordance with his choices well before polling day.

Karkar Local Government Council Rule No. 2 (1968) made it obligatory for each villager to devote two days a month to Administration work. Other rules dealt with marauding pigs, nonpayment of tax, truancy, and neglect of hygiene and plantations (cf. Parker 1966: 249-52). To all people, liability to perform forced labour must suggest their inferiority and the Marup resented it and renegued on it increasingly. Yet Kabug failed to make a single court charge, appealing instead through traditional methods of persuasion. This meant depending upon his wit, rhetoric and assumed authority over young men and women. It involved subtle bargaining with the use of the village truck and Kabug's own copra driers and with the general assistance he could organize through his extensive clan ties. Perhaps his greatest weapon was his power of inflicting public shame. Through his personal efforts at utilizing all available pressures, he ensured that Marup's contribution to communal work compared more than favourably with that of its neighbours, thus securing for it the reputation of being a progressive and well-kept village.

Above all, the councillor excelled as a mediator. A former policeman and *komiti* in Marup 2 commented with some satisfaction: 'Not much goes to the *kiap*. Kabug finishes all argument—he is the mouth of the Government'. Two things in particular facilitated his success: the people's dislike and disapproval of the kind of justice imposed by the *kiap* or by the indigenous magistrate (cf. Rowley 1965: 79), and Kabug's insistence that traditional methods of solving disputes be tried first. Thus, he only intervened after initial mediation at lineage or clan level had failed, and referred nothing but serious physical violence to the *kiap*. The Marup accepted his decisions and the penalties he imposed, partly because village opinion invariably supported him, and partly to avoid an impersonal and unfavourable verdict should he carry out his frequent threat to send offenders to court.

The nature of a complaint dictated to some extent how Kabug would tackle it. When the culprit was unknown, he dealt with the trouble at a public meeting, where he might obtain new evidence. Because everyone was suspect at this stage, people rarely withheld information. Such complaints mainly concerned pig stealing or damaging crops. Where there was an obviously guilty party, either he agreed to make compensation or, if this were impossible, Kabug punished him in such a way as to shame him. When it was proven that a Medan man killed a pig belonging to a Marup, he fined him $7 on the spot. There was no further argument. But when the aged foster parents of an unmarried woman accused her of vilely abusing them, the councillor, knowing she could not pay compensation, roundly upbraided her in public for her lack of respect and gratitude. Standing her in the middle of the assembly to embarrass her further, he told her that in ancient times, she might even have been put to death for her offence. Then he set her to work to dig for the item (her mother's vagina) to which she had referred in her abuse. Since this was an impossibility, the unfortunate woman became the laughing stock of all those who saw her as she dug throughout the day.

In complex disputes involving two or more parties and counter-accusations, the councillor took a consistent approach: he allowed the protagonists the catharsis of exhausting recriminations, only intervening when he had a reasonably good solution to offer and people were in a suitable frame of mind to consider it, for he had to be certain that his decision would be accepted (cf. Read 1959: 432). He preferred final mediation in serious disputes, where great loss of face might be involved, to take place in private. To make his solution more acceptable and at the same time stressing his position as a big-man in the extra-village context, he often placed the problem in the wider framework of national development. This practice frequently blanketed the niggling details which had prevented an earlier solution. Sometimes he made a Solomon's judgement, which either forced the guilty party to reveal himself, or at worst, left both contestants partially satisfied.

Here is an example of Kabug's adjudication. Old Salbung and his wife had quarrelled for over a year with their two daughters and their husbands after the latter had objected to their children living in their grandparents' house and demanded their return. In retaliation, Salbung ordered his sons-in-law to vacate his land on which they had long depended for gardens. They refused to go. The dispute came to a head at a village meeting, where, in spite of bitter and prolonged recriminations, no solution was reached. Later, Kabug went to Salbung's house, where he called both parties together. He kept them awake until 4 a.m. They begged him to let them sleep, the lamps went out, and there was no food. Unmoved, Kabug sent for more kerosene for the lamps, threatening to stay until the quarrel was settled. Using the need for economic development to support his argument, he explained to Salbung: 'Land is only yours when you use it. Times have changed and it cannot stay unused or someone from outside may take it. So let your daughters and their husbands clear your bush and plant food. This helps you prepare your land for cash crops—it improves it. In this way, you will help them, and they you. After that, you start planting.'

In a similar modern vein, this time with a dash of patriotic metaphor, he told the parents that their children were theirs only while they were small. Once they grew big, they would go away to high school and later perhaps to Lae or Port Moresby to work or study. 'Then they will belong to another man—this man is their country! You cannot fight over your children as if they are your own property.'

Thus the first meeting provided a medium for opening the discussion and relieving anger by public oratory, while the private meeting enabled Kabug to carry out the rest of his plan. By forcing the disputants to wear themselves out mentally and physically, by giving them metaphorical examples of their foolishness, suggesting how fleeting their problems were, and putting them into a wider, nationally significant framework, he eventually achieved a solution. The litigants gratefully closed the affair with honour more-or-less unimpaired.

In his role as host, the councillor aimed to achieve prestige through display and generosity. He operated at two levels, one for official visitors and the other for villagers. If a visit were a large-scale public affair, he called upon the Marup as a whole to provide food and labour. Otherwise he held himself responsible for hospitality. In March 1967 he showed his skill at organization when thirty delegates to the Third Madang District Local Government Councils' Conference, accompanied by a Local Government officer from Madang, visited Marup. With only two days' warning, he mobilized the entire village into cutting grass, cleaning, burning rubbish, killing pigs and chickens, hunting for game, scouring gardens and bush for delicacies, and cutting bunches of betel nut. A former mission cook baked bread and cakes; the women swept the area outside his house, arranged seating and set up his bakery with chairs, tables and vases of flowers in European fashion, for especially important guests. A massed choir greeted the visitors, with a well-rehearsed rendition of 'God Save the Queen' performed under a festooned archway. Kabug arranged for guides to take parties on an inspection of the immaculate village, before presenting as fine a display of food and oratory as most councillors had ever seen or heard. They departed with gifts of betel nut and tobacco, leaving the Marup with supplies temporarily depleted, but with self-confidence and prestige high.[5]

Even everyday hospitality required big gardens and a good labour supply, which in turn called for much ingenuity. Kabug drew upon his success as a councillor, and on his personal achievements as owner of a copra drier, manager of the village truck, and a store and bakery organizer. Skilfully manipulating these assets and his extensive kinship ties, he placed people under many obligations, which, according to custom, they had ultimately to honour. For example, he suggested that his invalid classificatory brother in Lul clan act as his trade-store clerk. This was a position conferring some status on its incumbent. Although unpaid, Bosei was grateful. When Kabug heard that he was not accurate in charging, he said: 'It does not matter. He is my brother'. Bosei's true brothers, delighted at his employment, were henceforth readily available when Kabug needed help.

In view of the traditional Karkar methods of solving disputes described earlier, it would not be surprising if Kabug were biased in favour of his kin. Although he was as often a concerned kinsman as a councillor, he claimed that he treated kin, big-men, church-leaders and ordinary villagers impartially. Actual events showed that he favoured people in special categories only to the extent that he spared them from public discussion of their affairs. While I lived in Marup, I discovered only one instance of his preference for close as opposed to more distant kin. This was a serious land dispute during demarcation between the sons of two brothers, Tubui (now dead) and Nabith. Although the accumulated evidence seemed to support the former, he adjudicated in favour of Nabith's family, reducing Tubui's land by exactly half in the process. Tubui's sons' long absence from the village at work and their defiance of village opinion by repudiating the church and refusing to participate in communal events may also have influenced his decision. Otherwise, rather than use his position in favour of his kin, he drew, in the traditional manner, upon his widespread cognatic network to pressure disputants into accepting his decisions in lieu of real official authority to enforce them.

The Marup appreciated the prestige Kabug brought their village. Only the previous councillor, Sei, consistently criticized his administration, largely because he realized when Kabug overreached his legal authority.[6] On the whole the councillor's presence aroused good-natured attention. People respected his ability, were swayed by the heroic terms in which he envisaged Karkar's expansion into national participation, and knew that neighbouring villages envied them. The results of the Multi-Racial Council elections in November 1968 testified to their satisfaction and his success. He was returned unopposed and his fellow councillors later elected him as a second vice-president of the Council.

NATIONAL POLITICS

Their introduction to national politics in 1964 provided an outlet for the Karkar people's felt need for change. More than five years had passed since local government began, and it was perhaps significant, in terms of Rowley's dichotomy, that an impressive cargo cult broke out in southern Takia early the same year.[7] Like many groups in New Guinea (cf. Bettison *et al.* 1965: 505), the Karkar did not comprehend the concept of centralized, representative government. As Wolfers (1968b: 50) suggests for other areas, they responded enthusiastically because of the novelty of the situation. In considering their four years of national political experience from 1964 to 1968, I make use of an analytical framework suggested by Lawrence (1964c: 10-15) in his contribution to a symposium on New Guinea's first national elections. He postulates two recurring themes in local and national politics, either or both of which impede change to a Western political system by their conservatism. They are the influence of traditional social structures and the influence of religious thinking, respectively.

Notably, the amalgamated Local Government Council helped people to identify themselves as Karkar, so that they frequently made the point that they were members of their village first, then of Takia or Waskia, and then of Karkar. Thus, they could vote without reservation for a Waskia, Suguman Matibri, in the 1964

House of Assembly elections, and a European, John Middleton, in 1968, because they regarded them as Karkar men. Furthermore, councillors could agree to the wisdom of limiting local nominations to only one local man to further his chances of success. Having arrived at these decisions, influential men used traditional kinship and local groups to ensure their widespread acceptance by voters.

If traditional groups were in fact a useful means of effecting political change, was religious thinking an impediment, as Lawrence suggests? It is most likely that religious influence in modern politics in this area would have been expressed through cargo beliefs or cargo cult. As Karkar was geographically isolated from the rest of its Open and Regional Electorates, cargoism in politics could only be activated by the emergence of a local chiliast with political ambitions, or by the deliberate efforts of mainland cult leaders. But political cargoism did not occur in 1964 as it did on the Rai Coast (Harding 1965: 207-11) and around Madang (Lawrence 1964c: 14-15) and Kainantu (Leininger 1964 and Watson 1964). Neither was it apparent in 1968 as it was again in Madang (Harding and Lawrence 1971). Yet cargo thinking may take many guises. Wolfers (1968b: 55) finds it no real advance that an expatriate, Middleton, should have succeeded a Karkar man in a long-contacted area like Sumkar. But most Karkar considered the election of a European representative, who would best be able to understand European political institutions, an advance on their previous thinking (when they voted for Suguman Matibri) and a practical solution to the alien situation in which they found themselves (cf. Bulmer 1964: 48). As well as his obvious advantage of being wealthy, people explained Middleton's presumed superior ability in non-empirical terms: by reason of being a European he automatically possessed the special knowledge denied them. Hence his co-operation was vital.

During the three months preceding the 1968 House of Assembly elections, I made a specific study of the people's knowledge of and attitudes towards the current official political structure (especially the House of Assembly), the elections themselves, and the post-election results. I observed their behaviour during village discussions and at the polls, and, as well as having informal discussions in seven Takia and six Waskia villages, recorded lengthy interviews with twenty men chosen at random from Marup 1 and 2. On the basis of this information, I drew up four roughly graded categories ranging from an *élite* of reasonably informed men[8] to people who seemed to have very little knowledge of modern politics beyond the most obvious village level. The *élite* comprised mainly councillors and former councillors, *komiti* men, trained clerks working for the missions or for co-operative societies, and teachers. Members of the least-informed group were educated at village Bible schools, if at all, and had never worked away from home.

In general, most people envisaged the House of Assembly as the Council writ large, and arrived at their choice of a representative by village consensus, as was the custom in the pre-contact situation described in Chapter 1. The Council reached agreement on a suitable person first, but the villagers had to agree to accept this. Since the *élite*, and in particular the councillors, informed the choices and political behaviour of others (cf. Leininger 1964: 31; Ryan 1964: 22), my comments are confined to this category.

People described the hierarchical political structure of the country as follows. At the grass roots level were the councillor, the Council committees, and the Council body as a whole. Then came the 'Government of the Madang District' (the Department of District Administration), whose responsibilities included agriculture, health and education, the 'Government in Port Moresby' (the Department of District Administration and the House of Assembly), and the 'Government in Australia' (the Australian Parliament). The villagers thought that ordinary local matters were the province of the Karkar Local Government Council, while the House of Assembly dealt with matters of magnitude or leading to national legislation. The role of the Department of District Administration was to guide, and to enforce the law (cf. Salisbury 1964: 232). Procedure in the House of Assembly was for members to discuss matters brought to their attention, to vote on them and, if accepted, to announce them as law to their constituencies.

At this stage, people were unaware of the power of veto held by the Governor-General of Australia acting on the advice of the Minister for External Territories.[9] Without exception, they applauded the establishment of the House of Assembly, seeing it as a vehicle for planning economic development, especially for less advanced areas in Papua New Guinea than their own progressive one, for utilizing ideas introduced by specific groups for the general good, and for bringing independence and international respect to Papua New Guinea.

Of the structural detail of institutions at levels above local government councils, the Karkar knew only that members of the House represented either Open Electorates comprising small areas like Sumgilbar in the Mugil area, and Karkar, or Regional Electorates consisting of a number of Open ones. They termed representatives 'big-men' in either the traditional or modern sense. Representation and responsibility was their role, not the expectation of privilege. In these respects their first representative, Suguman Matibri, failed to reach their expectations.

Suguman Matibri, the councillor of Langlang village and former vice-president of the Waskia Council, was the member for the Madang Open Electorate from 1964 to 1968. A Catholic who worked for ten years on the Lutheran plantation at Kurum, a Waskia who married a Takia, a businessman with stores in both Waskia and Takia, he was well-known throughout the island. He spoke both Karkar vernaculars and was literate in Pidgin. He attended meetings of the Fifth Legislative Council in Port Moresby with a number of other Papua New Guinea local leaders brought there to get some idea of its work. According to Suguman, the Karkar officer-in-charge, who arranged his visit, encouraged him to nominate in 1964.[10] The Karkar voted for him because he had traditional status as the son of a clan leader, because he was successful in modern skills, and above all, because he was a Karkar.

Suguman's conception of his role was to represent his electors by his presence in the House. He candidly admitted to being attracted to some extent by members' status and income. Some councillors and Europeans complained of his infrequent participation in affairs in the House, attributing it not to his lack of application but to his being put at a disadvantage by the many quick exchanges in English. In fact, he made eleven speeches and asked nineteen questions in the House of Assembly between 1964 and 1966 (Wolfers 1967: 35).

Although Suguman reported on affairs in the House of Assembly at Council meetings, his electors failed to see how he could carry out his responsibilities to them if he did not visit them in their villages. In 1968, during the campaign for the second national elections, they criticized him because he personally had not kept them informed, ascertained their needs and thoughts or initiated any local activities (cf. Bettison et al. 1965: 511-12). They accused him of using his member's income for unseemly ostentatious display, when he built a European-style house in his village. Actually, the Catholic Mission made him a loan for the building. Nevertheless, the villagers consistently praised his qualities as an individual. Like New Guineans generally, they deplored serious derogation (cf. Polansky 1965: 256), invariably beginning their criticism by saying, 'Suguman is a good man. I cannot give him a bad name'.

As mentioned, the three candidates for the Open Electorate in 1968 were John Middleton of Kulili Estates on Karkar, President Kaki of the Sumgilbar Council, and Wadau, a former policeman from Matukar village in the Sumgilbar area. The two other potential Karkar candidates, Council President Sibon and Vice-President Jongale, unwilling to oppose a respected European, whom they saw as a powerful figure in his own right, abandoned ideas of nominating. They also realized that three local candidates would split the vote and endanger Karkar's chances of success. Further, Jongale, who had no formal education, mistakenly believed that a standard VI education was a requirement for Open as well as for Regional Electorate candidates, and feared that there might be a good deal of English spoken in the House. In fact, the Regional qualification was the Territory Intermediate or its equivalent, which was a step higher than standard VI.

Council members unanimously agreed to accept Middleton's offer to stand, because of his life-long association with them, his superior knowledge, and his wealth, which would enable him to travel extensively during the campaign and afterwards in the course of his political duties. Other factors contributing to Middleton's solid block of support were Administration and Lutheran Mission approval of him, his generous contributions in the past to public services (especially health and education) on the island, the general belief that indigenous Karkar were not yet able to hold their own in national politics and the fact that mainland electors knew of him, as they could not know of a local villager.

As noted, the people's knowledge of and responses to the 1968 elections derived almost entirely from the local councillors. The Council adviser prepared them to act as political educators. As well as informing their own villagers, at least two of them accompanied every candidate on tour, introducing him and following his speech with a short address. The entire campaign for the Open Electorate occurred in an atmosphere of goodwill between the three candidates, and between them, councillors, and ordinary electors. Although he presented no policy, talking of economic development only in the most general way, Middleton was an outright favourite: all around Karkar, people accepted his assurance that he would keep them regularly informed, his opposition to self-government and independence in the very near future, and his identification with Karkar as sufficient reasons for electing him.

Other candidates had a courteous reception but aroused little interest. Unlike Middleton, they campaigned only cursorily: Kaki's one visit was curtailed by heavy rain; Wadau visited major coastal villages, but his diffident, almost apologetic manner and rumoured connections with Yali's post-war cargo cult killed any chance of success from the outset. The few people who admitted interest in him as a former Yali supporter were soon disappointed by his negative approach. Even so, people never criticized candidates in their presence or asked embarrassing questions. The Marup discussed Wadau's previous involvement in the Yali movement only after his departure, and only after getting me to turn my tape recorder off, so that 'outsiders should not hear a man "downed" '.

For most of the time, the Regional Electorate campaign was similarly uncomplicated. Of the three candidates, Garrett, a surveyor, Jephcott, a cattle rancher, and Whittaker, a store and bus owner, the Karkar preferred Garrett. They considered him a suitably mature family man, already familiar with them from the survey work he had done on Karkar, and mistakenly believed that he worked for the Administration, a point in his favour as opposed to private business. Furthermore, Middleton and Lloyd (of Dogowan) influenced the councillors, and therefore the villagers, to support him. For example, during his campaign, while explaining the mechanics of voting, Middleton gave Garrett's name as an example of a preferred candidate. Although he gave Jephcott transport and hospitality during his visit, he felt obliged to tell electors of his association with a political party,[11] implying that this made him an undesirable candidate at this stage of political development. Lloyd actively assisted Garrett in his campaign, distributing propaganda on his behalf, and keeping him informed in Madang of public opinion on Karkar.

The villagers' reactions on meeting Jephcott in person, three weeks before polling day, were those of lively interest, surprise, and confusion. His clear explanation of his background and the concrete ideas he offered, especially about solutions to land shortages, pleased them. What is more, Lutheran Mission representatives on Karkar came out unequivocally in his support partly because of his hospitality to participants in a Lutheran Conference near his property several years before.

Confusion arose when, having already arrived at a consensus of opinion in favour of Garrett, some people were tempted to change their choice in favour of Jephcott. In other words, for the first time in the elections they were faced with having to make a choice on an individual basis. A last minute visit from Garrett changed this uncomfortable situation. Warned by Lloyd, Garrett introduced the first aggressive campaigning, demolishing Jephcott's entire platform by emphasizing his connection with a political party, and the danger of having a cattleman representing copra and cocoa producers. He renewed his influence with the councillors, organizing some of them to visit mountain villages on his behalf. There, in their own words, they 'smoked' Jephcott, whom only a few days earlier they had willingly assisted, and popular opinion slipped back in favour of Garrett.

In spite of the drilling on voting procedure that the villagers had previously received from councillors and candidates, only a small minority among the *élite* understood preferential voting, and even they disliked the idea (cf. Wolfers 1968a: 78). The conviction that it was disloyal to the candidate of one's choice led to a widespread refusal to indicate preference other than the first, except among those who still felt attracted to Jephcott and thought it correct to record this preferentially.

Although councillors continually presented the themes of individual choice and secrecy of ballot, electors everywhere reached unanimous and known decisions in the process described for Marup village: voting blocs, while appearing to be kinship groups coincident with the villages, were, in fact, political units controlled by councillors. Where a councillor represented several villages, he managed to achieve a consensus whether these villages formed a phratry or not. Once he had influenced clan leaders to his point of view, he could depend on lineage, clan and subphratry unity for its total acceptance.

During voting I attended eight of the fifteen polling centres in Waskia and Takia catering for people from thirty-three villages, five European plantations, Miak Administration Centre, and Gaubin Hospital.[12] With one exception, where the councillor was a leader in name only, the host villages always presented an immaculate, gala appearance, with temporary palm shelters providing privacy for voting and relief from the sun or rain. Councillors or other appointed ushers kept electors moving along, maintaining the rule of secrecy for voters and prohibiting discussion within earshot of the booths for all but the very old; for example, one councillor, observing his old mother's confusion at the entrance of the booth, felt it proper to help her in view of her age; he showed her a picture of Middleton and Garrett again, getting her to repeat their names before she went inside. A clerk in Waskia began by trying to get people to vote preferentially, but firm opposition to it persuaded him to give up the effort.

Apart from the understandable confusion of old people and some young women, the only major discernible difference in voting behaviour among the Karkar was the greater number of Waskia than Takia who used the 'whisper vote'. This related to the clerks' demeanours. In Waskia, the clerk discreetly made himself available to everyone, encouraging even literate electors to use the 'whisper vote' but his less experienced counterpart in Takia merely asked people if they could write, walking away if they answered in the affirmative. Always proud of their literacy, the Takia would have been ashamed to draw attention to their need for help. Thus the Takia ballot box (which unfortunately for later analysis also contained Bagabag and Bunabun votes), contained 193 or 12·95% informal votes as compared with the Waskia box with 48 or 1·82% informal or invalid votes.[13]

Still caught up in the excitement of voting, the village *élite* and particularly councillors waited anxiously for news of the counting, to the extent that Councillor Kabug brought his radio to a mourning ceremony for his classificatory brother's widow so as to hear the results. But confusion about the station covering the event and delays in final results caused annoyance and a decline in interest (cf. Bettison *et al.* 1965: 313). When the news of Middleton's and Garrett's success[14] finally dribbled through, proposed plans for festivities on behalf of Middleton had collapsed and people were pre-occupied with other activities.

When asked their opinions, most electors expressed satisfaction with the results and relief that Europeans would be representing them with skill and knowledge. President Sibon and Councillor Kabug, however, preferred to wait for some activity before committing themselves. Sibon and a handful of educated Karkar had reservations about the desirability of having European members for both Electorates, all for roughly the same reasons. Sibon would have preferred a Karkar to represent the Open Electorate and a European, the Regional. Then both could have contributed to the common good, the European through his superior knowledge, and the Karkar through his rapport with the villagers. 'Only a native can sit down with the people and hear their true feelings and gauge their real problems', he said. 'They

are afraid of Europeans and will never be frank with them.'
Dinei, a Lutheran Mission head teacher, criticized the outcome as
an opportunity lost for training an indigenous politician. Nevertheless everyone infinitely preferred to have Middleton rather
than a New Guinean from the mainland represent them, their
parochialism being considerably stronger than their sense of
ethnic identification.

The Australian Government planned a progression from
national political participation, with increasing indigenous responsibility, to self-government and independence. In 1968, the
Karkar understood neither the difference between these two
words, nor their implications. As a Marup man commented:
'People know the name, but not the "work" of self-government'.
Believing that both self-government and independence must inevitably be accompanied by the withdrawal of Europeans, they
publicly opposed their introduction in the near future (cf. Hastings 1969: 172) and the settlers encouraged this opposition. During a meeting with a Visiting Mission set up by the United Nations Trusteeship Council in 1968, councillors protested about
the comments of a previous delegate from Liberia, who charged
Australia with deliberately withholding independence from
Papua New Guinea. Then President Sibon emphasized the importance of the indigenous people continuing to co-operate with
Australian businessmen to learn from them how to expand the
economy beyond agriculture. He believed that political and educational progress was being made at a reasonable pace, but that
more training was necessary before self-government could be
considered.[15]

In private, the Karkar whole-heartedly supported the idea of
self-government and independence, according to their various
interpretations, provided it occurred in the fairly distant future.
Some nominated twenty or thirty years' time when their small
children would be adults with education adequate enough for
them to manage their country's affairs. Although they believed
that self-government would be accompanied by equal status with
Europeans,[16] they feared its early arrival because of their own
perceived inadequacies and the suspicion that it might expose
them to unfriendly world powers. People recalled the shock of
being left to face unprotected the Japanese invasion. They wondered anxiously when Australia was going to help them build
their own factories to produce guns and planes in case of another
war. When Japanese interests financed a ship-building yard in
Rabaul, they questioned me about this in view of wartime

events. I explained that, as Australia and Papua New Guinea were Japan's neighbours, they could not sustain hostile attitudes to that country for ever. Immediately, Councillor Kabug translated this into terms of traditional post-war behaviour: 'The fight is finished, so you shake hands, exchange goods, and everyone is friendly'.

The Karkar's most constant fear of attack and invasion was by Indonesia. News broadcasts in Pidgin kept them informed of unrest in West Irian; a visiting councillor from Vanimo in 1967 described the arrival of refugees across the border with stories of atrocities; the Indonesian Ambassador to Australia made a fleeting visit to the island in 1968 as part of a general visit to Papua New Guinea. These events plus news about the conflicts in Vietnam and the Middle East (which they related to the suppression of Jews in Biblical times) made people feel more than ever the need for protection by a European power, and even less able to consider undertaking their own government.

These, then, were the main reactions to political development. Local Government and increased representation at the national level received full support. But in 1968 the Karkar opposed self-government and independence in the belief that Europeans would then withdraw, leaving them in a still unsatisfactory economic and socio-political situation and without the knowledge they needed to improve it. While the new formal political structures were based on Australian models, effective action and social control in the villages were still achieved largely by traditional means.

6

REACTIONS TO
EDUCATIONAL DEVELOPMENT PROGRAMMES (1952-68)

THE ADMINISTRATION, missions and planters all contributed to the learning of modern ways on Karkar. As noted, in 1957, the Administration established the first of its eight Primary T schools and imposed uniform and improved standards on ten central Lutheran and Catholic schools. For informal education in business enterprise, people drew heavily on the planters. In search of the knowledge that would bring them wealth, they pursued all available means of education, but because they still regarded technical and sacred knowledge as parts of the same complex, traditional beliefs and local interpretations of Christian teaching continued to influence their responses.

In 1968 it was too early to gauge the results of the Administration's formal education programme, hence I make no real effort to analyse its effectiveness, but simply give a general picture of the situation and the villagers' attitudes.

RESPONSES TO FORMAL EDUCATION

School Attendance

A total of 2,939 children attended primary school in 1968 on Karkar: 1,647 at Administration and 1,292 at mission schools. These occupied all the available places and constituted roughly three quarters of the school age children.[1] In the absence of records for village Bible schools, I estimated, on the basis of attendance in Marup, that these attracted at most some 500 children but had capacity for more. The remaining children did not attend school for a variety of reasons: some lived in villages remote from schools since sub-standard Lutheran ones had closed down; some were refused admittance because of limited space, after they failed annual examinations; others ran away from school; and parents kept some at home to care for younger children or because they could not or would not pay school fees.

Sixteen boys attended Taur Administration technical school,

and twenty the Lutheran vocational school at Anul. Tusbab Administration High School in Madang accepted sixty-four Karkar students; mainland mission high schools, sixty-six; and teacher training colleges, nineteen. Other formal training courses were undertaken by twenty technical school students, thirty-four nurses (in Karkar and mainland hospitals), sixteen Bible school teachers and two candidates for the Catholic Church and ELCONG. Four Karkar were at school in Australia. The following table sets out the above figures for Administration and mission institutions:[2]

TABLE V

Attendance of Karkar Students at Educational Centres in 1968

primary schools, Karkar:	Administration	1,647
	mission	1,292
village Bible schools, Karkar:	mission	500 (est.)
technical schools, Karkar:	Administration	16
	mission	20
high schools, Madang:	Administration	64
	mission	66
teacher training, mainland:	Administration	2
	mission	17
technical schools, mainland:	Administration	16
	mission	4
nursing training, mainland:	Administration	1
mainland and Karkar:	mission	33
religious training, mainland:	Lutheran and Catholic	18
Australian schools		4

Opinions of Modern Education

Attitudes towards education changed after 1957. Until then, mission education provided people with few practical means of improving their material situation (cf. Lawrence 1956), but because the Administration's teaching programme followed successful economic schemes and accompanied local political development, the villagers acknowledged its potentially useful and secular characteristics. They believed not only that it provided opportunities for well-paid positions and for achieving prestige, but also that it was a pre-requisite for the true knowledge that would bring them the European way of life and high status positions that white men would acknowledge.

Karkar adults claimed that because their own education had been so limited, they were now unable to attend adequately to

M

their own financial affairs or to comprehend what their children learned at school. Most hoped that the new formal education system would enable their sons to qualify for Administration positions which they rated highly, while only a minority appeared to realize its value in improving cash crop production and sales at home. This minority admitted its own vulnerability when it came to cash transactions with European cocoa and copra buyers, who, they believed, were not above cheating. Enlarging on the advantages of education in modern village life, President Sibon described himself as a mere 'workman' for his son, clearing the land and planting trees, but unable, through sheer ignorance, to supervise finances. He was hopeful that his son's education would overcome this drawback, not as a form of ritual to accompany secular activity as he had formerly believed, but as a secular contribution in itself, to the work. Gong of Marup 2, the father of academically promising children, summed up in Pidgin a majority (and, at the same time, traditional) opinion, when he said of his son: '*Em ikamap bilong kamapim mi*'. ('He is improving himself to improve my situation.')

What parents realized they could do to help their children was to make them attend school regularly. In Marup, two school *komitis*, both middle-aged men elected by the villagers, were responsible for marshalling children in the mornings and seeing them right to their destination.[3] Yet truancy still occurred and parents often searched all day for their erring sons. The councillor dealt with persistent offenders. I have seen him marching a lad, holding him firmly by the ear, through the centre of the assembled villagers on a Monday morning, to deliver him to school himself. One father, unable to control his son, called upon his wife's brother to discipline him. He explained that this was customary because a boy stood in awe of his *gai* or mother's brother as he did not of his father. Moreover, the *gai* would, if necessary, punish him physically, something the father avoided. This solution invariably proved successful.

Apart from the practical application of education, the Karkar believed that an educated man could gain prestige through being known as educated. Those who did not go to school would suffer the shame of being as ignorant as 'bush kanakas'. Parents too won prestige through their children's success at school. One form of advertising this was to give feasts when they left for secondary education on the mainland. These began with a religious service for the safety and success of the student, followed by speeches about the sacrifices parents made in sending their children away for advanced education, and about the role these young people must later play in their country's development. There was usually some discussion of education and politics at a general level. At one such feast in Mangar I, the student concerned addressed the villagers, at their request, on the history of local government in New Guinea, and a visiting Papua New Guinean teacher gave a comparative account of mission and Administration education. A lively discussion continued until 2 a.m.

Although the Karkar themselves argued that to achieve their goals they must reach European material standards and adopt European customs, only a small educated *élite* believed that this could result from formal school training. One of these was Dinei, the head teacher of Gulfuk Lutheran School, who said: 'A native's life must reach the stage of being the same as a European's before Europeans will mix with him'. He realized that his own limited training and comparatively traditional background prevented him from changing quickly enough to establish a European way of life, but he hoped that the present primary school generation could achieve it through education. Basenkei of Marup, a former policeman with twelve years' experience of working with Europeans, echoed Dinei's comments. He observed that all adults favoured having social relations with Europeans but simply did not understand what this would entail: they continued eating betel nut, smoking bush tobacco, trying to outboast each other, and thinking much as their ancestors had thought. He concluded that only formal education would help their children build up a way of life which would make them acceptable to white men (cf. van der Veur and Richardson 1966: 50, 85).

The majority of villagers, as mentioned, considered education as they knew it on Karkar and in Madang merely a preparation for the true knowledge they longed for. It provided intellectual concepts, but no guide to European material achievement. This is a common Madang District distinction. Intellectual concepts or perhaps spiritual concepts were referred to in Pidgin as *samting bilong het* ('something of the head or soul') and material goods as *samting bilong skin* ('something of the body'). Or, in the simple terms of one villager: 'School is all right, but we want something material'.

Even Kalei, an alert young pastor-elect of Marup, declared that he was puzzled because, although educated men were now fairly common, manufactured articles such as shorts, shirts, and shoes, in fact everything that made up a good way of life, had not come to the people and well-educated New Guineans still lived in a manner vastly inferior to that of Europeans. Kalei explained that all men believed in something: before, they believed in Yali's talk about cargo, then some began to believe in copra-growing as a means of achieving material well-being. But sacred rather than secular concepts about work remained, especially since some Europeans as well as New Guineans supported cargo cult ideas. Here, Kalei mentioned an Australian co-operatives officer found guilty of inciting the people to unrest in Madang[4] and whose actions, the Karkar claimed, indicated his belief in cargo cult.

Concluding that the Administration, by suppressing cargo cults, was deliberately concealing effective ways of obtaining European goods and power, people looked to the planters for the information they required.[5] For all that, only one Marup, Paliam, claimed to be on friendly terms with a local white man, the trader at Biabi. This, he believed, was a direct result of his education: 'He accepts me because I am educated. I wash, don't eat betel nut, and I put on a good shirt, trousers, shoes and socks. To be accepted by Europeans, you've got to adopt all their habits. To live like them is a good thing'.

In short, the Karkar saw education as significant in overcoming cultural biases. This view became more prevalent as they discovered that Europeans, who came to visit them in their villages to eat and talk with them on a basis of equality, were often attached to universities: there were the students who helped survey land during demarcation in 1967 and 1968, members of the Institute of Human Biology[6] stationed in Kaul village from 1968, myself, and my academic adviser. Some Takia explained in terms of advanced education the difference between these Europeans and planters and administrators who continued to maintain a separate social life on the same island. They hoped that, as education helped these visitors to adapt to village life, so it could help the villagers themselves attain a reasonable status in the eyes of all Europeans.

Attitudes towards Educated Karkar

In favour of education as they were, the people were not undiscriminating towards educated men. They based their opinions on whether the latter put their education into practice, and on the extent to which they syncretized it with persisting traditional values.

Largely because village and primary school life were two separate entities, primary school children were in no sense alienated from their parents or from children not attending recognized schools. Status in one sphere did not impinge on status in the other and, with few exceptions, children were no longer taken away from their villages. Each afternoon, they returned to more or less traditional activities, boys hunting or searching for nuts and fruit in the bush, and girls making string figures, gossiping in groups, or helping with gardening and household chores.

But those young people, usually youths, who had attended primary and sometimes technical school on the mainland and returned home without completing specific training, formed a group which appeared to have no recognized place in the eyes of their elders. They were usually considerably older than the current batch of students but not old enough to participate fully in village life. To some extent, they knew about the ways of Australian youths and tried to emulate them in dress, hair style and recreational behaviour. During the day they stayed about their villages, visiting in groups; at night they frequently met to play guitars and perform their own dynamic adaptations of Western dances. For them, there was no real niche until the economic demands of marriage forced them to accept traditional norms of communal work and co-operation. Councillor Kabug seized one of the rare opportunities on Karkar for boys in this group by sending his eldest son, a standard VI graduate from the Administration primary school in Madang, to be trained in Port Moresby as a road-grader driver. He returned in the permanent employment of the Local Government Council.

Young Karkar men working on the mainland included two groups whose education had been fairly complete within its narrow field. The first comprised technicians such as carpenters, bricklayers and electricians' assistants, holding permanent positions, usually in towns. But on returning to their villages on annual leave, they quickly adapted to traditional ways. The second group were relatively well-educated men, some of whom were influential at home, while others were not. This depended on the extent to which they followed traditional customs especially in relation to marriage and mourning, whether they attended communal meetings and used their skills and knowledge to help their village generally, and how much they were oriented towards their personal advancement in the modern world at the cost of village ties. Here are four brief case studies of educated Marup men in terms of these criteria.

Stahl Mileng was president of the Madang District ELCONG Circuit. He was an ordained pastor, a former teacher, and a member of the Madang District Advisory Council. He lived with his wife, also a former mission teacher, and his large family in a European-style house in Madang. New Guineans and Europeans alike respected him for carrying on traditions begun by his father, the first Pastor Mileng, for the important position he occupied, his devotion to his work, and his ability and empathy in both urban and village contexts. When he came to Karkar in 1967 to take the religious service at the opening of the new Gaubin Hospital, both Waskia and Takia people present welcomed him warmly. Although unable to visit Marup frequently, he kept in close contact with the people, informing them about his work, sending them itineraries of his frequent journeys abroad, welcoming them to his house in Madang, and in return, receiving regular food gifts from them.

Sob Bubun visited Marup fairly often in connection with his work. After he left high school his ambition was to be a doctor, but while working in the hospital in Madang, he was chosen to enter the Public Health Department and become a health educator. He endeared himself to the people by applying his knowledge to benefit them generally: during his annual leave in 1966 and 1967 he designed and built a pipe line bringing water from a spring up a steep bank to a point above the village. From here it would be a simple matter to channel it down to the houses.[7] When at home, he slipped easily into local activities, sitting at meetings, participating in demarcation negotiations with his father, and enjoying the society of other young men.

In creating an *élite*, there is always the danger of psychological as well as physical alienation from village society (Spate 1968: 128). One young man, with considerable educational and work experience in Australia, returned to live in Madang, where he was a member of five committees, including the Madang District Advisory Council and the District Education Board. Yet he maintained strong ties with his lineage, financing a trade store and encouraging members to form a 'company' for producing its own copra and cocoa and buying and marketing village copra. At the same time he developed other personal business interests on an individual basis. Some relatives, annoyed by his independent enterprises and self-possession, accused him of abandoning the concept of community good in favour of his own improvement. They questioned the advantages of a good education and fluency in English if it meant losing the true values of the village. Although in some respects he was an obvious choice as a candidate for national politics, a Karkar villager dismissed him with the comment: 'He should never be permitted to stand for the House of Assembly. He thinks only of business and of himself'.

The fourth case study refers to a graduate of the Administrative College in Port Moresby who now occupies a responsible Administration position. In the eyes of his kinsmen, he negated his successful academic career by eloping with a girl in a forbidden marriage category. For some years he lived on the mainland, returning to visit his home only after the birth of his children. He was greeted with bitter recriminations but, after lengthy discussions, his clansmen agreed to recognize the marriage because of the children. Yet relationships remained strained and his inability to accept traditional customs of mourning and feasting made his remaining few days of leave unhappy ones.

In short, people respected education as a new way of achieving both traditional results and new material needs. But they respected educated men only when they conformed to the old, institutionalized values. To them, personal secular achievement paled into insignificance beside loyalty to clan and village.

The Karkar were in favour of both Administration and mission schools. They knew that both followed the same syllabus and many particularly approved of the emphasis on teaching religion in mission schools. They readily admitted that their fear of European head teachers caused them to pay fees and to participate in parents' committees more promptly in Administration than in mission schools. But in the long run, the latter made heavier demands of money and labour, producing ambivalent feelings of resentment yet pride of ownership and achievement. For example, when the Lutheran missionary closed down the school at Gulfuk near Marup in 1967 because the villagers had failed to make necessary and major repairs to the buildings, the response was one of anger at what seemed a high-handed action, and annoyance at the need for yet more voluntary contributions. Gradually this response changed to one of shame at not having adequately maintained an institution of their own. Comforting themselves that they were not like the Catholics who sat lazily by while new churches and schools were built for them, the Marup undertook the considerable building required, thus restoring their faith in themselves as people able to conduct their own mission affairs.

Sometimes geographical proximity affected school enrolments, but more often parents' backgrounds dictated which school children attended. In Marup, a former mission teacher promised his first child to Gulfuk Lutheran Mission School because he felt that Karkar owed its first debt to the missionaries; Councillor Kabug, with his long and close association with the Administration, sent all his children to Administration schools; the aid post orderly, formerly a medical assistant at Gaubin Hospital and later trained and employed by the Administration, divided his children equally between Administration and mission schools. Occasionally, the antipathy of mountain for coastal people influenced the choice, as in Gamog. These villagers, fearing sorcery on the coast, refused all efforts to get them to enrol children at Dangsai Administration school, sending them instead to the mission school in neighbouring Boroman village.

Ignorance of the syllabus and school procedure prevented parents from influencing their children's educational careers. Although they wanted secondary education for boys in particular, they fatalistically accepted the teachers' decisions, for, as van der Veur and Richardson (1966: 52) discovered in their survey of parents' attitudes in Port Moresby, support for the education system derived more from faith than knowledge. In Marup, two factors influenced the beginning of change in this respect. First, as noted, land shortages put pressures on parents to ensure that their children were prepared for wage work. Second, the pass rate at nearby Namau Administration School decreased alarmingly: in 1967 only one and in 1968 only three children of a total of forty successfully completed standard VI. This meant that the rest were unable to continue their education because shortage of space in primary schools made it impossible for them to repeat the year. Their children's failure in 1967 shocked some Marup men into action. They blamed the teaching standards at Namau and vowed to send their children in future to Narer Mission School where, by contrast, the pass rate was increasing each year. Some of them took their problem to head teachers of several mainland schools, but again lack of space prevented their children being accepted.[8] With the proposed new Karkar high school offering convenient opportunities for secondary education, this kind of interest and initiative could be expected to increase.

Among some young people, particularly those attending Administration secondary institutions on the mainland, secularism of two sorts emerged. One was the tendency away from the Christian church. The other was the tendency to distinguish between sacred and secular spheres of life. This is not to say that these students became true secular atheists. Superficially at least, they accepted Christianity on their return to the village, but they seemed not to confuse the secular with the spiritual, or the Western world view with the traditional village one. It was the previous generation, the influential majority, which read more than obvious pragmatic advantages into modern education.

RESPONSES TO MISSIONS AND SETTLERS

In the 1963 and 1964 Karkar Circuit Reports, the Lutheran missionary on Karkar complained that the mediocre ability of current indigenous pastors helped perpetuate the long-standing belief that real knowledge derived only from Jesus. He blamed literal interpretations of the Bible for this theory. Such promises as 'Ask and it shall be given you' (Luke 11: 9-10) secured strong support for the cargo cults mentioned earlier and the participation of some congregational elders and pastors seemed to the villagers to give them religious validation. It is appropriate here to refer again to those returning home having failed to complete any specific training in the modern education system. Set somewhat apart from the mission ethos, traditional values and the general pre-occupation with economic development, they tended to be misfits in that they seemed to have no recognized position in their society, and this fact alone might make them vulnerable to cargoism. Worsley (1968: 255) suggests that such people will opt for secular orthodoxy in the Western sense. On the other hand, Lawrence (1964a: 269) works from the premise that cargo ideology provides feelings of self-respect under European domination, as do Burridge (1960) and Cochrane (1970). He suggests that involvement in new secular economic schemes would mean renewed dependence on white men, and would therefore be regarded unfavourably.[9] How much more would those who had failed in the European system turn to an independent means of success and of retaining their self-confidence?

In 1945, at least one Karkar Lutheran elder believed that the proposed English language programme in schools implied the imminent arrival of European material benefits (Lawrence 1964a: 271). As noted, by 1967, the fact that the new educational schemes still did not enable New Guineans to live like Europeans seemed adequate proof that formal education in itself would not lead to wealth, and that the Administration and the missions had deliberately concealed important information. The way in which they did this was spelled out to me by a Marup man and his Waskia visitor as we sat talking on a verandah a year after my arrival in Marup: if a European, working either for the Administration

or for the mission, entered into approved social relationships
with the villagers, visiting them, sharing their food, encouraging
their friendship, he was certain to be removed by his superiors.
This was especially true of missionaries of whom several had
endeared themselves to the people by such habits. This was
because the mission as a body did not want New Guineans to
learn all the secrets of the white man's superior way of life. Take,
for example, the attitudes of the Europeans to the white teacher
at Abisan Administration school and his Chimbu wife: such disapproval could only mean fear of these secrets being revealed.
They went on to say that the missionaries considered it enough
to give New Guineans the outline of the Bible, but the inside
details they withheld. They translated portions about Jesus,
Mark, Luke and John into Graged and Pidgin, but they never
translated the rest. Only in 1968 was the entire New Testament
published in Pidgin, for the local churches had all contributed towards the costs. Now, some people wondered whether the truth
that Jesus spoke was ever written in the Bible. When Pontius
Pilate washed his hands, he told the Jews that their burden
would remain with them for a long time. They sought refuge in
every country—in America, Australia, Germany—and most of
what Jesus really said remained in their heads. They kept the
secrets. Probably they were never written down.

As further evidence that knowledge was concealed, people
cited their continuing bewilderment over the financial affairs
of both the Council and the co-operatives. And some could not
comprehend the reason for repeated orders from the medical
officer at Miak and from Tscharke at Gaubin to fence pigs and to
send tuberculosis sufferers to hospital, when everybody knew that
fenced pigs did not prosper and that sorcery caused tuberculosis.

Informal education emanating from Gaubin certainly impressed people if it proved useful. Many women followed suggestions for improving their diet with vegetables and fruit readily
available and previously ignored, and they attended the infant
health clinic regularly. Both men and women were proud of their
constant awareness of the perils of flies on food—a legacy of
Tscharke's hygiene book written in Pidgin. How to deal with
official forms, banking, postage or dressmaking were only a few
of the useful bits of knowledge brought back to the village and
used regularly. But people continued to share their bowls of
food, their eating spoons, and above all, their lime sticks, thus
spreading bronchial illnesses and, in spite of the special ward at
Gaubin, tuberculosis. Moreover, in some respects, the improved

medical service available to them actually validated beliefs in the connection between some kinds of sickness and sorcery. Clearly if a sick person went to hospital for treatment and returned home cured, then the treatment was at least stronger than the sorcery that had caused the illness, or, to the acculturated, the disease was never brought about by sorcery. But if certain kinds of sickness were never cured by medical treatment, either on Karkar or in Madang, then they could only result from sorcery. The most common of these was advanced cirrhosis of the liver. It is called New Guinea sickness and is universally described as follows: the person's belly, face and legs swell up; he goes to hospital; the doctor does not know how to cure this illness, but he keeps him there trying all kinds of medicine. Eventually the patient dies. Believing that the disease is caused by sorcery, people emphasize that only by setting right the initial wrong, insult or argument, will the sorcerer remove his spell, and then if you cared to try, the hospital might be able to help you or good health would automatically occur.

In 1967, after two deaths from cirrhosis of the liver in Marup, a Dimer villager, said to have special powers of divining sorcerers, thieves and the sources of illness, was invited to Marup by some leading men. Known all over Karkar for his exceptional skills, he credited them to some power outside himself. This power, some Marup told me later, was God himself. In Marup, he walked at night along the main track, pointing out houses containing sorcery material. Then the councillor called a public meeting at which he asked the men whose houses they were if they possessed these things and they admitted it. He ordered them to cease practising sorcery and to destroy the materials. According to Kabug, there were no more problems of this sort.

I give this particular instance of belief in sorcery as only one aspect of a widespread and constant fear, in spite of the mission's persistent efforts to remove it. It seems that all the Karkar believed in the drastic effects of sorcery and that sorcery was all about them. Some claimed to have been victims, none admitted to having practised it, but everyone knew the methods used. People thought not to be true Christians were likely to be suspect as sorcerers and accusations to this effect were sometimes flung at an opponent in a heated argument or fight.

Under the circumstances just described, of dissatisfaction and disillusionment with what the Administration and mission taught, the only alternative was to involve the planters in education. As mentioned, the Karkar acknowledged the planters' frequently unintentional economic influence in the past. Now they appreciated their deliberate assistance, but criticized its incompleteness: 'It's only talk', complained Councillor Kabug. 'There is nothing useful.' Yet although the indigenous social ethic overrode Western economic considerations, the logic of the business principles the planters explained was gradually becoming clear to some villagers. Even so, they remained confused about the source and method of manufacture of the goods they bought and sold, arguing that if the explanations given them were true, there could be no acceptable reason for not producing these articles in New Guinea. They saw local manufacture as a means of overcoming the disparity between their own and the Europeans' material possessions. They put forward the reasonable view that the planters had come to New Guinea and made a lot of money from the land, but they brought all material goods from Australia, thus making them very expensive for local people to buy and achieving a second means of draining wealth away from New Guinea to Australia. At a feast in honour of Professor Peter Lawrence when he visited Marup, leaders asked him many questions about the New Guinean *vis-à-vis* the white man, including the following: 'When will factories be built in New Guinea to make tins, clothes and the things we now like to buy? We must have our own'.

Nevertheless, because of the planters' changed attitudes towards them, they were optimistic that they would soon share this knowledge with them. This was why Paliam of Marup, with seven years' experience as a store clerk in Madang, preferred to buy stock for his store from the Biabi trader rather than from the Lutheran Supply House, where he could have obtained a higher discount.

In short, although recognizing that a good secular education in either Administration or mission schools was a positive asset, the Karkar saw in it important limitations. They allied formal education with economic and political development, but subjected all three to traditional interpretations and extravagant expectations. The resulting syncretized body of traditional and Western knowledge they incorporated into their intellectual system, which is the topic of the last chapter.

7

THE INTELLECTUAL SYSTEM OF THE KARKAR

UNTIL 1952, Karkar society underwent little apparent change. In 1941 the people sought to realize their aspirations through the *Kukuaik* cult, which was based on traditional social values and beliefs. The movement was essentially an attempt to bring the colonial order into harmony with the old world view, first in quasi-spiritual and later in clearly cargoist terms. The new plural society of blacks and whites was to be made possible by equivalent access to European wealth, which would be guaranteed to both groups through correct relationships with the gods and spirits of the dead who created and delivered it. The implication was that the people would enjoy the new wealth in ways comparable with those of the past, distribute it through a network of social relationships of a kind in keeping with traditional social structure, and control it by the same kind of ritual as they had always used.

Although the villagers gained nothing materially from the *Kukuaik* cult, after 1945 they saw what they hoped would be great economic advances. Yet these turned out to be only agricultural changes—something the people could interpret as merely variations on traditional economic themes. Like later political and educational innovations, they did not revolutionize or seriously alter social life and intellectual concepts but could be relatively easily assimilated to the old world view. Hence cargo ideology, expressed in cargo cults and cargoism, remained the primary form of explanation of current events.

The Karkar conceived the events described in Chapter 4 as taking place within the universe now to be set out. From this the current intellectual system emerges clearly. However, a person's commitment to the following views was not usually overt but proportionate to his perception of his socio-economic deprivation. Further, punishment and ridicule from Europeans in the past induced caution in revealing true attitudes. Consequently, I obtained detailed and forthright information from only nine Takia villages with which I had fairly close contact, whose inhabitants felt that they could trust me not to mock their ideas. In Burridge's terms, they cast me in the role of 'moral European' (1960: 240). However, people frequently referred obliquely to this same system during my visits to six other Takia and four Waskia villages, Bakul Council Chambers and Gaubin Hospital. As the time approached for my final departure, their reticence decreased noticeably. From their point of view the time was running out for me to reveal, first my opinion of their beliefs about the world and about the sources of knowledge, and second the 'true' knowledge itself that Europeans had so far concealed.

As the villagers saw it, the world was inhabited by New Guineans,[1] Europeans and Asians, and deities and spirits of the dead. They derived these categories from two criteria, skin colour and material wealth, which, in their experience, were closely related. Like the Manam (Burridge 1960: 241), they conceived white men as people who made cargo and black men as those who could not. By grouping all white people under the common label of European, they reduced to manageable terms their perception of the world beyond New Guinea. Within this general term, they distinguished Australians, Germans and Americans (cf. Burridge 1960: 10). England's only significance was as the home of the Queen, who, people believed, controlled the Australian Government and had direct links with God (cf. Lawrence 1964a: 270). Councillors acknowledged her status and presumed power by hanging her picture with the Australian flag in a place of honour in the Council Chambers, and considered the Council boat in imminent danger until it 'was in the hand of the Queen'—in other words, until it flew the flag. She featured in a whole range of stories circulating in Takia, in which, after a series of adventures, people formerly in poor circumstances received high positions and wealth from her. Unlike Europeans, with whom the people maintained frequent and special relationships, Asians were not relevant to daily life, limited as their activities were in this area to the Chinese quarter in Madang.

The final dimension of the Karkar universe comprised the deities (who were a synthesis of Christian and pagan gods) and the ancestor spirits who could frequent the village environs but mainly lived on Mt Kanagioi above. Strictly speaking, Europeans belonged in this category, because people believed them to be returned spirits of the dead. But their constant physical presence and dynamic influence placed them apart from spirits still on Mt Kanagioi.

The Karkar perceived their universe as being tripartite and

more or less localized. The three areas comprised land on which New Guineans and Europeans (or returned spirits of the dead) lived, a second place underneath the ground, where the dead changed their skin colour and received important new knowledge, and a third, equivalent to heaven, where believers lived with God without worry, work or pain, after dying a second time. As much as possible, people conceived these areas as lying within the familiar local environment: the various kinds of Europeans originated in New Guinea, those who were sympathetic, helpful and egalitarian coming from Karkar.[2] Spirits of the dead went to live first in the volcanic crater, Bagia. Here, Kulbob, assisted by the ancestor, Karkar, supervised factories and workshops, whose sounds of production had long been a part of local legend (cf. Inselmann 1944: 115). Here, too, Jesus imparted 'real' knowledge, and Misken, the minor mountain deity, acted as guardian and companion of the spirits as she had done traditionally. Heaven was Kanagioi itself, the highest peak on Karkar. According to some Marup and Kumorians, a natural funnel, possibly the underground bed of a stream, which emerged with a rush of wind onto the open mountain slope further down, enhanced the special and fearful reputation of the area. Here, those who had died a second time lived in eternal happiness and comfort with God.

The Karkar saw themselves as the centre of their universe. Like their neighbours on Manam Island (Burridge 1960: 134-40) and the Wogeo further to the west (Hogbin 1967a: 34-5), they considered themselves superior to other New Guineans. To begin with, they believed their island to be the 'chosen place'. As the birthplace of Kulbob and Manub, it was the source of all men and all culture throughout Papua New Guinea and probably further afield. Moreover, Kulbob almost certainly returned secretly to live on Mt Kanagioi after distributing his gifts abroad.

But Karkar was not the island's true name. Europeans had concealed this, just as they had almost succeeded in hiding its outline on the map of Papua New Guinea. To illustrate the unimportance of the larger mainland compared to Karkar, an old man from Dumad held out his two fists, one clenched more tightly than the other. The smaller, representing Karkar, contained a stone, while the other, symbolizing the mainland, was empty. So it was with Karkar: 'Something is hidden here', he said meaningfully. 'God began here on Kanagioi and went away. Later he came back and hid. He lives now on Kanagioi, but

Europeans conceal this.' Clearly, he assumed that the Christian god and Kulbob were one.

People explained that Karkar was, in fact, the name of their ancestor. The island's real name was Paradise, for had not the early Lutheran missionaries themselves said as much?[3] This was proof that even Europeans believed that it gave rise to all humans and was superior to all other places. The villagers' own observations and experience bore out the latter: Karkar's superabundance of highest quality food, betel nut, and tobacco was equalled only in Rabaul. In modern achievements such as roads, schools and medical services, it led all but the mainland towns, which suffered the disadvantages of dusty streets, heavy traffic and large foreign native populations. Island life was pleasing and satisfying in that people walked on the land of their fathers, free from the pressures and embarrassment of permanent communities of outsiders. Further causes for self-congratulation were wholesale adherence to Christianity without which progress was thought to have been impossible, and the number of Karkar who became men of note in the wider New Guinea community. A final reflection of ethnocentricity was the continuing local opposition to marriages outside the island. Notwithstanding population pressures on land, if a girl insisted on marrying a mainlander, her relatives preferred her husband to reside in her village so that 'the blood would not be lost'.

Consideration of relationships with Europeans constantly preoccupied the Karkar. They believed white men to be spirits of the dead because of their apparent superiority. By way of example, they referred to situations where a European doing the same work as a New Guinean earned much higher wages, or where a European achieved better academic results than a New Guinean attending the same school. Such observations led Kabug of Marup 2 to say: 'There is something about a European that enables him to pick up knowledge quicker and better. We have the same face, eyes, nose and brain, yet he gets more and the New Guinean loses'.

From this kind of association of ideas, people deduced that Europeans were superhuman and they looked for supporting evidence from the scriptures and from white men themselves. As noted, they believed that the missionaries had deliberately concealed crucial knowledge (cf. Inselmann 1944: 108-10) by translating and printing only parts of the Bible into Graged and Pidgin[4] and refusing to clarify certain puzzling statements in the scriptures. They looked for clues in the first lessons the missionaries gave them, studying in particular the story of Jesus rising from the dead and the proposition that, when men died, the Devil put them to work, after which they returned to earth with Jesus, and eventually went to heaven. The first question to be settled was whether the body itself rose from the grave. They believed it did, referring to the physical return of Jesus from the dead. A number of problems followed from this: because Jesus rose and walked on the earth, did this imply that all the dead returned? Would they have a new appearance and new knowledge after death? Who would return with Jesus and when would they come? Would they all die a second time and go to heaven as Jesus did?

The story of Joseph seemed to answer the first two problems. Some Marup and Biu people agreed that it would have been unnatural, even impossible, for Joseph's brothers not to have recognized him when they begged for food in Egypt. Yet, according to the Bible, they did not. The explanation must be that Joseph, after being sold, died as a child and then returned to earth. He implied this by saying: 'So now it was not you that sent me hither, but God' (Genesis 45: 8). Since his brothers failed to recognize him, his physical appearance must have changed considerably. Moreover, he had achieved far greater riches, power and knowledge than they. Such startling inequality could only have been accomplished through his death and hence through God, as he himself suggested: 'For God did send me before you to preserve life . . . to preserve you a posterity in the earth and to save your lives by a great deliverance . . .' (Genesis 45: 5, 7).

In view of this apparent validation of the belief that the dead rose physically, returning changed in appearance, and with wealth, power and knowledge, it seemed a reasonable conclusion that the ancestors of New Guineans too could return with white skins and similar achievements. Like Joseph, their living relatives might not recognize them and they in turn might pretend ignorance of their kindred, and native tongue and customs.

Luke (21: 7-30) not only echoed people's questions about the identity of those who would return from the dead and when they would come, but provided the answers: the spirits of Christian believers would return with Jesus at the time of the millennium, which would be heralded by wars and signs in nature. Finally, if Europeans were returned spirits of the dead, one could be assured of dying a second time and, *ipso facto*, going to heaven, for everyone knew that Europeans did die. On Karkar they were buried at the early mission station above Kavailo and later in the white-fenced cemetery at Gaubin.

The Karkar satisfied themselves that Europeans were not only spirits of the dead but also spirits of New Guineans through their literal interpretation of the Bible in the context of their narrowly defined world view. The Bible said that all men were one great family—that they were brothers. This implied true kin ties between Europeans and New Guineans, and thus suited the concern for a close approximation to white men as a requirement for the new, desired way of life. As the villagers did not assign an important position to Asians, they omitted them from this kinship claim.

The second form of validation people looked for was evidence from Europeans themselves. They believed them to have given proof of their identity with New Guinean ancestors in the following ways: since contact, Europeans had shown themselves to be fearless of spirits of the dead and *masalai* (deities) by living alone in plantation houses, walking abroad after dark without carrying lamps, and, according to some, entering cemeteries at night dressed in black. At first such behaviour puzzled and frightened the villagers. Then they concluded that it could mean only one thing: white men were not afraid of creatures of the night as New Guineans were, because they were themselves spirits of the dead.[5]

Many stories existed to support this theory. Former ANGAU workers told me that some Australian soldiers claimed to have lived previously in New Guinea. In any case, how else could their egalitarianism be explained? Rare opportunities for close physical contact with Europeans showed that skin colour was, after all, the only observable difference and that some blood tie was therefore possible. In 1968 a Karkar man, recently returned from nine years' service with the Pacific Islands Regiment, related how an Australian in his regiment in Port Moresby showed him his bared hand and arm one day, saying: 'Look at my hand and arm. The muscles are just like yours'. 'And so they were!' exclaimed the Karkar. He claimed that when a soldier was going home on leave, from Port Moresby to Madang, this same European bought many goods, including clothes and bed sheets, and asked him to deliver them to his old New Guinean parents at Amele above Madang. He did so and, on his return, described the parents, their house, and their acceptance as a matter of course of their 'son's' gifts. My informant considered this to be a true proof that whites were former New Guineans returned from the dead.

Another startling event was the reported arrival by ship in Madang in 1960 of a European, who immediately searched out a Marup man working in a store, and embraced him with deep emotion. The storeman recognized him as his recently dead father but, before he could talk to him, the store manager reprimanded him and hustled the European back to the boat. The implication here was that powerful Europeans, as always, prevented New Guineans from developing such crucial relationships.

A relatively new phenomenon seemed to offer further supporting evidence of a blood tie between Europeans and New Guineans. A few Europeans now ignored the strict social barriers maintained between whites and local people since contact. They visited villages, sat in houses, and shared the people's food. Some returned the goodwill, a courtesy long ignored by white men. This was taken to mean that the time was close for them to declare themselves as spirits of Karkar ancestors.

So far it seemed to the Karkar in their efforts to come to terms with what they perceived as European superiority that, in accordance with traditional requirements for achievement, they held a number of necessary ingredients in common with white men, namely God, cemeteries and spirits of the dead. On the other hand, unlike Europeans, the great majority had actually seen neither pagan nor Christian deities.[6] Throughout Takia they described the sounds of factories, the lowing of cattle and crowing of cocks that used to emanate from Bagia before the missionaries made a number of visits there. Somehow the latter had caused these sounds to cease, but it was common knowledge that the work still continued. A few old people with special powers for calling up the ancestor spirits reported receiving whistled messages from them[7] to the effect that they were working as mechanics or carpenters in Bagia. One old woman in Marup who persisted in reporting this whistling was returned to her native village of Bafor because the villagers, although impressed by her messages, were embarrassed that she should behave in this way while I was living close by.

If, as tradition and the Christian Bible maintained, the deities revealed all knowledge and distributed all things to men, the 'true' knowledge of Europeans was proof enough of their death and sojourn in Bagia. Only Europeans had the wealth and power knowledge brought and only they had white skins. Thus, white skin must be either a precondition or a necessary accompaniment to knowledge. Takia villagers confided to me: 'We believe that if our skins turned white—if we lost our black skin— the white men's knowledge would surely be ours'. Should a change to white skin occur in some way without death, then black men could achieve real wealth and power in their present lifetime.

An example of the widespread concern and confusion over differences in skin colour is the case of a respected and hard-working man who, on two occasions, invited me to his house simply to discuss this problem with him. My attempts during two long afternoons to explain the relationship of climate and the evolution of skin colour proved beyond him in spite of his close concentration.

Paradoxes in the theory that Europeans were ancestor spirits require some discussion. First, there was the question of Australia. Although not Bagia, it was undoubtedly where many whites lived and they had relatives there as well as in New Guinea. Second, notwithstanding their great knowledge, most Europeans appeared not to recognize their New Guinean kin. Third, some continued to exploit New Guineans, who, in terms of this theory, were their own people. Fourth, the way the Karkar saw their universe could be expected to relate directly to their current ambitions. When I presented them with these problems, I found that the second and fourth had already occurred to them. Their solutions were as follows.

Although all Australians were spirit beings, Australia was not 'that second place under the ground'. Some people, aware of Australia's original black-skinned inhabitants, suggested that white men took over the country as spirits of the dead, applying their new knowledge to live in comfort there. They would return in the future to their birth places in New Guinea. No one offered opinions about the spirits of dead Aborigines. How was it possible for Europeans, being spirits of New Guineans, to have European parents and children? The Marup presented a hypothetical case: if a New Guinean baby died, its parents found it in Bagia when they died, living there with it until they went to Australia or returned to their birthplace. A single European could marry and have children in Bagia, in Australia, or after he returned to New Guinea. Some visited Bagia many times to get 'true' knowledge from Jesus. Having obtained it, they would return to live permanently with ordinary men in New Guinea, ultimately to die there. Thus the Karkar constantly reminded

Tscharke that he must die on the island. To me, they said that, because it was his birth place, he would die there.

People gave two main reasons why Europeans seemed unfamiliar with customary village life: like Joseph, they may have died in infancy or they may have deliberately concealed their identity. When a baby died in a village, he would not know the traditions and language of his people. Because he grew up elsewhere, his relatives frequently could not recognize him nor he them, when he returned as a European. As noted, some Karkar had recognized close relatives among Europeans; the Marup alone gave me four recent examples of this happening to them. But these Europeans usually denied the relationship, possibly because they had not yet obtained full knowledge from Jesus, or because of the Australian Government's prohibition on revealing important information. Perhaps, it was suggested, New Guineans should have a higher standard of education, including fluency in English, before the spirits would declare themselves and share their knowledge.

Clearly, some Europeans still meant to exploit New Guineans, instead of taking their places beside them as fellow planters. Planter opposition to the proposed cocoa marketing association in 1968 was mentioned as a case in point. People reasoned that these Europeans were either the spirits of Highlanders or Tolai, who could be expected to be unsympathetic,[8] or that they were forced into this position by the Government.

The Karkar world view related to current needs in two ways. First, it derived from experience, deliberate observation and Bible study; and second, it suggested a means of achieving social and material ambitions alternative to the secular and somewhat disappointing Administration schemes. In short, its function was to provide an intellectually acceptable explanation and setting for the syncretic way of life people desired (cf. Burridge 1960: 41; Lawrence 1964a: 260; Cochrane 1970: 141, 164 and *passim*). By incorporating all significant groups into familiar traditional categories based mainly on kinship, by concentrating on Europeans as the holders of 'true' knowledge, and by postulating local sources of wealth and power to which everyone deserved equal access, the Karkar emphasized communalism and materialism, and these derived logically from the belief in a divine source of knowledge.

Inevitably, this world view and these beliefs were co-ordinated into a cargo ideology aimed at achieving material rewards. Such an ideology was no innovation. As we have seen, movements of one form or another had arisen on the island since at least 1926 and those occurring during the long history of contact in Madang were well known. Nor was the ideology any longer put widely into practice. In general, the Karkar merely held it as relevant to their current social situation in respect to Europeans. The latter were the one group which continued to defy traditional concepts of egalitarianism by relegating them to positions of inferiority. Cargoism enabled the people to relate to Europeans in a comprehensible way which could be continued in spite of political changes in their favour and in spite of some continuing European off-handedness.

By the 1960s the Karkar had reformulated their cargo ideology from that held during *Kukuaik*. Earlier, they believed that Europeans obtained knowledge and wealth by performing ritual to the Christian deities and that they could do the same by meticulously carrying out the commands of the Bible. But they postulated no moral obligation on the part of Europeans to share their knowledge, and, as the movement gained impetus, its participants withdrew from contact with white men. The situation in 1968 was different: the people accounted for elements unsympathetic to themselves as temporary phenomena. Europeans who were friendly and co-operative in all other respects, yet refused to acknowledge their relationship to specific villagers, were merely waiting until they had received full knowledge from Jesus. Now, having drawn these Europeans into their kinship network and evaluated their past guilt, the Karkar conceived them as having no choice but to give their help. They synthesized pagan and Christian beliefs to avoid any crucial omissions, and localized all important humans and superhumans on Karkar itself. Even more than in the past, cargo thinking was a blend of the finite and anthropomorphic, incorporating traditional rules of reciprocity between man and man, and man and superhuman beings, with literal interpretations of Christian scriptures and the physical nature of the universe retained.

After watching my behaviour for more than a year, some of the Marup finally placed me as an ancestor spirit in their kinship structure on the basis of my special friendships, frequency of visits to certain households, joking relationships and so forth (cf. Burridge 1960: 36 fn. 1; Lawrence 1964a: 2-3). This set them at ease and they began to speak openly of cargo beliefs to which they had only referred obliquely before. Whereas earlier they had denigrated cargo cult in my presence as 'rubbish ideas', now they, like the people of the southern Madang District before them (Lawrence 1964a: 248), called it 'work'.

One afternoon in May 1968, a group of people from several Takia villages sent for me to join in discussion of a problem which had long worried them. They began with a prayer asking God for his goodwill towards them in their miserable state. Then the five men present explained their difficulty: experience had taught them that goods must be bought with money, yet, among all the cases of cargo they had seen arriving by ship for Europeans on Karkar, they had never seen a case of money. Under these circumstances, how did white men make their payments?[9] There must be a source of cash on Karkar itself, and the care Europeans took of their cemeteries, and their reputed visits to cemeteries at night, suggested that the graves themselves led to the source, which could only be Bagia. Since Europeans were spirits of the dead, this belief seemed acceptable, but, influenced by traditional concepts of equivalence, the people wanted everyone to have access to this money. They related how a certain European on Karkar, carrying a bag of money out of a village cemetery, offered to share it with some men who discovered him. They refused the offer because they wished to find the source itself. On another occasion, a European was said to have offered to take some villagers with him when he went into a grave, but, overcome with fear at the last moment, they fled.

The following beliefs were held generally in both Waskia and Takia: only accidents of history had kept New Guineans from their share of cargo; and the myth of the original brotherhood and equal endowment of all men through their common descent from Adam and Eve, and in turn from Noah, proved New Guinean entitlement. Syncretic religious beliefs provided further evidence of this: Noah, in his omnipotence after the Flood, symbolized God, and was one with the creator Kulbob. Both constructed superior sea craft, both distributed animals, plants and men on earth, and both divided mankind into black and white. The following Karkar story relating how this came about is also common elsewhere in north-eastern New Guinea: Hogbin (1951: 242) found it in the Morobe District, and Lawrence (1964a: 76 and fn.) in the Southern Madang District.

Ham, deriding Noah's nakedness, caused his father to relegate him to the role of servant to his brothers' servants (Genesis 9: 25) and to curse his heirs with black skins.[10] Shem and Japheth, covering Noah's nakedness, received his blessing in the form of the white skin and superior material possessions of

Europeans. Thus current inequalities were determined and the relationship of skin colour to knowledge and wealth was established.

At the same time, people claimed that Kulbob, after creating the components of both New Guinean and European cultures, sailed with them to Wadau on Karkar's east coast, then to Madang, Siassi, Rabaul and Australia. In their ignorance, New Guineans refused European cargo, receiving canoes instead of steamships, and spears rather than guns (cf. Dempwolff 1911: 77). Kulbob left the superior culture in Australia before returning to Karkar to live on Mt Kanagioi. Europeans, realizing at last that this rightfully belonged to New Guineans, were gradually returning to share it with them.

The important point emerging from these two myths was that, under their superficial differences, Europeans and New Guineans were in fact the same kind of people. Even so, as the Marup villager commented earlier, Europeans got more and New Guineans considerably less.

Another popular explanation of material differences, with some obvious similarities to the above, was that Europeans crucified Jesus in order to obtain his knowledge for themselves and to prevent it from reaching black-skinned people (cf. Hannemann 1948: 946; Lawrence 1964a: 93-4). The Biu villagers claimed that on his death the 'true' knowledge burst forth, and cars, factories and guns suddenly appeared.[11] Had Christ lived, his knowledge would gradually have spread among people everywhere. God's punishment of Europeans during the Pacific war made them aware of their guilt in keeping the secret of how to obtain material wealth to themselves and some were now beginning to teach New Guineans what should rightly have been theirs.

Thus, Karkar epistemology embraced four sources of knowledge without the obvious contradictions involved causing any embarrassment. What mattered was not the precise definition of the roles of Kulbob, God, Jesus and Noah, but the broad assumptions about them. By reducing their assumptions about these figures to a lowest common denominator, people were able to assimilate all four of them within a single system. From now on the aim was to cultivate Europeans by overcoming, as much as possible, elements of conflict and division. On the one hand, as noted, people removed the blame for concealing information from ordinary Europeans, placing it instead on the Australian Government and the Administration, which forbade them to divulge these secrets; or they excused them on the grounds that they had not yet acquired full knowledge from Jesus. On the other hand, they postulated the possibility of a new peaceful method of becoming like Europeans through miscegenation, while retaining the old theory of a violent upheaval at the time of the millennium.

Miscegenation involved Europeans declaring themselves spirits of the dead, returning to live permanently in their birthplaces and marrying local people, all of which would predispose them to share their knowledge, and would achieve a gradual change from black to white skins. To some extent, this proposition derived from the increasing rate of marriage between European men and New Guinean women, with the latter enjoying a higher standard of living than village women. Two such cases had occurred in Takia, the most striking being that of the Biabi trader and his Marup wife. Marriages between European women and New Guineans, although rare, created intense interest as the presumed working out of the above plan.

The alternative to miscegenation was divine intervention on behalf of the faithful. Jesus would return with all the spirits of the dead and there would be a gigantic upheaval, in which the island would turn upside down. Unlike the old *Kukuaik* prediction, this one foretold not that people would perish but that they would change. Those who believed in the cargo ideology would receive knowledge, wealth, white skins and eventually a place with God in heaven. The rest would remain for ever in Bagia manufacturing cargo. Two instances were cited in which God had already chosen some people for this experience: in the Gazelle Peninsula in New Britain and at Mt Lamington near Popondetta, he had caused violent upheavals of the earth,[12] from which the faithful emerged with new physical appearances, riches and a good way of life. Having long been aware of radical modern changes among the Tolai and their subsequent independent outlook, people presumed that the Mt Lamington earthquake indicated similar achievements for the Orokaiva.

Thurnwald (1936: 351) comments that the inhabitant of a country emerging into a Western technological stage wants to use the benefits of civilization 'in a rhythm of life and in a society that he has inherited'. Indeed, this is why the Karkar preferred the first solution described above as a continuation of an existing order. Apart from the obvious physical advantage of non-violence, it avoided dislocating established social institutions: Europeans could simply assume their former positions in society to which they would contribute their superior knowledge. The second solution provided for God to assert his power in a traumatic way. It derived from the story of the Flood. But even here, a new, benign interpretation was that the wholesale destruction of that time was nothing more than a metaphorical reference to the changes brought about in men.

Conditions for success in either case were obedience to the rules of Christian worship and appeals to the goodwill of Europeans and other spirits of the dead through care of villages and cemeteries. The reconstructed world view, by including Europeans in the local social and physical environment as spirits of the dead moving from their villages, to Bagia, to Australia, back to New Guinea and ultimately to Kanagioi, provided an adequate framework for access to the sources of power. These sources were conceived to be Kulbob and Jesus in Bagia and God on Kanagioi, and the vehicles of communication with them were spirits and returned spirits of the dead (or Europeans). That people believed sacred techniques necessary was apparent from their admission of increasing disillusionment with secular efforts, and concentration on pagan and Christian mythology. They considered that a ritual approach to the deities under the right conditions would bring them the material goods necessary for social and political equivalence with Europeans. Recent practising cultists used the old *Kukuaik* ritual of prayer, public confession and beautification of cemeteries. Others queried the efficacy of this because it did not include local Europeans who were clearly an integral part of the process. The exclusion of Europeans largely explained why, for the majority, cargoism remained only an ideology without a ritual cult—Europeans would be unwilling to participate in a cult. The most people could do was to continue to extend their network of relationships with white men who would, it was hoped, eventually confide the correct ritual.

It is worth emphasizing again that although the practice of cargo cults was confined to two major centres in recent years, cargoism, as described above, was widespread, ranging in intensity from fanaticism to equivocation. Even among those who denounced it, some invariably admitted that, like Thomas, they could not entirely disbelieve.

8

CONCLUSION

K ARKAR REACTIONS to Administration programmes must be seen in terms of continuing traditional values, beliefs and customs, with the people adopting Western institutions into their own intellectual framework. The new schemes were undertaken with enthusiasm and apparent success. But, in over seventy years of contact, although arriving at a satisfactory explanation of presumed European superiority, the villagers had been unable to achieve it for themselves. On the whole, Europeans had recognized neither their dignity nor their society's integrity. Nor had they permitted them to enter white society. Hence, when the economic and political innovations of the 1950s occurred, tradition provided the only charter of action and belief.

The main characteristic shared with Europeans was materialism. One of the important differences was the Karkar merging of economic, political and educational institutions into one generalized social system oriented towards the traditional value of local communalism as against European specialization and compartmentalism. Not only did Europeans practice economic specialization and competition—one man one job and each man for himself—but they divided their social system into distinct hierarchical institutions. The Karkar, working mainly on the basis of kin groups in modern economic enterprise, practised cooperation, reciprocity, equivalence and distribution to secure prestige and its accompanying social and political benefits. Participation in the new political system was characterized by a preference for consensus of opinion in all matters, and for solution of disputes by mediation at village level. Formal education, although it brought a measure of prestige and seemed to be a prerequisite for social relationships with Europeans, had only limited usefulness: it did not lead to European wealth. People believed that the knowledge they really wanted derived from a sacred source: by incorporating white men into their universe as potentially benign ancestor spirits, and by introducing a new element of moral obligation for Europeans to share their knowledge, they felt that they were ensuring their ultimate economic, political and social success. Furthermore, the emphasis on the old belief that whites were spirits of the dead made intelligible their special attributes and powers.

Two things combined to make the Karkar villagers' expectations of the introduced programmes wildly extravagant: their lack of understanding of the premises underlying these new institutions, and their belief that the way of life of the relatively wealthy and powerful Europeans they knew was the norm for white men. But the unique conditions of the past in New Guinea and of current rapid modernization have resulted in many expatriates earning incomes well beyond the reach of even the majority of their countrymen in Australia. It follows that the villagers aimed to change from a subsistence society to a consumer society representative of an especially favoured minority group of one of the world's richest countries. This was beyond even the most industrious New Guinean, who, as Fisk (1972: 46) points out, 'can only hope to act out a charade of such wealth or to acquire it by non-economic means'. Such a situation of unrealistic expectations may well result in a dangerous state of increasing frustrations. As I have shown, at a certain temporarily static level of achievement, the Karkar began to question the usefulness of their experiments with the Western concept of hard work for modest returns, in favour of traditional expectations of achieving wealth through divine intervention. Their expectations of finite and instantaneous rather than preplanned and evolutionary achievement threatened the consolidation and expansion of changes so far, possibly by the replacement of secular with ritual methods.

That people have clung to the traditional belief system suggests that it continued to promise them economic and consequently political and social gains. Their epistemology, based on traditional religious beliefs, indicated the source of knowledge and hence of material goods. The ritual forms of old times provided, they thought, a means of obtaining them. Belief in this ritual as a necessary technology was the inevitable result of their goals being attainable. It follows that realizable goals today would tend to restore the balance of sacred and secular techniques, as in the past, when although ritual was emphasized, secular efforts were never neglected. Yet it is precisely these goals that are most unlikely to change without an ideology appealing to mass rejection of the European life-style.

Thanks to their cultural conservatism yet flexibility, the Karkar appeared to have suffered neither psychological nor social dislocation to any serious extent as a result of recent changes. Karkar traditional cosmology, organizing the world into a composite and stable system, assured them of maximum security. It defined their interaction with nature and with humans and extra-humans as one of harmony and balance. This method of organizing the diverse parts of their environment proved adequate for organizing its even more diverse components after European institutions were imposed. As in the past, it provided for everybody in the new situation who was liable to prove significant.

Given that the perpetuation of some of the old beliefs had obvious psychological and practical benefits, the question arises: can there be any actual worth in beliefs not based on scientific fact? The answer lies in the degree of fit between this society and its environment. Karkar belief in a sacred source of knowledge, like the Karkar world view, acted as a restraint on the exploitation of one's fellows. Since only deities and ancestor spirits were thought to have access to the sources of material wealth, everyone had the right to share in it. This belief involved ritual and respect towards extra-humans in return for equitable shares of goods to fulfil perceived needs. Individual grasping and economic conniving to obtain more of the prize than one's fellows was excluded from this concept. To become a big man one might manage other people's produce, but one did not own it.

Concerning the question of the value of behaviour based on non-scientific beliefs, the Reverend Percy Chatterton (1968: 17-18), from his experience of forty years as a missionary in Papua, warns that, if non-secular ideas appear in the people's own plans for change, they may not necessarily derive from cargo thinking. Rather, they may be aimed at influencing people to carry out new projects with integrity and at emphasizing the respectable and stable nature of such undertakings. 'A Blueprint for Survival' (1972: 43) supports Chatterton's argument:

> . . . if we realized that the object of cultural information is to mediate the behaviour that will lead a society to adapt to its particular environment, it then becomes apparent that whether or not this information constituted 'scientific' knowledge is irrelevant . . .

From these points of view, placing Europeans in the world order as spirits of the dead permitted satisfactory social adaptation to a situation of alien control and presumed alien superiority; the belief that the disruption of social relationships caused illness encouraged social harmony; attributing true know-

o

ledge to an extra-human source discouraged exploitation of man and nature and consequently maintained a high degree of social equality. In sum, the traditional world view and epistemology, maintained in its expanded form into the present, promoted complementary, self-renewing interrelationships with both the social and the eco-system.

At the crossroads the Karkar have reached, they have the undoubted psychological advantage of feeling that they can influence the outcome of their confusing and frustrating situation through reference to their traditional belief system. They have shown the traditional culture to be a valuable platform for their modern emergence so far. Whatever the outcome of their current predicament, as they undergo increasing change, some of the old beliefs and their accompanying customs will be found wanting and abandoned, while the rest may well endure as a stable cultural base—as roots for the continuing society.

NOTES

INTRODUCTION

1 Following the Oxford English Dictionary's definition of intellect, I take the intellectual system to be the formal and established body of ideas by which one knows and reasons. It includes epistemology, which the same source defines as the theory or science of the method or grounds of knowledge.

1 KARKAR ISLAND AND THE TRADITIONAL WORLD VIEW

1 1972 was also a drought year on Karkar and the adjacent Madang coast.

2 By June 1973 the total population was close to 20,000 (Administration Census 1972-3).

3 The Yam of Madang also ascribe their origins to Kulbob (Hanneman n.d.: 14). For a brief summary of the Kulbob-Manub myth on the mainland (Madang and Rai Coast), see Hagen (1899: 281-4), Hanneman (n.d.: 15; 1934: 11-29), Schmitz (1957: 257-80) and Lawrence (1964a: 21-4). For an account of the geographical extent of varying forms, see Riesenfeld (1950: 368-71) and Bodrogi (1953: 120-9). The pronunciation of the names of Kulbob and Manub varies slightly from district to district. Thus Lawrence (1964a) spells them Kilibob and Manup.

4 Finsch described this pattern of residence in *Nachrichten uber Kaiser-Willhelmsland und den Bismarck Archipel* 1885 *1*: 5-6.

5 S. T. Epstein (1968) and Salisbury (1970) report the existence traditionally of a profit motive and capital investment among the Tolai, and Pospisil (1958) among the Kapauku. The factors leading to these apparently atypical concepts in two such disparate societies are conjectural. A detailed investigation and comparison of their religious systems and epistemological assumptions with those of the Karkar might throw some light on this problem.

6 A discussion of the impact of change on the traditional technology and the implications this had on Karkar culture generally, is beyond the scope of this study. The topic, with reference to the Siane, is admirably treated by Salisbury in his book, *From Stone to Steel* (1962).

7 Here I take examples from current usage.

8 Hogbin, however, based membership in the cluster on filiation, or being the child of either father or mother and consequently inheriting that parent's land rights. As described below, non-agnatic land inheritance also accounted for some cognatic elements in descent groups on Karkar, but it was not considered the norm.

9 Mager (1937: 2) also records this custom. Although he wrote about Waskia, his information, as noted, applies equally well to the Takia.

10 A comparison with Dravidian and Iroquois systems as set out by Scheffler (1971: 231-254) shows Karkar terminology to bear some resemblances to the former, especially in that it distinguishes between male and female matri- and patri-cross cousins, which the Iroquois does not. However, the equation of cross-cousins of the opposite sex to ego with siblings and parallel

cousins of the opposite sex is atypical in both Dravidian and Iroquois. Terms for the generation below ego follow the Iroquois pattern. Hence I label it an Iroquois variant until further research is possible.

11 As Scheffler (1971: 247, 252) emphasizes, inferences about marriage rules cannot validly be drawn from kinship terminology of this general type. Certainly this Karkar assumption does not apply to all societies along the Madang seaboard. The Ngaing in Aiyawang village and the Sengam and the Som on the Rai Coast littoral, with the same terminology in ego's generation as the Karkar, ideally prescribe marriage with cross-cousins, but permit only classificatory relationships (Lawrence 1973: 282 and fn. 7). The Karkar permit (but do not prescribe) marriage of descendants of a common ancestor who is at least five generations distant.

12 Again, this pattern occurs in the case of cross cousin marriage.

13 The Karkar believed that pseudo-kin relationships were established to facilitate trade, but Harding (1967: 176) points out that, among the Sio, successful exchanges were the medium through which such ties evolved.

14 In reconstructing Karkar religion I have drawn mainly on versions of myths and descriptions of ritual from contemporary villagers and verified this information where possible from secondary sources. Apart from the villagers' general confusion about the identity and role of 'Maklai' (the Russian Baron Mikloucho-Maclay who visited the Rai Coast three times between 1871 and 1883), myths varied only slightly from village to village. Such similarity and the frequent total absence of any mention of Maclay persuade me to omit him from this description. His experiences are described in Greenop, *Who Travels Alone* (K. G. Murray, Sydney, 1944) and in *Mikloucho-Maclay: New Guinea Diaries 1871-1883* translated by C. L. Sentinella (Kristen Press, Madang, PNG, in press).

15 Hagen (1899: 285), Hannemann (1934: 20) and Riesenfeld (1950: 371) refer to a third creator deity on Karkar called Anut. The Karkar told me that this was a mainland deity of no significance to them, whose name was introduced by the Lutheran missionaries as a term for the Christian god.

16 According to Bodrogi (1953: 126) Kulbob was taller and fairer than Manub, but this information may derive from cargo ideology in which Kulbob features in connection with Europeans.

17 Technically, Kulbob and Manub, having sailed away and no longer having ritual performed to them, were culture heroes (cf. Lawrence and Meggitt 1965: 8), but this distinction is not made here, especially in view of modern cargo cult beliefs described in Chapters 4 and 7.

18 These spirits appear to have many characteristics in common with the Wogeo souls of the dead, *lewa* and *nibek* (cf. Hogbin 1970: 55-81).

19 My understanding of the Karkar traditional world view approximates that described by Lawrence (1964a) for the southern Madang District. Worsley (1968: xx), in his introduction to the second edition of *The Trumpet Shall Sound*, criticizes Lawrence for presenting a cosmic order so inflexible as to make the people's later adaptation to European contact impossible. I agree with Salisbury (1970) and others that change (and the ability to handle it) in village society cannot conceivably be denied. Yet my personal experience of Karkar 'categories of thought', to which I refer especially in Chapters IV and V, showed that the values and beliefs which I have described above still persisted. However, I must stress that the people showed great imagination, ingenuity and logic in explaining new factors within the framework of their old cosmology.

2 THE HISTORY OF EUROPEAN CONTACT

1 The German New Guinea Company's joint administrative and commercial role until 1899 was an exception to the general rule.

2 The policies of the various Administrations in New Guinea are described by Lawrence (1964a) who drew mainly on Rowley (1958) for events during the German and Australian Military Administrations.

3 Lawrence (1964a) excuses the Imperial German Administration to some extent on the grounds that it drew up measures to facilitate indigenous participation in the cash economy prior to 1914, but these were never implemented by its Australian successors.

4 The Australian New Guinea Administrative Unit.

5 The gradual return of political power to Papua New Guineans in the national elected House of Assembly culminated in the achievement of independence on 16 September 1975.

6 *Luluai* and *tultul* are both Tolai words. A *luluai* was a war leader (Salisbury 1964: 226) and a *tultul* was a 'messenger and servant of a great man' (Rowley 1954: 779).

7 *The Pacific Islands Monthly* (1937, 7: 46) gives this information but the relevant ordinance does not appear in official lists of land ordinances.

8 The Production Control Board (P.C.B.) was set up under National Security Regulations to achieve full production of urgently needed copra and rubber (ANGAU War Diary 27.5.1943). See also Stanner (1953: 83-4).

9 Details of the Japanese occupation of Karkar, the landing of the 37/52 Infantry Battalion, and subsequent ANGAU activities are from ANGAU War Diary 27.5.1943, 'G' Original War Diary 1-30 September 1944, Extracts from the General Report of ANGAU activities on Karkar Island by W. O. Monk F.O. 2-30 June 1944, and the Monthly Report, Medical Services ANGAU August 1944.

10 For a general account of this period see Stanner (1953: 112-129).

11 An Administration plan in 1968 to offset their loss with a co-operative marketing society collapsed when the villagers failed to contribute the required share capital of $30,000. A joint venture, with the three major European planters providing half the required capital and the villagers the remaining half, began trading successfully in 1970 under the registered name of the Karkar Kompani (being Pidgin for Karkar Company).

12 By 1974 a number of loans had been granted to Karkar villages but no information on their number or the amount of money involved was available from Development Bank officials in Madang or the area's head office in Lae.

13 A third such election in 1972 took place after this study was completed.

14 Karkar women ceased to pay tax in 1966. This did not interfere with their right to vote.

15 Harding and Lawrence (1971) include this material in their paper on the elections in the southern Madang and northern Morobe Regional Electorates. They give backgrounds and platforms of all candidates in the Regional and Open Electorates (pp. 173-9).

16 The Karkar High School was opened in 1969. By 1974 it catered for 410 students.

17 Complications arising from Western compartmentalization after ELCONG was incorporated as a public body have so far foiled LMNG attempts to hand over control of Lutheran plantations. Further, ELCONG itself has

been unable to decide where control should be vested: in congregations, circuits, districts or ELCONG itself (Grosart 1969: 11, 13).

18 Areas seem to have been confined to Karkar. Grosart (1969: 4) lists congregations, circuits, districts, and ELCONG or Church Conference or General Synod for Lutheran organization in general.

19 The preceding information is from interviews with Mr E. Tscharke and from Gaubin Hospital records and personal observations at the hospital and at village clinics. From 1967, the Public Health Department had accepted Gaubin hospital's aid post orderly training programme for the first two years of the three year course. In August 1973, Gaubin was accredited and registered as the aidpost orderly training school for the whole of the Madang District, thus contributing considerably to rural medical work.

20 Personal communications from the Reverend R. Pech (Lutheran Mission) and Father J. Tschauder (S.V.D.).

21 In other areas, trading in coconuts had long been a lucrative business for European planters (cf. German Annual Report 1900-1901: 13-4; Salisbury 1970: 112-3).

22 Epstein (1968: 120-1) describes a similar situation in the Gazelle Peninsula where the Tolai Cocoa Project was threatened by competition from European and Chinese traders.

23 On the other hand Reay (1969b: 66) notes Administration disapproval in 1965 of a suggestion by expatriates in the Wahgi Valley to establish a multi-racial private company. As mentioned, the Administration's plan for a new co-operative marketing association on Karkar failed, possibly partly because of the planters' opposition, and was ultimately replaced in 1970 by the multi-racial Karkar Kompani. Although it was the suggestion of a local planter, the potential European participants were noticeably unenthusiastic.

24 This may also have been caused in part by the sudden cancellation of all indigenous labour indentures in October 1945, which, according to Stanner (1953: 134-5), although probably a gesture of sympathy for the villagers who had suffered considerably during the war years, wrought such havoc that most rubber and copra production collapsed overnight. In parts of Madang, the order was at first ignored, so that almost the only copra produced in the entire country in 1946 came from that area. Ultimately, of 999 labourers paid off in Madang, only twenty re-engaged. See also Mair (1948: 210-12), and Lawrence (1964a: 51).

25 W. M. Middleton retired in favour of his sons, one of whom managed Kulili Estates generally, while the other managed Kaviak Plantation.

26 This was largely because of district parochialism in an extremely large electorate, Middleton polling as well on Karkar as he did on subsequent occasions.

27 Since then, Lloyd has insisted on better husbandry of some of the larger village plantations, but he created ill-will by consistently opposing the Council in its support of the now abandoned cocoa marketing association proposal. He declared his intention of speeding up decision-making at Council meetings and introducing a more practical note into Council affairs. Similar European impatience with traditional discursiveness has been reported in the Multi-Racial Council of the Markham Valley (personal communication from S. and H. Holzknecht).

3 KARKAR REACTIONS TO EUROPEAN AND JAPANESE CONTACT TO 1952

1 The information in this and the following chapters derives largely from villagers in both Waskia and Takia, with material from around Marup, where I lived, outweighing the rest. Wherever possible I have drawn as well on the meagre secondary sources on Karkar, especially for figures and dates. These are all acknowledged in the text.

2 According to Lawrence (1964a: 94) participants in the Letub cult in the Madang District between 1933 and 1945 destroyed their goods in a deliberate attempt to gain the sympathy of the cargo deity and the spirits of the dead for their poverty. The Karkar denied this suggestion. Nevertheless, their idea of destruction as an act of faith could also be seen as a moral pressure on God (cf. Mead 1956: 16-17).

3 *Totol* is a Graged word meaning messenger. This boat was lost during the bombing of Madang (Jericho n.d.: 23).

4 In fact, as noted earlier, these contracts were officially cancelled in 1945.

5 Although £.s.d. were the currency in use at the time, I have converted all sums of money to dollars in keeping with contemporary Australian nomenclature.

6 Kubai, *Kukuaik*'s eventual leader, assured me that at this time only the *luluais* and *tultuls* were friends of the Government.

7 This situation reflected Rowley's theoretical reconstruction of the effect of the *luluai* system (1958: 772-82).

8 Similarly, in 1968, the Madang people regarded the mace in the House of Assembly as the source of power (Harding and Lawrence 1971: 182).

9 'And there shall be signs in the sun, and in the moon, and in the stars; and upon the earth distress of nations, with perplexity . . . And then shall they see the Son of man coming in a cloud of power and great glory . . . your redemption draweth nigh.'

10 In his paper, The Australian New Guinea Administrative Unit (1968), Ryan notes that in September 1944, P.C.B.'s request for a reduction of rations was approved. He continues: 'No doubt it produced the appropriate economic benefits. It produced other things too . . . "Natives will readily engage for work in ANGAU labour lines, but the response is not good, when they are called upon to sign for plantation work" '.

11 See Worsley (1957: 197), Lawrence (1964a: 51) and Mair (1948: 216-7).

12 Yali of Sor village on the Rai Coast was a controversial leader who emerged in 1945 in the Southern Madang District. With the Administration's approval he carried out a post-war programme aimed at village rehabilitation and improvement. Through people's misinterpretation and exaggeration of his speeches, a series of cults comprising the widespread 'Yali movement' began at the end of 1945, reached a peak in 1948 and subsided in 1950, when Yali was arrested and imprisoned. For a detailed account of Yali's career see Lawrence (1964a: 116-221).

13 A loose English translation of the Pidgin is as follows: 'We worked for nothing until we were just bones'.

14 For a detailed discussion of the concept of knowledge in New Guinea, especially in the Southern Madang District, see Lawrence 1964a and 1965.

15 When Mr and Mrs E. Tscharke made a journey around Karkar in 1947, they were accommodated in Takia in well-kept 'Yali houses' complete with gardens, lawns and fences after the European fashion. He could not recall the situation in Waskia and the Takia were unwilling to speak for them.

Councillor Suguman Matibri implied that interest in Yali and belief in the Yali movement was rife in Waskia during the mid 1940s.

[16] Information from E. Tscharke.

[17] By 1974 political changes had caused the Company to revoke this policy.

[18] Similar stories have been heard on the Rai Coast (personal communication from P. Lawrence).

[19] The New Guinean's concept of religious ritual as work is discussed by Burridge (1954; 1960) and Lawrence (1964b).

[20] The Takia word *Kukuaik* can be translated as 'Look out!' or 'Tread carefully!' It is interesting to note the similarity between this and Melchior Tomot's translation of *Mataungan* as 'being alert', 'watchful', and Kaputin's as 'be prepared' in Gunther (1970: 28).

[21] Lawrence's records show only one European to have arrived in Madang by canoe in the 1930s (personal communication from P. Lawrence).

[22] They were in fact, Australian airmen returning from a patrol, who landed at Kurum in the hope of obtaining fuel. Their skin was sunburnt and they were short in stature (personal communication from A. Barnett).

[23] As noted, the Lutheran Mission in Madang sent the Reverend F. Henkelmann to investigate *Kukuaik*. The Karkar, who respected him highly, welcomed his enquiry, giving him much detail and many personal opinions which appear in his undated report, *Kukuaik*. Some Marup villagers were among those who saw him imprisoned and taken away by the Japanese at Amele near Madang. He is presumed to have been killed.

[24] In his examination of the medical and psychiatric aspects of human sacrifice in cargo cult, Burton-Bradley (1972: 668) notes that human sacrifice generally is associated with efforts to establish rewarding relationships between men and extra-human beings.

[25] My information from the villagers does not quite agree with Yali's claim that he visited Karkar to arrest *Kukuaik* leaders in 1942, or that the Administration sent him to address local headmen in 1946 (Lawrence 1964a: 122, 144-5).

4   REACTIONS TO ECONOMIC DEVELOPMENT
PROGRAMMES (1952-68)

[1] For a consideration of requirements for local enterprises see 'Some Problems of Indigenous Businessmen', by Jackman (1967: 10-16).

[2] Personal communication from Mr R. Bentinck, co-operatives officer then.

[3] This name, a combination of the initials M.A.N.S. and the Pidgin word for ship (*sip*), was suggested by the then Madang Co-operatives officer, who later discovered that the Karkar would have liked to call it *Kanagioi*.

[4] This information is from D.D.A., Co-operatives Department and D.A.S.F. reports, from personal communications from officers of these departments, and from initial enquiries I made among members on Karkar.

[5] As Mead (1967: 6) points out, the collapse of local enterprises through corruption and embezzlement often results from the efforts of people to occupy new roles without 'sufficient protection against the normal demands of other members of the kin group'.

[6] As noted, despite the enthusiasm they had initially shown for the proposed scheme, the majority of producers failed to take out their shares. They told me in 1970 that they were suspicious of any venture in which Europeans did not participate as well: 'If the Europeans come into this it will succeed. If they stay outside, it will fail'.

7 Personal communication from Mr I. Wiseman, co-operatives extension officer on Karkar at this time.

8 The same fear in regard to Indonesians was current on the Rai Coast in 1956 (personal communication from P. Lawrence).

9 By the 'Salum family' I mean Salum and his three eldest sons, and, after his death, the three sons alone.

10 A villager in Biu described to me a similar experience which caused him also to change his way of life.

11 In 1970, having eventually become unpopular in Boroman, Mileng deserted his wife and child and moved to the neighbouring village of Did. Here he gained the support of all the young people and increasing numbers of older ones in a fully fledged cargo cult in which he encouraged people to abandon cash cropping. The European councillor for Did, in an effort to discredit Mileng in the eyes of his followers, secured his imprisonment for failing to pay Local Government Council tax for four years. Thereupon the cult subsided. (Personal communication from Mr W. Lloyd.)

12 Both private planters and missions kept trade stores.

13 The place of Europeans in the Karkar world view is discussed in the last chapter.

14 From Vehicle Registration, D.D.A., Karkar Island, 1967-68.

15 In 1970, the Kulili planter personally recommended a number of Karkar for Development Bank loans for the purchase of trucks. Consequently, more vehicles were operating in Waskia than in Takia, and Development Bank agents were responsible for seeing that loans were repaid (personal communication from the Manager, Commonwealth Bank, Madang).

16 Hide (1971: 48) notes that Chimbu demarcation committees saw their function as one of deciding claims rather than marking customary boundaries.

17 In May 1970 the Land Titles Commissioner called for work to resume, with particular emphasis now on marking individually-owned areas.

18 From December 1973 to March 1974 during research among Karkar migrants in Madang, I asked the fifty-two married males available at that time what they thought of Karkar as a place in which to live. Of these, twenty-eight gave quarrels over land as a reason for disliking life at home, twenty-one (or 40%) giving this as their main reason.
In 1973 Mr Barnett offered shares in Dogowan to the Local Government Council and the Karkar people. But as both Council and people had shares in the Karkar Kompani, it seemed better for the Kompani to make the investment. In June 1974, Dogowan was offered for outright sale and the Karkar Kompani took it over in March 1975.

19 The Lutheran Mission was sympathetic towards the question of contraception in areas of over-population. Supplies permitting, Gaubin staff fitted women with intra-uterine devices on request (personal communication from E. Tscharke).

20 During a visit to Marup in May 1970, I found that some serious disputes had indeed been solved through exchange of land, payment of cash and pigs, division of land, and marriage arrangements. This of course did not solve the potential problems inherent in establishing fixed boundaries.

21 A description of four new land bills distributed to members of the House of Assembly in March 1971 appears in Alualua (1971). On 3 June, before the debate came up in the House, Ward (1972) distributed a critical paper to Members, with the result that the bills were withdrawn on 16 June. In his

paper, Ward questions the basic assumptions underlying the bills that wholesale conversion to Australian practice must of necessity precede progress. More recently, Papua New Guinea's Improvement Plan for 1973-74 gives assurance that traditional land use has its place in contemporary rural life.

22 The 1973-74 Improvement Plan (p. 6) acknowledged the persistence of kin groups in modern enterprises when it promised a new company law 'to make it possible for people to organize business along traditional group lines and get the benefit of incorporation and legal recognition'.

5 REACTIONS TO POLITICAL DEVELOPMENT PROGRAMMES (1952-68)

1 The first exceptions to this rule occurred with the election of a copra buyer employed on Dogowan Plantation and a school teacher from Narer to the Multi-Racial Council in December 1968.

2 For a discussion of their secret regard for the creator deity, Kulbob, see chapter 7. This was not incompatible with their acclaim for Christianity, since many suspected that God and Kulbob were one and the same. On the other hand, to force a logical connection between all the theories the people postulated to explain their confusing, changing environment is 'to neglect the capacity of men happily to believe many contradictory things at one time' (McRae's Introduction to Martin 1967:8), provided the contradictions fit basic assumptions or are not perceived as contradictions.

3 Having reached this decision, some councillors went to great lengths to enforce it. In 1970, a group of Karkar told me that they and other villagers had been threatened with 'court' if they supported any but the two favoured European candidates.

4 But after a year's experience of a multi-racial Council, some councillors voiced their disappointment: the European members had not, after all, shared their knowledge with them. They still felt a great sense of imbalance between what they themselves could cope with and what Europeans could achieve. Now they believed that only self-government would equalize things yet they were apprehensive of their country's ability to cope with it.

5 This Marup entertainment was famous at Bogadjim as late as 1972, as well as among the Garia in 1968 (personal communication from P. Lawrence).

6 As on the occasion already mentioned, when Kabug threatened the Marup with court charges should they vote for a European in the 1968 Multi-Racial Council elections.

7 See p. 109 above.

8 By this I mean at the rather superficial and general level resulting inevitably from inadequate political education and the socio-cultural environment of village life. For a discussion of political awareness of both local and national institutions see Hastings (1969: 138-207), Bettison, van der Veur and Hughes (1965) and Epstein, Parker and Reay (1971).

9 People were better informed in 1970 after a visit to Karkar of a Select Committee on Constitutional Development to ascertain opinions on self-government and independence, when this matter must have been raised. Both the Marup councillor and the komiti from Biu used the existence of this power as a good reason for voting in favour of self-government in the near future, rather than supporting it in theory but avoiding it in fact until they felt more confidence in their local politicians' ability to cope with it.

10 Although Bettison *et al.* (1965: 506) claim that the Administration made no attempt to induce observers at the Legislative Council to nominate, this does not seem to have been the case on Karkar.

11 This was, in fact, a perfunctory and unsolicited association with the People's Progress Party founded by J. Mackinnon of The Middle Ramu, but it was sufficient to be a distinct liability at that time, as Wolfers (1968a: 9-18) notes for some other Electorates. Jephcott's success in the 1972 elections, again as a member of the People's Progress Party, showed this no longer to be the case.

12 Since voting occurred simultaneously at Waskia and Takia polls I was unable to visit them all.

13 A third box for one Takia and two Waskia villages had 11 or 4·86% informal votes, implying that the informal votes in the main Takia box could not be attributed to Bagabag or Bunabun.

14 Middleton, winning on the first count, received roughly five times as many votes as his nearest opponent, Kaki Angi. Garrett defeated Jephcott by almost twice as many votes, winning on a second count.

15 Councillors put forward these same points during the visit to Karkar in 1970 of the Select Committee on Constitutional Development. Of a large crowd attending the meeting, only three people, including a Council clerk from Manus, voted in favour of self-government and these were heavily criticized by the villagers present.

16 As noted, the Marup told me in 1970 that when self-government came the Europeans would give them their *tingting*. Lawrence (1964a: 271) implies that the people use this term to mean sacred knowledge.

6 REACTIONS TO EDUCATION DEVELOPMENT PROGRAMMES (1952-68)

1 By 1974 the eighteen Primary T schools could offer places to all children whose parents wanted them to attend. An estimated 85% chose to do so (Education Department, Madang).

2 This information comes from the Department of Education and Lutheran and Catholic schools' supervisors in Madang, and from records of high schools and other educational institutions on the mainland.

3 Ultimately, problems about children attending school were brought to the councillor. These two men were regarded as his helpers in this context and the term *komiti* was borrowed to give some sort of formality to their positions.

4 *Regina* v. *Cooper*, Supreme Court of the Territory of Papua and New Guinea at Port Moresby, 23 January 1961. Cooper's application for leave to appeal against the verdict was dismissed in the High Court of Australia in Sydney in April, 1961 *(Commonwealth Law Reports: High Court* 1960-1961, vol. 105: 177-87).

5 This attitude may be compared with two of Yali's early beliefs. The first was that cargo came from God to the Administration and hence to the New Guineans. If they could obtain it through the Administration, then they could forget about God. The second was that white men opposed cargo cults because they saw them as an attempt to steal their property (Lawrence 1964a: 139).

6 Now known as The Papua New Guinea Institute of Medical Research.

7 The project was completed in 1973 with Local Government Council finance, every three or four households then sharing an outdoor tap.

8 In 1969 these men eventually managed to get their children accepted to repeat standard VI in mainland schools. These students entered high school on Karkar in 1970 and did well.

9 We have seen that both Mileng of Kumoria and Ulel of Kevasob discouraged cash crop planting.

7   THE INTELLECTUAL SYSTEM OF THE KARKAR

1 People used the words 'New Guinean' and 'New Guinea' to refer indiscriminately to the entire country and to New Guinea *per se* and to the inhabitants of both Papua and New Guinea unless they wished to distinguish between the two.

2 At the same time people secretly believed that Karkar was the birthplace of all men—or Paradise, as I describe later.

3 As frequently reported to me, this impression certainly resulted from new arrivals' praise of the beauty and tranquillity of Karkar.

4 The New Testament appeared in Graged after 1956, but it was not until 1968 that the Lutheran press in Madang published it in Pidgin on behalf of the British and Foreign Bible Society.

5 Some Marup constantly tested me about my attitude to the dark, asking me if I would be willing to walk from Marup to Kevasob without carrying a lamp, and if I would walk past the village cemetery alone at night.

6 Exceptions I knew of were Ulel of Kevasob, Mileng of Kumoria, both of whom claimed to have seen God, the old Kevasob man who described his childhood view of the guardian deity, Kaulok, to me and an old Kumorian who claimed to have seen Kulbob/God on the mountainside during *Kukuaik*. It is worth noting that the Garia thought that Europeans saw God and Jesus Christ in Sydney (Lawrence 1964a: 251fn[1]).

7 In 1968 a Manus Islander arrived on Karkar and stayed with the Manus co-operative storeman in Mangar village. He claimed that his brother's ghost always accompanied him (cf. Fortune 1935). The people from Marup and other neighbouring villages told me that, after he visited them, they always heard a whistled 'Goodnight' from this being as the two left the house.

8 This concept was an old one in the Madang area. In 1904 the Yam people considered the acquisitive and exploitative whites to be 'reincarnated spirits of inimical people who had come to enrich themselves at the expense of the natives' (Hannemann n.d.: 27).

9 According to Jackman (1967: 10) even some members of the House of Assembly believed that creating currency was either a magical process or a mechanical technique which Europeans concealed from New Guineans.

10 There is an obvious connection between this belief and the *Kukuaik* leaders' warning that those recruited labourers who did not abandon their work and return to their villages to participate in the ritual would remain slaves forever.

11 In 1961, in the fairly widespread belief that a black Jesus would have to be crucified before New Guineans would receive cargo, Lagit, *luluai* of Abar near Madang, slit the throat of a willing victim, who stood with arms outspread in the form of a cross before him while he did so (Lawrence 1964a: 267). Another instance of this belief concerns a Catholic Mission catechist, Godfried Tataige, who, during the campaign for the 1964 national elections, told the Maprik people that if he were elected he would

bring back cargo from the House of Assembly and would later be crucified as Jesus was (Dewdney 1965: 185). The same man promised, during the 1968 elections, to go as a member to the House of Assembly in Canberra where he would be crucified in order to discover the source of cargo (Wolfers 1968c: 8). In the same campaign, Yali's supporters claimed that he would go as a member to the House of Assembly where his (second) death would cause cargo to arrive to benefit New Guineans (Harding and Lawrence 1971: 182).

12 Mt Ulawun in the Gazelle Peninsula erupted in 1961, 1963, 1967 and 1970. Mt Lamington erupted in 1951. (Personal communication from the Chief Government Geologist, Port Moresby). In 1973-74 and again in January 1975, Mt Uluman on Karkar itself became increasingly active. The island has been divided into zones of varying degrees of potential danger and evacuation centres publicized (personal communication from Mrs R. Middleton). Some people interpreted these phenomena in terms of their cargo cult theory, but there was no great general reaction.

BIBLIOGRAPHY

Agricultural Reports 1956-67, Department of Agriculture, Stock and Fisheries, Port Moresby.

ALUALUA, 'Four new land bills', *New Guinea and Australia, the Pacific and South-East Asia*, 6 pt. 2 (1971), pp. 41-7.

Allied Geographical Section Special Reports Nos. 44 and 59 South-West Pacific Area, Appendix D, Australian War Memorial, Canberra.

Annual Report on New Guinea 1900-1, Imperial German Administration (translated by H. A. Thomson), Library of the Australian School of Pacific Administration, Mosman, N.S.W.

Australian Mandate Administration Annual Report on New Guinea 1931-2 and 1932-3, Government Printer, Canberra.

Australian New Guinea Army Unit (ANGAU): ANGAU War Diary 27.5.1943; Extracts from the General Report of ANGAU Activities on Karkar Island by W.O. II Monk F. O., 2-30 June 1944; Monthly Report, Medical Services, ANGAU, August 1944, Australian War Memorial, Canberra.

BARNES, J. A., 'African models in the New Guinea Highlands', *Man* 62 (1962), pp. 5-9.

BARNETT, H. G., *Innovation: the basis of cultural change* (McGraw Hill, New York, 1953).

BERNDT, R. M., *Excess and restraint (social control among a New Guinea mountain people)* (University of Chicago Press, 1962).

————, 'Warfare in the New Guinea Highlands', *American Anthropologist* 66 (4), pt. 2 (1964), pp. 183-203.

————, 'The Kamano, Usurufa, Jate and Fore of the Eastern Highlands', In *Gods ghosts and men in Melanesia*, eds. P. Lawrence and M. J. Meggitt (Oxford University Press, Melbourne, 1965), pp. 78-104.

BETTISON, D. G., van der VEUR, P. W. and HUGHES, C. A., eds. *The Papua-New Guinea elections, 1964* (Australian National University Press, Canberra, 1965).

'A blueprint for survival', in *Ecologist*, volume 2, no. 1 (January 1972). This document was produced by collaborative efforts and was supported by leading British scientists including Sir Julian Huxley.

BODROGI, T., 'Some notes on the ethnography of New Guinea', *Acta Ethnographica*, 3 (1953), pp. 91-184.

BROOKFIELD, H. C. and BROWN, P., *Struggle for Land: agriculture and group territories among the Chimbu of the New Guinea Highlands* (Oxford University Press, Melbourne, 1963).

BROWN, P., 'Non-agnates among the patrilineal Chimbu', *Journal of the Polynesian Society* 71 (1962), pp. 57-69.

————, 'From anarchy to satrapy', *American Anthropologist*, 65 (1963), pp. 1-15.

————, 'Enemies and affines', *Ethnology*, 3 pt. 4 (1964), pp. 335-56.

————, 'Social change and social movements', In *New Guinea on the threshold*, ed. E. K. Fisk (Australian National University Press, Canberra, 1966), pp. 149-65.

————, 'Chimbu transactions', *Man*, n.s. 5 (1970), pp. 99-117.

BROWN, P. and BROOKFIELD, H. C., 'Chimbu land and society', *Oceania*, 30 (1959), pp. 1-75.

BULMER, R., 'Hagen and Wapenamanda Open Electorates: the election among the Kyaka Enga', (part of a symposium, New Guinea's first national election), *Journal of the Polynesian Society*, 73 pt. 2 (1964), pp. 40-7.

BULMER, R., 'The Kyaka of the Western Highlands', In *Gods ghosts and men in Melanesia*, eds. P. Lawrence and M. J. Meggitt (Oxford University Press, Melbourne, 1965) pp. 132-61.

BURRIDGE, K., 'Race relations in Manam', *South Pacific*, 7 pt. 13 (1954), pp. 932-8.

————, 'Disputing in Tangu', *American Anthropologist*, 59 pt. 5 (1957), pp. 763-80.

————, *Mambu: A Melanesian millennium* (Methuen, London, 1960).

————, 'Tangu, Northern Madang District', In *Gods ghosts and men in Melanesia*, eds. P. Lawrence and M. J. Meggitt (Oxford University Press, Melbourne, 1965), pp. 224-49.

————, 'Tangu political relations', *Anthropological Forum*, 1 pts. 3-4 (1965-6), pp. 393-411.

BURTON-BRADLEY, B. G., 'Human sacrifice for cargo', In *The Medical Journal of Australia*, 2 (1972), pp. 668-70.

CHATTERTON, P., 'The Missionaries: working themselves out of a job', *New Guinea and Australia, the Pacific and South-East Asia*, 3 pt. 1 (1968), pp. 12-18.

COCHRANE, G., *Big men and cargo cults* (Clarendon Press, Oxford, 1970).

COGGER, H. G., 'Expedition to Karkar Island', *Australian Natural History*, 15 pt. 7 1966), pp. 212-15.

Commonwealth Law Reports 1960-1961, vol. 105, pp. 177-87 (The Law Book Company of Australia Pty. Ltd.), Library of the London School of Economics.

Co-operatives Reports 1952-68, Madang, Department of Trade and Industry, Co-operatives Section.

CROCOMBE, R., 'That Five Year Plan', *New Guinea and Australia, the Pacific and South-East Asia*, 3 pt. 3 (1969a), pp. 57-70.

————, 'Crocombe to his critics', *New Guinea and Australia, the Pacific and South-East Asia*, 4 pt. 3 (1969b), pp. 49-58.

CURTIN, P. W. E., 'How to be inconsistent', *New Guinea and Australia, the Pacific and South-East Asia*, 4 pt. 4 (1968), pp. 19-24.

Custodian of Expropriated Property, Catalogue of New Guinea properties. Second Group (Sale of Expropriated Properties in the Territory of New Guinea), (Government Printer, Melbourne, 1926). Government Gazette No. 58, 1965.

DEMPWOLFF, O., 'Sagen und Marchen aus Bilibili', *Baessler-Archiv*, 1 (1911), pp. 63-102.

Deutsches Kolonialblatt. Amtsblatt für die Schutzgebiete des Deutschen Reiches, 1905, Vol. XVI (2).

Deutsches Kolonialblatt. Amsblatt für die Schutzgebiete in Afrika und in der Sudsee, 1912, Vol. XXIII (1).

DEXTER, D., 'The New Guinea offensives', *Australia in the war of 1939-1945*, Series 1, Army Vol. VI. (Australian War Memorial, Canberra, 1961).

EPSTEIN, A. L., *Matupit* (Australian National University Press, Canberra, 1969).

EPSTEIN, A. L., PARKER, R. S., and REAY, M., eds. *The politics of dependence: Papua New Guinea 1968* (Australian National University Press, Canberra, 1971).

EPSTEIN, S. T., *Capitalism, primitive and modern* (Australian National University Press, Canberra, 1968).

————, 'Indigenous entrepreneurs and their narrow horizon', *New Guinea Research Bulletin*, 35 (1970), pp. 16-26.

————, 'The Mataungan affair', *New Guinea and Australia, the Pacific and South-East Asia*, 4 pt. 4 (1969-70), pp. 8-14.

————, 'The Tolai "Big Man"', *New Guinea and Australia, the Pacific and South-East Asia*, 7 pt. 1 (1972), pp. 40-60.

FAIRBAIRN, I., 'Namasu: an innovation in economic organisation', *New Guinea Research Bulletin*, 20 (1967), pp. 77-88.

FINNEY, B. R., 'Bigfellow man belong business in New Guinea', *Ethnology*, 7 pt. 4 (1968), pp. 394-410.

————, 'New Guinea entrepreneurs', *New Guinea Research Bulletin* 27, (1969).

FIRTH, R., *Elements of social organization* (A. C. Watts & Co. Ltd, London, 1951).

FISK, E. K., 'Cold comfort farm', *New Guinea and Australia, the Pacific and South-East Asia*, 7 pt. 1 (1972), pp. 28-39.

FORTES, M., *The web of kinship among the Tallensi* (Oxford University Press, London, 1967).

FORTES, M., and EVANS-PRITCHARD, E. E., *African political systems* (Oxford University Press for the International African Institute, London, New York, 1940).

FORTUNE, R., *Manus Religion: an ethnological study of the Manus natives of the Admiralty Islands* (The American Philosophical Society, Philadelphia, 1935).

Functions of the Land Titles Commission, 24.4.1966, Land Titles Commission, Port Moresby.

'G' Original War Diary 1-30 September 1944, Appendix C, Australian War Memorial, Canberra.

Government Gazette No. 52, 1957, Department of District Administration, Port Moresby.

GREENOP, F. S., *Who travels alone* (K. G. Murray Publishing Company, Sydney, 1944).

GROSART, I., Disengagement in New Guinea: the ELCONG-LMNG paradigm, Paper presented at a colloquium in the Department of Government, University of Sydney, N.S.W., 1969.

GUNTHER, J. T., 'Trouble in Tolailand', *New Guinea and Australia, the Pacific and South-East Asia*, 5 pt. 3 (1970), pp. 25-37.

HAGEN, B., *Unter den Papuas* (C. W. Kreidel, Wiesbäden, 1899).

HANNEMANN, E. F., Village life and social change in Madang society, mimeographed paper, n.d.

————, *Tibud: New Guinea legends* (New Guinea Section of the Board of Foreign Missions of the American Lutheran Church, 1934).

————, 'Le culte de cargo en Nouvelle-Guinea', *Le Monde Non-Chrétien*, 8 (1948), pp. 937-62.

HANSEN, P., 'He should have been a millionaire', *Pacific Islands Monthly*, 28 (1958), pp. 86-7.

HARDING, T. G., 'The Rai Coast Open Electorate', In *The Papua-New Guinea elections*, eds. D. G. Bettison, *et al.* (Australian National University Press, Canberra, 1965), pp. 194-211.

————, *Voyagers of the Vitiaz Strait* (University of Washington Press, Seattle and London, 1967).

HARDING, T. G., and LAWRENCE, P., 'Cash crops or cargo?' In *The politics of dependence: Papua New Guinea 1968*, eds. A. L. Epstein, R. S. Parker and M. Reay (Australian National University Press, Canberra, 1971), pp. 162-217.

HASTINGS, P., *New Guinea: problems and prospects* (Cheshire, Melbourne, 1969).

HENKELMANN, F., *Kukuaik*, unpublished manuscript, n.d.

HIDE, R., 'Land demarcation and disputes in Chimbu', *New Guinea Research Bulletin*, 40 (1971), pp. 37-60.

HOGBIN, H. I., *Transformation scene: the changing culture of a New Guinea village* (Routledge & Kegan Paul, London, 1951).

————, *Social change* (A. C. Watts & Co. Ltd., London, 1958).

————, 'Land tenure in Wogeo', in *Studies in New Guinea land tenure*, eds. H. I. Hogbin and P. Lawrence (Sydney University Press, 1967a), pp. 3-44.

————, 'Tillage and collection in Wogeo', in *Studies in New Guinea land tenure*, eds. H. I. Hogbin and P. Lawrence (Sydney University Press, 1967b), pp. 45-90.

————, *The Island of menstruating men* (Chandler Publishing Co., Scranton, 1970).

HOLMBERG, A. R., 'The wells that failed: an attempt to establish a stable water supply in the Vini Valley, Peru', in *Human problems in technological change*, ed. E. H. Spicer (Russel Sage Foundation, New York, 1952), pp. 113-26.

P

HOLY BIBLE, The Book of Genesis, The Gospel according to St. Luke, Authorized Version, 1611.

HORTON, R., 'A definition of religion, and its uses', *Journal of the Royal Anthropological Institute*, 90 pt. 2 (1960), pp. 201-26.

House of Assembly Debates 1964, vol. I, no. 1.

INGLIS, K., 'With their fuzzy wuzzy hair', *New Guinea and Australia, the Pacific and South-East Asia*, 3 pt. 3 (1968), pp. 23-38.

INSELMANN, R., Letub, the cult of the secret of wealth (mimeographed M.A. thesis, Kennedy School of Missions, Hartford Seminary Foundation, 1944).

JACKMAN, H. H., 'Some problems of indigenous businessmen', *New Guinea Research Bulletin*, 20 (1967), pp. 10-16.

JERICHO, E. A., *Seedtime and harvest in New Guinea* (New Guinea Mission Board, U.E.L.C.A.), n.d.

KABERRY, P. M., 'Political organization among the Northern Abelam', *Anthropological Forum*, 3-4 (1965-6), pp. 334-72.

————, 'The plasticity of New Guinea kinship', in *Social organization*, ed. M. Freedman (Frank Cass & Co. Ltd, London, 1967), pp. 105-23.

Karkar Census 1967 and 1972-3, Department of District Administration, Madang.

Karkar Circuit Reports 1954-64. Lutheran Mission, Narer, Karkar.

KENT WILSON, R., 'Village industries in Papua-New Guinea', *New Guinea Research Bulletin*, 20 (1969), pp. 30-49.

Koloniales Jahrbuch, 1898, Vol. II.

KRIELE, E., *Das Kreuz unter den Palmen* (Verlag des missionshauses, Barmen, 1927).

KUNZE, G., 'A letter from Island Karkar', in *Rheinische Missionsberichte*, 39 pt. 6 (1892), pp. 196-207.

————, 'Allerlei Bilder aus dem Leben der Papua', *Rheinische Missionsschriften 3*, Barmen, 1897.

————, *Im Dienst des Kreuzes auf ungebahnten Pfaden*, Vol. 2. (Verlag des Missionshauses, Barmen, 1925).

LAWRENCE, P., 'Lutheran Mission influence on Madang societies', *Oceania*, 27 (1956), pp. 73-89.

————, 'The educational conflict in Papua and New Guinea' (Mimeographed, Library of the Australian School of Pacific Administration, 1958).

————, 'The background to educational development in Papua New Guinea', *South Pacific*, 10 (1959), pp. 52-60.

————, *Road belong cargo: A study of the cargo movement in the Southern Madang District New Guinea* (Melbourne University Press, 1964a).

————, 'Work, employment and trade unionism in Papua and New Guinea', *Journal of Industrial Relations*, 6 pt. 2 (1964b), pp. 23-40.

————, 'The social and cultural background to the election' (part of a symposium, New Guinea's first national elections), *Journal of the Polynesian Society*, 73 pt. 2 (1964c), pp. 10-15.

————, 'The Ngaing of the Rai Coast', in *Gods ghosts and men in Melanesia*, eds. P. Lawrence and M. J. Meggitt (Oxford University Press, Melbourne, 1965), pp. 198-223.

————, 'The Garia of the Madang District', *Anthropological Forum*, 1 pts. 3-4 (1965-6), pp. 373-92.

————, 'Research into regional economic, educational and political development', in *Behavioural science research in New Guinea* (Publication 493, National Research Council, Washington D.C., 1967a), pp. 72-6.

————, 'Land tenure among the Garia', in *Studies in New Guinea land tenure*, eds. H. I. Hogbin and P. Lawrence (Sydney University Press, 1967b), pp. 91-148.

————, 'Politics and "true knowledge": when God is managing director?', *New Guinea and Australia, the Pacific and South-East Asia*, 1 pt. 2 (1967c), pp. 34-49.

————, 'The state versus stateless societies in Papua and New Guinea', in *Fashion of Law in New Guinea*, ed. B. J. Brown (Butterworths, Sydney, 1969), pp. 15-37.

————, 'Marriage rules and kinship terminology among the Ngaing', in *Festschrift zum 65. Geburtstag von Helmut Petri*, ed. K. Tauchmann (Bohlau Verlag, Cologne, 1973), pp. 271-88.

LAWRENCE, P., and MEGGITT, M. J., Introduction to *Gods ghosts and men in Melanesia* (Oxford University Press, Melbourne, 1965).

LEININGER, M., 'Kainantu Open Electorate: (2) a Gadsup village experiences its first election', (part of a symposium, New Guinea's first national elections), *Journal of the Polynesian Society*, 73 pt. 2 (1964), pp. 29-33.

LEPERVANCHE, M. de, 'Descent, residence and leadership in the New Guinea Highlands', *Oceania*, 38 (1967), pp. 34-158.

LEVI-STRAUSS, C., *Elementary structures of kinship* (Beacon Press, Boston, 1969).

Local Government Council Reports 1958-68, Department of District Administration, Madang.

LUANA, C., 'Buka', *New Guinea and Australia, the Pacific and South-East Asia*, 4 pt. 1 (1969), pp. 15-20.

LYNG, J., *Island films* (Sydney Cornstalk Publishing Co., 1925).

MCCARTHY, J. K., 'The Rabaul strike', *Quadrant*, X (1959), pp. 55-65.

MACKENZIE, S. S., 'The Australians at Rabaul', *Official history of Australia in the war of 1914-1918* (Angus and Robertson, Sydney, 1942).

MAGER, J. F., 'Educational and social change in a New Guinea society' (M.A. thesis, Chicago, 1937).

————, *Graged English dictionary* (Board of Foreign Missions of the American Lutheran Church, Columbus, Ohio, 1952).

MAIR, L. P., *Australia in New Guinea* (Christophers, London, 1948) .

MALINOWSKI, B., *Crime and custom in savage society* (Kegan Paul and Co. London, 1926).

MARTIN, D. A., *A Sociology of English Religion* (Heinemann, London, 1967).

MEAD, M., *New lives for old* (Victor Gollancz Ltd, London, 1956) .

————, Introduction to *New Guinea Research Bulletin*, 20 (1967), pp. 3-9.

MEGGITT, M. J., 'The Enga of the New Guinea Highlands', *Oceania*, 28 (1958), pp. 253-330.

————, *The lineage system of the Mae-Enga of New Guinea* (Oliver and Boyd Ltd, London, 1965a).

————, 'The Mae Enga of the Western Highlands', in *Gods ghosts and men in Melanesia*, eds. P. Lawrence and M. J. Meggitt (Oxford University Press, Melbourne, 1965b), pp. 105-31.

MIKLOUCHO-MACLAY, N. N., *Mikloucho-Maclay: New Guinea diaries 1871-1883* (Kristen Press, Madang, in press).

MILES, J. A., 'Some factors in New Guinea history', *South Pacific*, Vol. 8 (1955-56) , pp. 105-9.

MOORE, W. E., *The impact of industry* (Prentice Hall, New Jersey, 1965).

MORAWETZ, D., 'Land tenure conversion in the Northern District of Papua', *New Guinea Research Bulletin* 17, 1967.

MORRIS, G., 'The co-operative as a means of economic education', *South Pacific*, 10 pt. 2 (1958), pp. 30-7.

MURDOCK, G. P., *Social structure* (Macmillan, New York, 1949) .

Nachrichten über Kaiser-Willhelmsland und den Bismarck Archipel 1885, Vol. 1 (2); 1887, Vol. 3. *Koloniales Jahrbuch* 1898, Vol. 11.

NADEL, S. F., 'Social control and self-regulation', *Social Forces*, 31 (1953), pp. 265-73.

Pacific Islands Monthly, vol. 4 pt. 2 (1934); vol. 7 pt. 10 (1937); vol. 8 pt. 5 (1937).

Papua New Guinea House of Assembly Debates (1964) vol. 1 no. 1, Government Printer, Port Moresby.

Papua New Guinea's Improvement Plan for 1973-4. Prepared in the Central Planning Office by authority of the Cabinet Committee on planning, Port Moresby (Sept. 1973).

PARKER, R. S., 'The advance to responsible government', in *New Guinea on the threshold*, ed. E. K. Fisk (Australian National University Press, Canberra, 1966), pp. 243-69.

————, 'The emergent state', *New Guinea and Australia, the Pacific and South-East Asia*, 6 pt. 4 (1972), pp. 35-51.

Parliamentary Debates (Hansard) n.s. 1960, vol. H. of R. 226, 1019-21, by the Hon. Paul Hasluck (Government Printer, Canberra).

Patrol Reports 1944-1962, Department of District Administration, Port Moresby and Madang.

PHILLIPS, J., Judgement: delivered at Madang on Wednesday 25th May, 1932.

POLANSKY, E. A., 'Rabaul Open and West Gazelle Special Electorates', in *The Papua-New Guinea elections, 1964*, eds. D. G. Bettison *et al.* (Australian National University Press, Canberra, 1965), pp. 242-63.

POSPISIL, L., *Kapauku Papuans and their law* (Yale Publications in Anthropology, New Haven, 1958).

RAPPAPORT, R. A., 'Marriage among the Maring', in *Pigs, pearlshells, and women*, eds. R. M. Glasse and M. J. Meggitt (Prentice-Hall, Inc., Englewood Cliffs, New Jersey, 1969), pp. 117-37.

READ, K. E., 'The effects of the Pacific war in the Markham Valley', *Oceania*, 28 (1947), pp. 95-116.

———, 'The political system of the Ngarawapum', *Oceania*, 20 (1950), pp. 185-244.

———, 'Morality and the concept of the person among the Gahuku-Gama', *Oceania*, 25 (1955), pp. 234-82.

———, 'Leadership and consensus in a New Guinea Society', *American Anthropologist*, 61 (1959), 423-6.

REAY, M., 'Present-day politics in the New Guinea Highlands', *American Anthropologist*, 66 (4) pt. 2 (1964), pp. 240-56.

———, 'Women in transitional society', in *New Guinea on the threshold*, ed. E. K. Fisk (Australian National University Press, Canberra, 1966), pp. 166-84.

———, Land tenure as a system of political change, paper presented at the Third Waigani Seminar, Port Moresby, 1969a.

———, 'But whose estates?', *New Guinea and Australia, the Pacific and South-East Asia*, 4 pt. 3 (1969b), pp. 64-8.

Regina v *Cooper*. Supreme Court of the Territory of Papua and New Guinea, Port Moresby 23.1.1961.

Regional Local Government Report 42-75-1.

Report to the Council of the League of Nations 1928-9, Brisbane Public Library.

Report to the Lutheran Mission by G. Reitz, n.d., Lutheran Mission, Narer, Karkar.

RIESENFELD, A., *The megalith culture of Melanesia* (E. J. Brill, Leiden, 1950).

ROWLEY, C. D., 'Native officials and magistrates of German New Guinea 1897-1921', *South Pacific*, 7 pt. 1 (1954), pp. 772-82.

———, *The Australians in German New Guinea, 1914-1921* (Melbourne University Press, 1958).

———, *The New Guinea Villager*, (Cheshire, Melbourne, 1965).

———, 'The villager and the nomad', *New Guinea and Australia, the Pacific and South-East Asia*, 2 pt. 2 (1967), pp. 70-81.

RYAN, D., 'Lakekamu Open Electorate: the election at Uritai' (part of a symposium on New Guinea's first national elections), *Journal of the Polynesian Society*, 73 pt. 2 (1964), pp. 21-3.

RYAN, P., *Fear drive my feet* (Melbourne Paperbacks, 1959).

———, The Australian New Guinea Administrative Unit. Paper presented at the Second Waigani Seminar, Port Moresby, 1968.

SACK, P., 'Land law and policy in German New Guinea . . . the native version', *Australian External Territories*, 3 pt. 2 (1971), pp. 7-19.

SAHLINS, D. M., 'Poor man, rich man, big-man, chief', *Comparative Studies in Society and History*, 5 (1963), pp. 285-303.

————, 'On the ideology and composition of descent groups', *Man*, 65 (1965), pp. 104-7.

SALISBURY, R. F., *From stone to steel: economic consequences of a technological change in New Guinea* (Melbourne University Press, 1962).

————, 'Despotism and Australian administration in the New Guinea Highlands', *American Anthropologist*, 66 (4), pt. 2 (1964), pp. 225-39.

————, *Vunamami* (Melbourne University Press, 1970).

SCHEFFLER, H., 'Dradivian-Iroquois: the Melanesian evidence', in *Anthropology in Oceania*, eds. L. R. Hiatt and C. Jayawardena (Angus and Robertson, Sydney, 1971), pp. 231-54.

SCHMITZ, C. A., 'Zum Problem des Balum—Kultes in Nordost—Neuguinea', *Paideuma*, 6 (1957), pp. 257-80.

SCHWARTZ, T., 'The Paliau movement in the Admiralty Islands, 1944-1954', *Anthropological Papers of the American Museum of National History*, 49 pt. 2 (1962), pp. 211-421.

————, 'Systems of areal integration: some considerations based on the Admiralty Islands of Northern Melanesia', *Anthropological Forum*, 1 (1963), pp. 56-97.

————, 'The co-operatives', *New Guinea and Australia, the Pacific and South-East Asia*, 1 pt. 3 (1966-7), pp. 36-47.

SHILS, E., *Political development in the new states* (Mouton, The Hague-Paris, 1962).

SPATE, O., 'Education and its problems', in *New Guinea on the threshold*, ed. E. K. Fisk (Australian National University Press, Canberra, 1968).

STANNER, W. E. H., *The South seas in transition* (Australasian Publishing Co., London, 1953).

STEWARD, J. H., *Contemporary change in traditional societies: introduction and African tribes*, ed. J. H. Steward (University of Illinois Press, Chicago, 1967).

STRATHERN, A. J., 'Despots and directors in the New Guinea Highlands', *Man*, n.s. 1 pt. 3 (1966), pp. 356-67.

Traders Licences, Karkar Island 1967-8, Department of District Administration, Karkar.

TO ROBERT, H., 'Credit and indigenous businessmen', *New Guinea Research Bulletin 20* (1967), pp. 23-9.

THURNWALD, R., 'Price of the white man's peace', *Pacific Affairs*, 9 pt. 3 (1936), pp. 347-57.

VALENTINE, C. A., 'The Lakalai of New Britain', in *Gods ghosts and men in Melanesia*, eds. P. Lawrence and M. J. Meggitt (Oxford University Press, Melbourne, 1965), pp. 162-97.

VEUR, K. VAN DER and RICHARDSON, P., 'Education through the eyes of indigenous élite', *New Guinea Research Unit Bulletin 12* (1966).

Vehicle Registration, Karkar Island 1967-8, Department of District Administration, Karkar.

WAGNER, H., A field study of the Bongu-Buged Circuit (mimeographed paper, Lutheran Mission New Guinea, Lae, 1963).

WARD, A. D., 'Agrarian Revolution', *New Guinea and Australia, The Pacific and South-East Asia*, 6 pt. 1 (1972), pp. 25-34.

WARUBU, K., 'With malice towards some', *New Guinea and Australia, the Pacific and South-East Asia*, 3 pt. 3 (1968), pp. 60-1.

WATSON, J. S., 'Kainantu Open Electorate: a general analysis of the election at Kainantu' (part of a symposium on New Guinea's first national elections), *Journal of the Polynesian Society*, 73 pt. 2 (1964), pp. 23-8.

WILLIAMS, F. E., *The drama of Orokolo* (Oxford University Press, 1940).

WOLFERS, T., 'Politics and the House: how they voted', *New Guinea and Australia, the Pacific and South-East Asia*, 2 pt. 2 (1967), pp. 28-36.

————, 'The elections', *New Guinea and Australia, the Pacific and South-East Asia*, 2 pt. 4 (1968a), pp. 67-70.

————, 'The 1968 elections', *New Guinea and Australia, the Pacific and South-East Asia*, 3 pt. 3 (1968b), pp. 50-9.

————, 'The 1968 elections-III: campaigning', Institute of Current World Affairs Newsletter EPW-14, 7 July 1968, p. 8.

WOLFF, R. J., 'Modern medicine in traditional culture: confrontation on the Malay Peninsula', in *Human Organization*, 24 pt. 4 (1965), pp. 339-45.

WORSLEY, P. M., *The trumpet shall sound (a study of 'cargo' cults in Melanesia)* (MacGibbon & Kee, London, 1957, second edition Schoken Books, New York, 1968).

Zeitschrift für Kolonialpolitik, Kolonialrecht und Kolonialwirtschaft 1904, Vol. 6.